DECISION-MAKING IN DENG'S CHINA

Studies on Contemporary China

Studies on Contemporary China

DECISION-MAKING IN DENG'S CHINA

PERSPECTIVES FROM INSIDERS

CAROL LEE HAMRIN and
SUISHENG ZHAO, Editors

With a Foreword by
A. Doak Barnett

An East Gate Book

M.E. Sharpe
Armonk, New York
London, England

An East Gate Book

Library of Congress Cataloging-in-Publication Data

Decision-making in Deng's China: perspectives
from insiders / Carol Lee Hamrin
and Suisheng Zhao, editors.
p. cm.
"East gate book."
Includes index.
ISBN 1-56324-502-7.— ISBN 1-56324-503-5 (pbk.)
1. China—Politics and government—1976–
I. Hamrin, Carol Lee, II. Zhao, Suisheng, 1954–
JQ1508.D43   1995
320.451'09'045—dc20
94–33141
CIP

Printed in the United States of America

The paper used in this publication meets the minimum requirements of
American National Standard for Information Sciences—
Permanence of Paper for Printed Library Materials,
ANSI Z 39.48-1984.

BM (c)   10   9   8   7   6   5   4   3   2   1
BM (p)   10   9   8   7   6   5   4   3   2   1

To our children
Eric, Kira, and Krista Hamrin;
and Lillian, Sandra, and Justin Zhao.

Contents

About the Editors
and Contributors

The Editors

Carol Lee Hamrin is adjunct professor at the Nitze School of Advanced International Studies (SAIS), the Johns Hopkins University, and a Chinese affairs specialist at the U.S. Department of State. She is the author of *China and the Challenge of the Future: Changing Political Patterns* (1990) as well as book chapters and journal articles on Chinese politics and foreign policy, and co-editor of several books on Chinese intellectuals and the state.

Suisheng Zhao is assistant professor of government at Colby College in Maine and founder and editor of the *Journal of Contemporary China*. He is the author of *Power, Position, and Institutional Design: Constitution-Making in Nationalist China* (forthcoming) and has taught at Beijing University and the University of California–San Diego. A research fellow at the Economic Research Center of the State Council and the Institute of South and Southeast Asian Studies of the Chinese Academy of Social Sciences (CASS) before 1985, he has published widely in both Chinese and English on Chinese politics, foreign policy, and East Asian international relations.

The Contributors

Timothy Cheek is an associate professor of history at the Colorado College. His research focus is on the role of intellectuals in the modern transformation of China, particularly their role in the CCP. His books include *China's Establishment Intellectuals* (1986), edited with Carol Lee Hamrin; *The Secret Speeches of Chairman Mao* (1989), edited with Roderick MacFarquhar and Eugene Wu; and *Deng Tuo and Intellectual Service in Mao's China* (forthcoming).

Chen Yizi is the former director of the State Council's Economic Reform Institute in China and participated in the political reform decision-making process in 1986–89. He is currently president of the Center for Modern China in Princeton.

Cheng Xiaonong was director of the Comprehensive Studies Department at the State Council's Economic Reform Institute in China and is currently a Ph.D. candidate in the Department of Sociology, Princeton University.

Joseph Fewsmith is associate professor in the Department of International Relations at Boston University, and author of *Party, State, and Local Elites in Republican China* (1985) and *Dilemmas of Reform in China* (1994).

Ching-chang Hsiao was a columnist for the *World Economic Herald* (1986–89) and a reporter for the *Wen Hui Daily* (1957–86) in Shanghai. In 1984–85, Mr. Hsiao was a Nieman Fellow at Harvard University. He is currently an independent consultant and scholar, affiliated with the China Times Center for Media and Social Research, School of Journalism, University of Minnesota.

Hsiao Pen was involved in high-level reform policy research both in the provinces and in Beijing in the 1980s and is now working in the financial field in Hong Kong.

Kam Yiu-yu was director of the Policy Research Office of the Xinhua News Agency in Hong Kong, party secretary of the Propaganda Front in Hong Kong, and editor-in-chief of *Wen Wei Po* in Hong Kong from 1949 to 1989. He currently lives in Los Angeles.

H. Lyman Miller is currently associate professor and director of the China Studies Program at the Nitze School of Advanced International Studies at Johns Hopkins University in Washington, D.C. Professor Miller has written articles on Chinese history, politics, and foreign affairs and is the author of *The Politics of Knowledge: Ideology, Science and Liberal Dissent in Post-Mao China*. His current research includes two book projects: an examination of national and cultural identity in China as seen from evolving trends in historical and popular culture depictions of China's place in world history; and an analytical history of the international relations of East Asia, 1550 to the present.

Ruan Ming was deputy director of the Department of Theoretical Research at the Central Party School in Beijing and worked closely with Hu Yaobang from 1977 to 1982. He is currently a visiting scholar at Princeton University. He is the author of *Deng Xiaoping: Chronicle of an Empire*, translated and edited by Nancy Liu, Peter Rand, and Lawrence R. Sullivan (1994).

Su Shaozhi is former director of the Marxism-Leninism-Mao Zedong Thought Institute at the Chinese Academy of Social Sciences. He has served as a visiting professor at several American and European universities, including the China Times Center for Media and Social Studies at the University of Minnesota. He is currently an independent scholar affiliated with the China Initiative at Princeton University.

Tong Zhan served as a staff member in the United Front Work Department in Beijing through the 1980s.

Wang Lixin was head of the Agricultural, Forestry, and Irrigation Department of China's State Planning Commission before 1990.

Guoguang Wu, currently a Ph.D. candidate in the Department of Politics at Princeton University, was a speechwriter in the late 1980s to Premier Zhao Ziyang and a chief editor in the Editorial Department of the *People's Daily*. He is a contributor to *The China Quarterly* and other English publications, as well as the author of books and numerous articles in Chinese.

Yan Huai was a section chief of the Young Cadre Bureau in the Central Organization Department (1982–86); director of the Beijing Institute of Organizational and Personnel Studies (1986–88); and a research fellow at both the French Fondation Nationale des Sciences Politiques (National Foundation of Political Sciences) and at the East-West Center, Hawaii. Since 1992 he has been a research fellow at the Institute of East Asian Political Economy in Singapore.

Yan Jiaqi was director of the Institute of Political Science at the Chinese Academy of Social Sciences. From 1986 to 1987, he was a member of the Central Political Reform Office. Yan was the founding Chairman of the Federation for a Democratic China in 1989–90. He now lives and writes in New York City.

George Yang is a former division chief at the Ministry of Foreign Affairs in Beijing, now living in the United States. He is currently involved in foreign trade.

Meirong Yang was a columnist for the *World Economic Herald* (1986–89) and a reporter for the *Liberation Daily* (1953–86) in Shanghai. From 1984 to 1985, Ms. Yang was a Nieman Fellow at Harvard University. She is currently an independent consultant and scholar affiliated with the China Times Center for Media and Social Research Studies at the University of Minnesota.

Fang Zhu received his Ph.D. in political science from Columbia University, and continues to research the role of the military in China.

Zhu Xiaoqun, a former CCP official, is currently a graduate student at the University of Illinois at Chicago.

Foreword

A. Doak Barnett

This unusual and valuable book is special for several reasons.

The Chinese contributors to the volume are intellectuals and former officials who held significant party and government positions in China before the Tiananmen crisis of 1989. Their posts and responsibilities varied, but all had intimate knowledge, from personal participation in the Chinese political system, of important aspects of policy-making and implementation. Some played active roles in the efforts to initiate reforms in the 1980s. The analyses in the chapters that make up the bulk of this volume draw from the authors' personal knowledge of the organization and functioning of political institutions in China.

Since coming to the United States, these knowledgeable and able individuals have had the opportunity, and the freedom, to reflect on and begin to write about their experiences, using their accumulated knowledge and expressing their views about China's political system, about the country's political predicament and problems, and about its future prospects. They also have begun to broaden their contacts and interactions with Western scholars and political analysts, and in a variety of conferences and workshops they have had the opportunities to exchange views with non-Chinese specialists—as well as among themselves. The resulting dialogues on Chinese politics clearly have contributed significantly to the analyses contained in this volume.

The result is a book that is unique in many respects. It sheds new light on political institutions and processes in China and makes a valuable contribution to the ongoing effort to raise our level of understanding of the evolution of the Chinese political system. Some chapters focus primarily on the organization and functioning of particular political institutions. Some reinforce, elaborate on, or fill in gaps about many of the fundamental authoritarian characteristics of the structure and functioning of the political system.

Others analyze changes over time in the roles, responsibilities, and relative power of top leadership groups, decision-making bodies, and bureaucracies. In many chapters, the authors provide revealing data drawn from their own experience about how certain specific policy decisions were made; information about particular cases help illustrate and bring to life abstract generalizations. Although some chapters touch on the Maoist period, the most interesting new data and insights in the volume are those that relate to the Deng era of economic, social, and political change in China. Discussions deal with the changes in the leadership dynamics at the top of the regime in the Deng era compared to those during the Mao era; the factional struggles between relatively conservative leaders and the leading reformers; the great generational differences between the surviving party elders and the next generation of technocrats; and many other important changes and trends.

The authors in Part III present important new data and insights about the efforts of reform leaders to introduce limited but nevertheless potentially significant steps to begin internal political reform of the overall system in the years immediately preceding the Tiananmen crisis of 1989. Drawing on their own experience as active participants in the reform process to illuminate the objectives of the reforms attempted at that time, the debates about them, the backers and the opponents of particular political reforms, the partial short-term successes of some reform efforts, the major failures of others—and the setback to basic aims of political reform resulting from the Tiananmen tragedy and the purges of key reform leaders.

Because many of the authors were themselves involved in reform efforts in these and other fields, they clearly considered many of the steps attempted or proposed potentially significant, and most were deeply alienated by the political clampdown after the Tiananmen tragedy. But it is apparent that many still believe that political reform will certainly come in China—and seem to believe that the important questions concern when, how, and in what form political reform will come, not whether it will come.

At several points in the book—especially at the beginning and at the end—some of the authors, and the editors, identify key political issues, and put forward their judgments or hypotheses about the main directions of likely future changes and possible evolution of the political system. Each reader will doubtless find particular new data or insights to be of special interest, because they fill gaps in outsiders' knowledge, or because they provide unique "insider" perspectives, or because they highlight important issues and questions about the future as well as the past.

These important issues will be a focus for continuing discussion and debate for many years to come—among intellectuals within China as well as those abroad, among reform-minded Chinese leaders as they grapple with the country's immense problems in the period ahead—and also among scholars and leaders in other countries who must try to understand and deal with China. This book—and the dialogues from which it has emerged and the future dialogues to which it could contribute—should make a valuable contribution, both to the task of understanding the past and present, and to thinking about the future of the Chinese political system.

Acknowledgments

This book is largely the product of a workshop on "Leaders, Institutions and Politics in the People's Republic of China," convened in La Jolla, California, on August 28–30, 1992. The workshop was sponsored jointly by the Center for Modern China, the University of California–San Diego, and the U.S. Department of State, Office of Research. As the conveners of the workshop and editors of this book, we owe enormous thanks to Chen Yizi, president of the Center for Modern China, Susan Shirk of the University of California–San Diego, Thomas Fingar and Susan Barnes of the State Department's research offices. We appreciate their encouragement, ideas, and practical support, including funding from the Center and the Department. Douglas Merwin of East Gate Books and his colleagues at M.E. Sharpe have encouraged and guided the publication progress. We thank Matt Flynn, Tina Valdecanas, Zhou Yiru, Tian Chen, Alvin Yam, and Michael Zee for their valuable technical assistance.

The workshop, in turn, was part of a two-year project (October 1991–October 1993) on "The Chinese Political Process in Comparative Perspective," cosponsored by the State Department and the Nitze School of Advanced International Studies (SAIS) at the Johns Hopkins University. This book includes several chapters and many ideas gleaned from other workshops and interviews in the larger project. For their major contributions we thank H. Lyman Miller, director of China studies at SAIS and codirector of the project with Dr. Hamrin; Mike Finnell, director of International Studies at Meridian House International, the location of most of the workshops; as well as Kenneth Roberts, director of the State Department's Office of Research.

Several others deserve thanks for their critical part in the first stage launch of the project, Joseph Fewsmith of Boston University, who organized a workshop on "The State Council and Economic Development," Timothy Cheek of the Colorado College, organizer of a workshop on "The Changing Propaganda System," and Huan Guocang and Jia Hao, whose help in brainstorming and networking brought high-quality contributors to the project.

Finally, we thank each other for an enjoyable working relationship on the workshop and on this book, as well as for new friendship.

Washington, D.C., and Waterville, Maine
May 1994

Introduction: Core Issues in Understanding the Decision Process

Carol Lee Hamrin and Suisheng Zhao

The demise of European and Soviet communism in 1989–92, following hard on the heels of the violent clash between Chinese society and the party-state in June 1989, raised considerable controversy over the Chinese Communist Party's (CCP's) future prospects. "Will the CCP follow the way of the Communist Party of the Soviet Union? If so, why? If not, why not?" Convincing arguments were made both for China's similarities to the Soviet Union and for China's uniqueness, with different prognoses for the future. What the debate most clearly revealed, however, was that outside observers did not share a consensus about how the Chinese political system was structured and how it operated sufficient to make judgment calls with any great degree of certitude.[1]

Meanwhile, the June Fourth, 1989, tragedy brought to the West a large number of former high- or middle-ranking Chinese government officials and prominent intellectuals who had participated in important reform policy decisions of the last decade in various official and semiofficial capacities. Some of them obtained academic positions in the United States as teachers or graduate students; others continued research and writing in Chinese language forums. But all were motivated by the events of 1989 to reflect analytically on the nature of politics in the People's Republic of China (PRC), in order to discern a strategy for the future, both for themselves as individuals and for the nation.

From October 1991 to October 1993, a project on "The Chinese Political Process in Comparative Perspective" brought together Chinese who had worked within the political system with Western-trained China scholars and U.S. government political analysts, using simultaneous interpretation to allow full and clear communication. The project sought to establish a new baseline or template, presented in this volume, for understanding the dynamics of the political system as of the end of the 1980s, criteria by which ongoing change could then be measured.

One inspiration for this project was A. Doak Barnett's classic study of the PRC after its first decade, *Cadres, Bureaucracy, and Political Power in Communist China,* which through fortuitous timing was published on the eve of the Cultural Revolution and thus provided a benchmark for analyzing the bewildering, radical systemic changes in the 1960s.[2] We do not mean to assert that China necessarily is headed into cataclysmic change, but rather that the Chinese people (and China analysts) have been experiencing "future shock" from rapid socioeconomic change for some time now, and since early 1992 the pace of change has been accelerating once again. The passing of the founding generation of revolutionaries is likely to accelerate political change as well. We want to discern how much of that change is superficial and how much is fundamental to the system.

The Project Design

The immediate precursor for the project and this volume was the 1988 conference on PRC bureaucratic behavior organized by Kenneth G. Lieberthal and David M. Lampton, who edited the results published in *Bureaucracy, Politics, and Decision Making in Post-Mao China.*[3] Our focus, like theirs, was on the policy process that encompasses both decision-making and implementation and reflects the dynamic interaction of formal institutional structure with informal personal actions. We sought to build on the excellent, cutting-edge findings of that volume, by learning more about the noneconomic sectors, the role of party institutions, and the nature of politics at the highest level of the system. Explicitly, we tested the hypothesis, suggested by the Lieberthal/Lampton findings, that the nature of politics differs in different sectors and at different levels of the system, and found that the case studies bore this out. Our findings on this are spelled out in the concluding chapter.

The project began with an introductory conference on comparative political systems, to identify the right questions to ask. Several workshops on specific functional sectors, and interviews on individual organizations followed. A workshop on case studies in decision-making was then convened to view the dynamics of politics across the spectrum of sectors and levels in the system.

Former Chinese practitioners at the workshop presented detailed case studies of policy decisions or detailed descriptions of the structure of important institutions. To shape their contributions, the workshop organizers provided them with specific questions in advance, including: How was authority structured as viewed from the position of the author? How did both institutional roles and personal leadership influence play into the policy-making process? What were the strategies and tactics of leaders of the decision arena in question? How did officials and staff use key institutions and information flows in the policy-making process? How were leaders' decision-making abilities constrained by the institutions and information available? How did the institutional framework for decision-making evolve? When and how did leaders organize or use social group interests and actions in the political process?

Western political analysts, chosen purposely to represent different disciplines and fields of study, then commented on the case studies based on their own theoretical and empirical findings. The dialogue produced surprises for both groups. "Outsiders" quickly came to realize that they had underestimated the personalistic elements in decision-making and the fluidity of institutional structure. "Insiders" were challenged to take into account more fully the actions of other groups and institutions in decisions they were involved in, and to be aware of the institutional and regulatory constraints on individual political strategies.

This volume, as a product of a complex and collaborative effort, is not a typical academic study. Rather, it is a compilation of descriptive and analytical accounts of personal experience, subjective by definition, corrected and enriched by commentary from other participants in key episodes and from Western-trained political analysts. Rather than using footnotes to document published evidence for these case studies, which for much of this material does not exist, we have relied on the built-in correctives provided by the authors' personal notes taken at the time, and by comments of other discussants and the editors who had either experience in or research knowledge of the same decision-making processes. As the editors, we take final responsibility for any errors that remain.

Given the continued political sensitivities and uncertainties in China, the project was unable to shed much light on the military and security sectors, and a few of the authors chose to use pseudonyms and obscure their exact positions and responsibilities while in China. Each author chose the spelling and order (Western or Chinese, surname last or first) for his or her name, as reflected in the Contents, but the text follows standard pinyin usage for Chinese terms and names.

Organization of the Book

Our approach as editors was to condense the heart of each "insider's story," incorporating corrections and additions inspired by commentary and discussion into case studies that form the main body of this volume. The first two parts focus on structure and process, illustrated by mini–case studies of decision-making. The third presents detailed case studies of policies from the point of initiation through research, document drafting, review and formal approval, to actual implementation. We then highlighted the dialogue on key systemic issues in this introductory chapter, our methodological and comparative findings in Dr. Miller's chapter and theoretical offerings in Dr. Zhao's concluding chapter, both in Part IV. These two chapters point the way for a future research agenda.

The division of the main text into three parts reflects our finding that the very nature of politics is different at different levels in the system, which not coincidentally correspond to different stages of the process—high-level decision, mid-level administration, and local implementation.

Part I examines the central decision-making level, where nonroutine policy and personnel initiatives originate. It explores the highly personalistic dynamics of power politics at the top and describes the relatively fluid roles of the party's Politburo and Secretariat, their ad hoc working groups, and the key subordinate executive departments for oversight of elite cadre and institutions (the Organization Department), the state economy (State Planning Commission), the nonparty elite (United Front Work Department), and information (Propaganda Department). The 1980s was characterized by a shift from personal dictatorship to oligarchical consensus-building at this level.

Part II analyzes the administrative level, characterized by the interaction of personalistic power politics and institutional bureaucratic politics in the making and supervision of specialized routine policies. Through the 1980s, this level became increasingly regularized and professionalized in terms of cadre, institutions, and procedures. Besides central government institutions, we have included a look at two special localities directly under central control; the Beijing Garrison Command and the Xinhua (New China News Agency) office in Hong Kong.

Part III reveals the "feedback" role of local implementing bodies and even of society in the process of introducing radical reform policies—reforms in the political system pursued in 1986–88 and a closely related reform of the price system in 1988. Together, these case studies highlight the importance of the continued involvement of the supreme leader to press forward with controversial policy initiatives, as well as the probability of dilution or even defeat of such policies at the stage of implementation.

Notable by their absence in this volume are the autonomous or semi-autonomous arenas of electoral politics and media politics that characterize more democratic political systems. Both elections and the media are important to Chinese politics, but as adjuncts to rather than correctives or limitations on the political process we sketch here. The increasing role of money politics at provincial and local levels of society in 1993–94 is also outside the purview of this study, though it will have increasing influence on the political process over time.

Core Issues: The Nature of the System

Under the influence of reform through the decentralization of authority and opening up to outside resources, Chinese society in the 1980s gradually was outgrowing its Leninist system of party-state governance, even though the basic structure and processes remained intact. In order to hasten economic development, the central party-state made concessions to lower-level administrators and local producers, granting them more material benefits through profit retention and more functional autonomy through greater decision-making authority. Similar but smaller concessions were made to noneconomic units. Like the gangly limbs of an adolescent body protruding from a child's overcoat, the relatively marginal sectors of the economy and society (the arms and legs) were allowed to go their own way, even as the key economic sectors, administrative organizations, and personnel (the stomach, heart, and lungs) were kept under wraps.

This purposeful delegation (not sharing) of authority, combined with the supplement of foreign resources, was intended to restore regime legitimacy and efficiency, that is, to strengthen the party-state. The unanticipated result, however, was the emergence of a hybrid system wherein the Leninist center maintained its monopoly on policy-making authority as described here but found itself "persuading," "consulting," or "bargaining" with a multitude of lower-level actors over the implementation of its policies. The party-state looked quite strong from the perspective of the top level of analysis, while from the grass-roots level, it appeared quite weak. Given the durability of this system despite both the failed popular uprising of 1989 and the recentralization efforts of 1988–91, we need to reach a common understanding of the nature of this decentralized, horizontally segmented, and loosely integrated structure, which nevertheless is still dominated by party-state authority.

Bureaucratic Authoritarianism

The project participants insisted that China remains a command system in terms of the top-down flow of authority (however negotiable the contents and terms of command may be), and party leadership directives are the primary means of regulating (*zhi*) the whole system. The politics of articulating and mediating conflict between different interest groups is carried out entirely within the party-dominated bureaucratic hierarchy through the process of creating policy (political) directives. There is no separate electoral process or legislative process.[4] This volume therefore closely examines the central policy-making process precisely in order to understand Chinese politics and society more broadly. Analysis of decision-making illuminates the larger issues of the nature of the political system, the sources of legitimacy and the flow of authority, and the direction of systemic change by the late Deng era.

In comparing our findings to the body of theoretical literature, we do not find a perfect fit between theory and reality. We are most comfortable with the concept of "bureaucratic authoritarianism" to describe the overall Chinese political system in the Deng Xiaoping era.[5] "Bureaucratic" pinpoints the CCP's attempt to incorporate all social organizations within the party-state structure, exemplified by the 1989 decision to repress the autonomous worker and student organizations, as well as by the post-1989 efforts to organize entrepreneurs within the united front system. "Authoritarianism" captures the corresponding retention of ultimate, unlimited authority by the central party-state. Key concepts from several other theories nevertheless indicate major aspects of the evolving Chinese political system.

Communist Neotraditionalism

Literature on how Leninist regimes degenerate into "Communist neotraditionalism" looks at state-society relations and highlights the shift from totalitarian mass mobilization to network-based clientelism in the way party organization shapes and manages society.[6] This conception captures an important echo of premodern politics in the granting of spheres of autonomy by a central party-state unwilling to share power. Feudal imagery for how "plenipotentiaries" parcel out "fiefdoms" aptly describes rule by China's elders, the remaining revolutionaries who created the system. They share the solidarity of a war band of "heroes," each having earned a say in the affairs of state and a share of the spoils. Each has his own fiefdoms (functional and geographic bases of power) to use in distributing privileges to loyal followers. Each is a clan patriarch, jealous of turf, prerogatives, and personal honor (face). Once the elders are gone, however, the system will have difficulty replicating an equivalent higher moral authority above the law and outside the regular bureaucratic channels, and leaders eventually will be forced to find new means of legitimation.

The term *neotraditionalism* itself, however, implies something of an inertial relapse into premodern structure and culture, and some of its proponents tend to view neotraditionalism as an alternative to modern society, rather than a transitional stage of development. The analytical framework has a static rather than dynamic quality that makes it difficult to account for trends in the late 1980s and early 1990s in China.

Fragmented Authoritarianism

Another body of literature, on "fragmented authoritarianism," looks at the mid-level bureaucracy and focuses creatively on the shift from bureaucratic central command through the planning apparatus to interunit bargaining in economic governance.[7] "Fragmentation" captures the disorderly nature of the Chinese bureaucratic system, which resulted from the decades of weakened central power under Mao Zedong followed by an incomplete reconstitution of the central party-state in the early 1980s. It points the way to an understanding of the state's evolution from dictatorship to coordinator or referee in an increasingly differentiated society.

But the phrase also leaves something to be desired in that it implies an uncontrolled process whereby autonomy is being seized by subunit actors against the will of the state. This does not evoke the state's complicity in its own devolution and overstates the weakness of the center. The focus on economic dynamics leads to a rather vague conception of the state structure, as reflected in the suggestion that China "is in transition from a traditional hierarchical system toward a more modern, market-oriented system."[8]

State Corporatism

Literature on state corporatism, focused on state-society relations, appears most promising for explaining our findings on change toward the end of the Deng period. This approach, as adapted to China in several recent articles, has the important advantage of fitting into even broader theoretical constructs of corporatism for comparison of Communist to noncommunist states. The original definition of corporatism is as follows:

> Corporatism can be defined as a system of interest representation in which the constituent units are organized into a limited number of singular, compulsory, noncompetitive, hierarchically ordered and functionally differentiated categories, recognized or licensed (if not created) by the state and granted a deliberate representational monopoly within their respective categories in exchange for observing certain controls on their selection of leaders and articulation of demands and supports.[9]

With a further refinement of definition as to the relationship between the state and its constituent units, the theoretical fit with Leninist states was even more clear. State corporatism was to be distinguished from societal corporatism on the basis of whether the units were a product of state imposition or of general socioeconomic development and voluntary arrangements, as well as whether state controls on selection of leaders and interest articulation were a product of state imposition or reciprocal consensus.[10]

If we apply corporatist theory, the evident retreat of the state under Deng may be understood as a totalitarian state evolving toward a corporatist state by granting material concessions to induce compliance from lower-level units in order to overcome the inefficiencies of a command economy. A totalitarian state aims to maximize political and economic dominance; it uses all-intrusive power to reshape society for state purposes. But a corporatist state accepts its own limits and allows limited autonomy and benefits to its constituent parts, so long as these interests remain subsidiary. Economic imperatives drive this change, resulting in the irreversible segmentation of public power.[11]

China has not reached an advanced stage of state corporatism, which would require full recognition of the legitimacy of subunit autonomy. This, in turn, would require open rather than tacit repudiation of the Leninist myth that the party-state represents the interests of the whole society and would also provide moral justification for legal protection of such subunit interests. In other words, full state corporatism would probably follow (or immediately precipitate) the demise of the Communist Party's monopoly on power.

What is essential to understand is that the development of state corporatism should not be mistaken for societal corporatism, much less a pluralistic society, whatever degree of pluralization may appear within the bureaucratic structure. "Interest-licensing" by the party-state is not interest articulation and representation by subsidiary units of society. Administrative delegation of power is not the same as acknowledging legal and political rights. Ultimate authority remains in the hands of the top party-state leaders, and who among them shall wield what authority is determined through elite factional competition. Authority does not emanate from the bottom up through elections.

Whether China experiences a relatively peaceful and gradual evolution from totalitarianism through bureaucratic authoritarianism to full state corporatism and on to democratic pluralism is yet to be answered either theoretically or experientially.[12] The workshop discussion of the case studies in this volume would suggest that skepticism is in order. If China's politicians balked at sharing power outside the official bureaucracy in 1989, the transfer of ultimate authority from the pinnacle of the system to society likely would be even more traumatic.

Core Issues: Centralized Authority

Workshop discussion of the set of chapters in Part I quickly focused on the issue of authority. Since accountability in any system is imposed by the person on whom one must depend to remain in office, whose view of a Chinese official's work performance counted most? To whom was he accountable? Who therefore had de facto "authority"? This approach helped to highlight the key question of the source of authority in the Chinese system.

In China there was no electorate as the fundamental source of authority, but rather a "selectorate" with the authority to choose leaders, and therefore to whom they were accountable. Was it one person at the top (a dictatorship as under Mao), or a small group of elders and leaders (an oligarchy as under Deng)? Did the Central Committee as a whole body have some indirect, informal authority, and therefore play a role in the selectorate?[13]

Politbureaucracy

All discussants emphasized the monopoly on basic authority within the integrated party-state of a tiny elite—a small group composed of the top leader, other elders, and members of the Politburo Standing Committee. At most, Politburo members, not the Central Committee as a whole, shared some of this ultimate authority. From the Mao era to the Deng era, one could discern a shift from autocracy toward oligarchy. But the role of the Central Committee remained largely that of providing symbolic legitimation for decisions made elsewhere. As Yan Jiaqi's chapter on the nature of Chinese authoritarianism indicates, power struggles erupted over the right to choose Central Committee members, thereby ensuring majority approval of decisions. Power struggles between factions thus were revealed most openly in the period of preparation for a new party congress. The propaganda apparatus was used to prepare the "political climate" most suited to the choice of certain types of candidates and the agenda of a congress.

Dictatorship and Oligarchy

Most discussants agreed with Yan's suggestion that a fundamental systemic dynamic was cyclical swings between small group oligarchy and one-man dictatorship. The theoretical norm was collective leadership, which helped to maintain a balance of power and thus limited destabilizing factional purges. But the system allowed one main player to emerge as first among equals, based on the systemic requirement for an ultimate authority to arbitrate final policy decisions as well as the appointment of the top two dozen officeholders and their membership in and duties as Politburo members. The dictator's power thus rested on ultimate power of appointment and policy decision; the power of the Standing Committee rested on control over the next one hundred senior leadership posts and supervision of functional policy sectors. The scope of authority for personnel and policy diminished progressively down the hierarchy.

The constant interplay and uneasy tension in the central decision-making process between individual leadership prerogatives and norms of collective leadership came through consistently in the course of the project. The project overall revealed a continuing high degree of dominance and unlimited authority by each level of leadership over its subordinate levels, with collective norms coming into play among leaders at the same level. Chapters by Chen Yizi and Cheng Xiaonong both underscore the extent to which Zhao Ziyang sought out Deng Xiaoping's views to guide every stage of the process of research and review of draft policies. A former official of the Science and Technology Commission described the science and technology policy process in the 1980s as one of "fleshing out" informal, simple remarks first by Deng to foreign visitors and second, by Hu Yaobang or Zhao in meetings or ceremonies.[14] Yet Deng had to take into account the views and interests of his peers to a greater extent than did Mao. Collective norms may have been used with greater effect by veterans to constrain the independent authority of the successive generation of leaders.[15]

Nevertheless, collective norms remained weak in the face of logrolling tactics by leaders taking advantage of a cultural aversion to confrontation. According to discussants, Zhao often biased Politburo discussion by opening with the comment, "I have just discussed the agenda with Comrade Deng and he says . . ." and then dominating the discussion.

Hierarchy and the "Loyalty Imperative"

In seeking the functional equivalent in China of the American "electoral imperative," wherein the desire for reelection means politicians must seek to please the electorate, discussants underscored that in China, any official must follow closely both his patron and his patron's faction, since they are the source of his authority. This explained the key political role of the personnel system, characterized by a very strict hierarchy, a monolithic grid covering the entire regime bureaucracy (party-government-military).[16]

Discussants observed that loyalty was everything. There were no constraints on this imperative and no alternative to "following"; even retirement was dependent on this. Yet at the same time, an official had to cultivate more than one patron to ensure survival. Therefore, conflicting loyalties inevitably arose in the system.

This loyalty imperative was strengthened by both party principles and the bureaucratic ethos. Concepts of "party spirit" (*dang xing*) and "democratic centralism" (no questioning after a decision comes down) reinforced the tendency to "follow the leader," to obey without questioning. Combined with Chinese conflict avoidance, this produced very indirect and oblique communication from subordinates to superiors, and an absence of direct argumentation in meetings, in deference to status.

According to one discussant, Vice Foreign Minister Liu Huaqiu was a good example of how to rise quickly up the ladder by following, in his case following former Foreign Minister Ji Pengfei and impressing leaders such as Hu Yaobang during travel abroad. Compared to this following ability, cultivating good relations within the ministry, while relevant, was unimportant.

Some noted there had been changes within the elite since the Cultural Revolution, especially among liberals who followed Hu Yaobang only because they thought he was right, not because they wanted a promotion.[17] Before, intellectuals followed the party and Mao without question. They woke up only after the Cultural Revolution, when they began to search for blame, including their own; a new conflict of loyalty resulted—whether to follow the party or to follow Truth? Others commented that there has been a similar change in the dependency culture of the broader society as well, with dissent reflected indirectly in social unrest. For the most part, however, the "loyalty imperative" prevailed; officials were always "looking up," accountable mainly to those above. Only secondarily could they afford to look across or down the system in response to other pressures.

At the higher levels, the system was characterized by factional struggle for supreme (undivided) authority over lower levels, the right to set the strategic direction (the party line) and make the key appointments in the system (nomenklatura). The "selectorate" was a small group ruling through self-legitimation. The top leaders took on themselves the role of interpreters of the mandate of history, to be affirmed by pledges of loyalty to the leader and his line and obedience to central directives. This contrasted with legitimation from below via popular election or even limited elite election, such as elections within the Central Committee would be.

Power Float

Ruan Ming's chapter on the Secretariat highlights the changing distribution of power among even the highest formal CCP institutions. To what extent changes in the 1980s were motivated by inner-party competition or by desire for inner-party democracy was a matter of controversy during discussion. Nevertheless, the ability to restructure institutions emerged as a key lever of power, along with personnel appointment, control over propaganda, and policy initiative. For example, Wang Lixin emphasized the power competition between conservative and reform factions involved in the 1988 incorporation of the State Economic Commission into the State Planning Commission (SPC), depriving Zhao Ziyang of the SEC's authority, staff, and resources and giving a red light to reform. Similarly, a green light came from the post-1992 piecemeal reversal of this centralization of power in the planning commission.[18] Such formal restructuring, however, had to be authorized by formal party or government meetings and documents. More informal means of shifting power thus were preferable.

At the very top, the key power distribution was that among elders, Politburo, and Secretariat. Decisions were enacted from 1980 through at the Twelfth CCP Congress in 1982 to promote younger, more educated leaders and reintroduce a measure of institutional separation of powers in the party. These changes were intended both to improve inner-party democracy and effectiveness and to complete the shift of power from Hua Guofeng's group to Deng Xiaoping and Chen Yun, in part by giving full executive power (under the Politburo Standing Committee) to the Secretariat rather than the Politburo. The new generation of leaders nevertheless remained under heavy constraint from Deng and Chen on the standing committee and other elders who began to fill the Central Military, Discipline Inspection, and Advisory Commissions.

The golden age of the Secretariat occurred in 1982–87; membership included key leaders from all three bureaucracies, except the premier, who nevertheless also attended the meetings held twice weekly. The Politburo rarely met. Later, State Council work conferences meant that State Council members attended only the first weekly meeting of the Secretariat, so Hu Yaobang used the second to discuss purely party affairs. A division of responsibilities emerged between the Secretariat (political affairs) and the State Council (administrative affairs), which was confirmed by the Thirteenth CCP Congress.

Some discussants suggested that the Secretariat's power perpetuated the relative weakness of the State Council, setting up obstacles to further political reform and leading to a backlash in 1987, when Hu Yaobang was removed from power. Wang Lixin pointed out how Hu Yaobang intervened in the economy in ways that provoked the anger of the SPC. Under the principle of party leadership, he intervened in economic affairs primarily through two channels: giving instructions and approving projects while on tour in the provinces, and requiring reports to the Secretariat from the party groups (*dangzu*) in State Council organs. In the case of policy on the Special Economic Zones (SEZs), Hu Yaobang used the Secretariat to bypass not only the Politburo but also its Finance and Economics Leading Group and the State Council, both under Zhao Ziyang.

Ruan Ming's chapter, a fascinating case study of the ins and outs of SEZ policy, counters such criticism by arguing that Hu's actions were necessary in both political and policy terms. Because Zhao's influence over the government was weak, Hu used the Secretariat to fight valiantly for the zones against Chen Yun's followers throughout the state apparatus. This study reveals the judicious use of different meeting formats, memberships, and agendas in the policy battle.

In any case, it would seem that while the introduction of a division of functions or powers or measures of institutionalization may look like system democratization, in fact they may strengthen party dictatorship over the system, so long as the source of authority remains at the top rather than at the bottom.

Policy Initiative

The power float was even more evident among the informal personal mechanisms that coexisted with the formal bureaucratic institutions. In this shadow government, leaders divided up responsibility for specific functional spheres, in which other leaders were not to intrude. All discussants agreed on the importance of these functional duties in distributing authority at all levels. Yan Huai's chapter in Part I contains many references to the *guikou* (proper channels) system of making decisions according to assigned sector.

A common conception in the literature on Chinese bureaucracy is that problems caused by strict compartmentalization in the Chinese system provided the raison d'être for leading groups as coordinating bodies; there was a need for final decision-making authority. But our discussion suggested this conception might better be turned on its head; leaders enforced strict compartmentalization so as to preserve their authority as final arbiters and initiators.

Highly personalistic authority was exercised through the Politburo's commissions for military or political-legal (security and judicial) affairs, and leading small groups (*lingdao xiaozu*) for subsectors of party and government work, as explained in Yan Jiaqi's chapter. These groups, some relatively permanent and others temporary, initiated and brokered key policies. Notably, the functional authorities at the top were termed "central" commissions or groups and were conceived of as joint party-military-government or party-government organs, reflecting the party's absorption of military and government authority at the top. It was not clear in discussion whether in the periods when the Secretariat was powerful, with members having functional oversight of all sectors, whether another layer of authority was added, or if the Secretariat competed with and weakened the authority of these Politburo groups. The latter seems most likely.

Leading groups did not exist as ongoing institutions; rather, they were task forces composed of individuals with other formal responsibilities and institutional bases meeting together for coordination and decision-making purposes. A prime example was the Political Reform Research Group discussed in Chen Yizi's chapter in Part III; composed entirely of high-level leaders, it met frequently in 1986–89 to make decisions on the highly sensitive and secretive political reform initiative. Politburo involvement came late in the process and mainly as official endorsement. In lengthy discussion, many questions were raised about how leading groups actually function. This is an important area for further research.[19]

Given the power float at this level, what a leading group could or could not decide depended on the issue, the personal power and work style of its leader, and the circumstances—crisis or routine. Even leading groups would push tough decisions to the top to avoid responsibility. And they often were bypassed by the elders; Ruan Ming described how in 1979, Peng Zhen did not hold a meeting of the Political-Legal Commission to discuss Wei Jingsheng's case but just sent his personal recommendation to Deng Xiaoping, who decided on the fifteen-year sentence. When Hu Yaobang's aides tried to report mass opinion on the issue to him, Hu said it was too late; Deng had already decided.

Documentary Politics

The whole project on China's political system underscored the extent to which it remained a command system, that is, the essential mechanism of party governance was by central directive. Guoguang Wu's rich chapter posits the concept of "documentary politics" as the means by which an oligarchy rules, in distinction to autocratic systems based on purely personal fiat by a dictator or democratic rule by elected officials through constitution and law. There was an important process in China wherein a group of leaders built consensus, formalized personal preferences, and gained ideological legitimacy through formulating political documents that represented the collective will of the leadership.

The requirements of the directive system served both to enhance the power of hegemonic leaders and to constrain individual leaders' actions. On one hand, what a top leader said was highly important, as reflected in what Chen Yizi calls the "head-scratching" approach to policy initiation, and what Yan Jiaqi means by staying within the "speech space" of the top leader. On the other hand, a leader's views had to be shaped into a directive with ideological "dressing" and formal approval to be authoritative. In a recent example of this process, Deng's pro-reform comments on his early 1992 trip to South China first had to be verified by Politburo discussion and decision before circulating widely as a fully legitimate policy directive.[20]

The directive process also required leaders and officials to take some measures to build at least a minimum of consensus. Consensus was built through the process of coordination of policy, often on paper being circulated for comment rather than face to face in meetings. In an example familiar to those who have worked in a government bureaucracy, at the Foreign Ministry level vice ministers would cosign a policy document, which then was sent to the State Council and then on to the Politburo member in charge of foreign affairs, who in turn sent it to other Politburo members for signature. If there was a military component, it was sent to the People's Liberation Army chief of staff; similarly, if a military decision such as an arms sale had foreign affairs significance, it was to be sent to the Ministry of Foreign Affairs (MFA) for signature. This required coordination was called "policy control."

According to Chen Yizi, the bottom line of the coordinating process was not so much achieving real consensus as building support, that is, obtaining the minimum balance of forces needed to prevent the "overthrow" of the document in question. This process consisted of various stages of "struggle," beginning with choosing members of the responsible leading group, members of the drafting group, and members of the discussion group. The case studies in this book suggest there was less real bargaining over interests involved than persuasion or even intimidation. Politicians carefully gauged the timing and atmosphere for pushing or countering policy initiatives.

Guoguang Wu provides a close, detailed study of the stages of document-making, with important case studies, and argues persuasively that this was central to the Chinese political system. It was the "nervous system" for China's state-run society and economy—the body, with the party as the brain in command. Case studies in Part III also confirm the centrality of the process of creating central directives.[21]

If power struggles were functional equivalents of the electoral process in choosing decision-makers, perhaps the drafting of central directives in a command system was the equivalent of the legislative process in an electoral system. Political aides (*mishu*) to Chinese leaders functioned in part like legislative aides to members of the U.S. Congress.[22] In China, the shift from using personal instructions of leaders to party directives and then to government regulations, and finally, legislation in the governing process was important evidence of system transformation. The corollary shift from personal "brain trusts" to political research organs throughout the system in the 1980s, and government think tanks under Zhao Ziyang—all used for document drafting—also reflected this progress.

Growing Limits to Central Authority

Trends in authority in the Deng era, discussed further in our concluding chapter, might be summed up as "individual pluralism" (more than one elder involved) in arenas of major decision, and "institutional pluralism" at lower levels affecting more routine or technical issue areas of minor decision. The former trend produced political cycles; the latter produced incremental progress toward institutionalized decision-making. Good examples of the distinction between policy types can be found in chapters by George Yang and Cheng Xiaonong.

Core Issues: Executive Power

Beneath the top-level decision-making institutions were the central bureaucratic agencies, including the executive departments of the party Central Committee and the administrative commissions and ministries of the State Council. These agencies had nationwide hierarchies and exercised supervisory powers.

According to their function and scope of authority, they could be grouped into two types: comprehensive (*zonghe*) and specialized or professional (*yewu*) institutions. Although these precise terms were most often used to distinguish among types of government organs, the distinction was a useful one in looking at organs across the whole party-state-military bureaucratic grid. Both main types played important roles, but comprehensive institutions held broader administrative jurisdictions reaching into the whole system and, unlike specialized institutions, had authority over other central institutions in certain aspects of their operation. The dynamics and atmosphere of operation within the former type tended to be more political, the latter more professional.

While political leaders had to rely on the expertise of specialized institutions to deal with sophisticated economic, cultural, and foreign-policy problems, they had to use the authority of the comprehensive institutions to ensure execution of their policies. Those leaders who controlled key comprehensive institutions usually stood at the vantage points in the policy-making arena, and heads of these agencies often were Politburo or Secretariat members.

Throughout the project, it became apparent that Chen Yun's indirect control over key comprehensive units during much of the Deng era gave him a powerful institutional base in the leadership. Hu Yaobang and Zhao Ziyang were continually frustrated in attempts to win cooperation from the central bureaucracy in general and from these institutions in particular. For example, according to Wang Lixin, Zhao's orders to the State Planning Commission (SPC) via the Finance and Economics Leading Group were considered nominal, discussed in a pro forma fashion and ignored in practice, while every word from Chen Yun was taken very seriously.

Comprehensive Institutions

The most powerful of these were the Central Organization Department (COD) and the State Planning Commission. The former supervised the nominations and appointments of ministers and vice ministers of the State Council and departmental directors and deputy directors of the Central Committee, while the SPC was known as the "small State Council" with much authority over economic agencies. A common saying among bureaucrats was "Economic units are afraid of the Planning Commission and all units fear the Organization Department." (Actually, the SPC also supervises planning in noneconomic organs.) To understand the Chinese political system, one had to understand these two organizations.

Chapters in Part I by Yan Huai, and by Wang Lixin and Joseph Fewsmith, show in detail the large size, wide scope of authority, and political importance of these key organs. Staff members in such organs were carefully screened and disciplined, with political loyalty outweighing education or expertise; many children of high-level leaders had found employment here.

The Organization Department's extraordinary power came from its function as a gatekeeper whose ultimate veto power resided over the selection process for some 30 million cadre nationwide, at all levels, including nonparty as well as party officials, and including the selection of reserve cadre being groomed for future leadership. Also known as "the first department under Heaven," the COD took a very serious attitude toward this heavy responsibility, conducting investigation and approval procedures before final appointments. Yan Huai insisted that "there is no pro forma approval, even for personal recommendations from Deng Xiaoping or Chen Yun."

In Chapter 4 Yan Huai explains both the scope and the import of the nationwide hierarchical grid that fixed in rank all party-state organizations as well as state cadre. The resulting bureaucratic culture led to a rigid, but also highly stable party-state system, despite political volatility among leaders and factions and despite social dissension.

The SPC, the primary organ for drawing up and implementing state economic policy, was responsible for the secretariat work of the Central Finance and Economics Leading Group. A huge organization with more than thirteen hundred staff members at the end of the 1980s, it had a powerful vested interest in the planned economy and was a major obstacle to marketizing economic reforms.

The power and scope of the authority relationships held by both the COD and the SPC can be seen in their structure; a specialized section would directly interact with its counterpart (*duikou*) sector. For example, the COD's economic cadre bureau directly managed the personnel issues regarding ministries and vice ministries of economic units in the State Council, as well as principal leaders of large-scale state-owned enterprises. The SPC's finance bureau controlled the banks; its bureau for rural and agricultural policies discussed and approved every stage of the rural reform. In both organizations, a section chief in the comprehensive unit did not hesitate to call a vice minister in a specialized unit to request information or discuss a problem; bureau chiefs contacted ministers.

Given the extensive authority of these comprehensive institutions, it was no surprise that control over them was a major focus of political competition. The top job at each was always highly contested. Yan Huai also gives us a particularly fascinating glimpse into the political origins and operation of the Young Cadre Bureau, known as the "Organization Department No. 2," tasked with choosing the "third echelon" of future leaders to be placed on reserve lists.

Two other traditionally powerful central institutions that were comprehensive in nature managed the broad functional arenas of united front work (control over the noncommunist social elite, including entrepreneurs) and propaganda (media, education and culture, research, sports and health, and educational curricula and ideological training). Every party core group or committee in every work unit, no matter what its functional system, would have a secretary in charge of these matters.

Tong Zhan's valuable study of the central United Front Work Department contains new information about the scope of responsibility, operational structure, work style, and mindset of united front work. The department managed—solely or jointly—a wide range of state organs: the Chinese People's Political Consultative Conference and the State Council's Religious Affairs Bureau, Nationalities Affairs Commission, and Offices for Hong Kong and Macao Affairs, Overseas Chinese Affairs, and Taiwan Affairs.

Through these administrative arms, it controlled the leadership, material resources, and policies of ostensibly nongovernmental social organizations, including the eight democratic political parties and the five official "patriotic" religious organizations. CCP control over "mass work" through the Communist Youth League and Trade Union and Women's Federations was carried out along similar lines and supervised by the same leader in the Secretariat or Politburo.

The chapter by Ching-chang Hsiao and Timothy Cheek on propaganda reveals the largely unknown wide scope of influence of the Propaganda Department due to the secret, internal reporting function of the media, which was the focus of their essay. The project conference "The Changing Propaganda System," convened by Professor Cheek in November 1991, also confirmed the highly politicized nature of the propaganda system.

Within the military bureaucracy, the three main "general" departments for political affairs, logistics, and staff work, may have been the functional equivalent of such comprehensive institutions, under the policy direction of the Central Military Commission.

Specialized Institutions

The specialized administrative agencies included in Part II are found mainly in the government but also exist in the party and military. Examples were the Central Party School and military academies. In contrast to comprehensive organs, these had no authority over other central institutions, only over directly subordinate units at lower levels. They are responsible for implementing guidelines from higher levels and making concrete policy in only one narrow sector. This was reflected in the organizational structure; bureaus corresponded to professional functions rather than to the work of other linking agencies.

The problems dealt with were specialized, and there was a strong emphasis on professional education and expertise among staff, whose job assignments were also specialized. Although the policy process at this level did not completely avoid the impact of power politics, it was relatively professional and consensual in nature. The leaders and staff members in these institutions tended to see themselves as professionals rather than political workers; their influence on policy stemmed from the technical knowledge they could offer, which leaders lacked. As George Yang asked rhetorically, "If the MFA drafted all Zhao Ziyang's speeches on foreign policy, who was directing whom?"

Yang's study of the MFA spotlighted the regularization of procedure in the 1980s, with clear-cut channels for consultation and a strict chain of command. This trend corresponded with a generational turnover of MFA leadership from veterans of the revolution to those trained in foreign affairs colleges in the early 1960s. Without the informal, personal coordination possible among widely connected veterans, there was a greater need for supraministerial coordinating bodies. Policy tended to become less ideological, more pragmatic, with greater consensus. All these trends were also evident in economic and technological sectors covered in the project conference "The State Council and Economic Development," convened by Professor Fewsmith in October 1991.

Yang underscored the uniqueness of national security policy involving the United States, USSR, and Europe (NATO), in that decisions remained highly centralized in the hands of a few or even one top leader, with very little delegation of decision power to the MFA or other foreign affairs agencies. This was also true of Taiwan policy and of Hong Kong policy, which touched on the sensitive issue of sovereignty, as Kam Yiu-yu's chapter on Hong Kong underscores.[23] In such areas, implementation was carefully monitored with a high level of discipline; subversion of a decision was not easy. Nevertheless, there was still a broad scope of "recommending power" (influence) for the many sections of the foreign ministry involved in research, analysis, and operations regarding China's most important bilateral relations—its immediate neighbors, especially Korea and Vietnam, and border issues.

Personalistic Politics

The trend toward professionalism in foreign and economic affairs was less evident in our other case studies in Part II, which were chosen precisely to explore other, less well-studied and more politically sensitive sectors. Reunification policy as conducted in Xinhua–Hong Kong; supervision of the Marxism-Leninism Institute by the propaganda system; and political work procedures in the Beijing Garrison Command were all highly politicized and nonprocedural in nature. For the Garrison Command, the explanation appeared to lie in the party's alertness to avoid or nip in the bud the slightest problems in the PLA. For the others, the fluidity of structure and policy was strongly shaped by residual long-standing personal rivalries within the older revolutionary generation. The persistence of their influence in these sectors was in itself evidence of the reluctance of top leaders to delegate authority in sensitive areas.

More than personalities was responsible, however; as Kam Yiu-yu pointed out, dual lines of control and communication, and fluidity of structure and personnel, were intended to serve the systemic goal of maintaining final authority over political matters in the hands of top leaders. Su Shaozhi believes that the propaganda and organization systems were especially vulnerable to personal interference by top leaders, factional politics, and the vagaries of political campaigns. Nevertheless, as his case study shows, regulations and procedures that were ignored or overridden by policymakers could be used by subordinates pushing "counterpolicies," and thus did shape politics.

Fang Zhu's valuable study of political work in the PLA confirms his creative conception of the fusion of party and military leadership, wherein military involvement in politics was a systemic feature, not an aberration. He provides an explanation of the personnel system, including recruitment and professional schooling, and case studies of political campaigns in the Beijing Garrison Command. His chapter illuminates the shadowy party-military side of the "party-state" system. The resulting picture was of a symbiosis in which the military elite was absorbed into the party, just as was the government elite. In both bureaucracies, the key was party control over personnel, with the General Political Department (GPD) being the functional counterpart of the Central Organization Department for the civilian part of the system.

Core Issues: Restructuring the System

Part III of this volume highlights major attempts in the late 1980s to introduce reforms in political structure, in the press, and in the price system that together would have brought about fundamental systemic transformation. Both the willingness and the ability of the leadership to actually research, plan, and draft such reforms and their unwillingness or inability to implement them are worthy of the close review given here.

Each type of reform played out differently in terms of origin of initiative and institutional arrangements. In the case of the political reform decision, high-level temporary institutions and personnel (led by the equivalent of a leading small group) were created alongside the formal bureaucracy. The whole process, depicted in Chen Yizi's chapter, was kept secret. Persuasion among the top leadership was greased by constant attentiveness to the personal wishes signaled by Deng Xiaoping. With Deng's imprimatur at every stage, there was no legitimate basis for opposition based on special interests or even ideological qualms. Hsiao Pen pointed out that severe and constant political pressure on Zhao during the 1987 anti–bourgeois liberalism campaign, which endangered the very existence of the Political Reform Office, led Zhao to push through highly controversial reforms in one big leap, without any stages of experimentation or implementation.

The resulting wind of reform at the top fanned a tide of complementary "bureaucratic entrepreneurship" at the middle levels, as detailed in other chapters in this section. Zhu Xiaoqun's chapter shows how a powerful organization like the Beijing City Party Committee thought it in its interests to signal its support early, offering the city as a political reform model, in order to win Zhao's favor—despite qualms about the practical interests involved. One discussant stressed the importance of this role of localities in providing political capital to leaders. Leaders on the defensive would go to the margins of the system—the localities or foreign actors—to shore up support. Going to society, the masses, was always a risky last resort.

Yan Huai's chapter on public service reform, chapter 14, tells a delightful tale of conspiracy among young reformers in mid-level posts in different organs of the central party apparatus, working to get around conservatives put in charge of planning personnel reform. They used a mix of formal channels, personal connections, semiautonomous organization, razzle-dazzle with "scientific" charts and lingo, and the internal media as they lobbied to win over elders who could single-handedly block major change. Their target in this case was Song Ping—the godfather of the organization-personnel network. As Yan put it, this successful strategy represented the "art of 'following' or the art of being 'led' by the leadership . . . Who is leading whom?"

Such were the dynamics that allowed the political reform plan to be drafted, vetted, and adopted in a remarkably short period beginning in the summer of 1986, in time for the thirteenth party congress in late 1987. Subsequent implementation of key parts of this reform, however, met with immediate and widespread resistance and ultimate defeat at the hands of vested strong interests who had gone along in the formulation stage. Still unable to "oppose" Deng's reform in principle, implementers at this later stage of the process nevertheless were able to point to "problems" that required "delay" or modification. The Beijing Party Committee, in its search for dependable patronage, shifted allegiance to Zhao's enemies led by Li Peng. Hsiao Pen and Yan Huai detail the failure of efforts to separate party and government and establish the public service system; yet they also reveal how the residual ideas and practices remained and even resurfaced as key democratizing trends in the 1990s.

In the case of press reform, as explored by Meirong Yang, the driving force came from below—from the determined, able, and well-connected editor of Shanghai's *World Economic Herald,* rather than from above. China's first influential, semiautonomous paper was born from the central systemic dynamic of "seeking autonomy." This effort illustrated the difficulty of breaking out of the enmeshment of party-state controls, given state control over resources. The *Herald* had to borrow office space from the CASS, the printing capacity from the party paper, and obtain the authority of the local propaganda department. But the case also showed the potential for success through the judicious use of higher-level factional ties, foreign connection, and favorable public reputation. When it was shut down in 1989, the *Herald* was literally on the verge of signing a joint venture agreement that would have created an independent media outlet for the first time since 1949. It was in this gray world of semiautonomous or quasi-official organization and operation that the potential for system evolution lay.

In the highly interesting case of price reform, as related by Cheng Xiaonong, the push for radical reform came from the very top of the system, Deng Xiaoping himself, in near-total isolation from even his loyal lieutenants. Deng's insistence on price reform kept Zhao Ziyang and his aides scrambling to incorporate it within a package of comprehensive reform that might give it a chance of success. Meanwhile, opponents of radical reform in the planning system under Yao Yilin's direction drafted both a watered-down version of price reform that might meet Deng's minimal expectations and a retrenchment plan they knew would gain Chen Yun's approval.

The failure of the price reform was foreordained given its highly politicized and polarizing nature, leading to disunity among top leaders and decision-making on the basis of political rather than economic criteria. Cheng points out several typical results of such involvement by the elders in economic decision-making: irregular communication outside normal channels, usually via informal comments by Deng or Chen in private sessions; discussion of issues as simplistic political formulae that ignored the complexities of economic reality; indirect "debate" between the two sides via unpredictable and sequential commentary by leaders as events unfolded, leading to incoherent and discontinuous policy; and finally, unreliability of implementation as second-level officials redefined or reinterpreted vague and confusing policies. Meanwhile, Cheng's case was an excellent example of how societal forces also affected decision-making, in this case with the August 1988 run on the banks and panic buying by consumers.

Discussants made important observations on how the process of decision-making during the political reform effort of 1986–88 differed from that during the earlier economic reforms. The early rural reforms were initiated at the margins of the system by local farmers and officials trying to stave off starvation. Throughout the mid-1980s economic and administrative reform process, many people became involved who spoke openly of their special interests and bargained for gains, resulting in a greater element of compromise and consensus. But when later radical reforms impinged on the basic political system, there was no legitimate basis for arguing special interests. Meanwhile, with leadership division, it was harder to win agreement at lower levels. The point was made that economic reform could lead to development that would make the pie bigger and everyone would gain, but politics was a zero-sum game.

Conclusion: Outgrowing Communism

The evolution of the Chinese bureaucratic authoritarian state was entering a new stage in the 1990s. Whereas the 1980s reform program redistributed authority to lower levels of the bureaucratic grid, a new dynamic began to change the very nature of system authority. Under Mao (and among the remnant post-Mao elders) authority had been charismatic and personal; the party (personified by its leaders) claimed its right to rule based on the victory of the revolution and its seizure of effective power. Party identity and loyalty outweighed all others (institutional or familistic or factional). Even in the 1980s, the "coin of the realm" still was political power, albeit based more on status within the party-state hierarchy.

By the mid-1990s, the coin of the realm increasingly was money. As party-state actors scrambled to exchange their power for money, even the key internal organs were beginning to experience change. State-sponsored commercialization of the Chinese elite and society proceeded rapidly during the 1992–94 economic boom, and some segments of the bureaucratic elite became more assertive about protecting their interests. New structures of interest prejudiced officials' attitudes in favor of capitalism and eroded discipline in the party and army. The commercialization of officialdom was producing a kind of bureaucratic capitalism.[24]

Three main forces seemed to drive the 1992 reorientation of the reform program to full-blown marketization, as articulated by Deng during his visit to the south and later endorsed by the fourteenth party congress. These forces were the accelerating interdependence of Chinese society as well as economy with the outside world; generational turnover to a more professional elite at all levels and in all arenas of leadership; and a profound transformation of China's external environment in terms of both expectations and rules because of the demise of the cold war strategic confrontation. The resultant marketizing process was beginning a more basic transformation of the Leninist system than the 1980s reforms were able to accomplish. Chinese "*danwei* socialism" became history; something new was emerging in its place.

Workshop discussants cited Taiwan as the most approximate model for future peaceful change in the Chinese political system. There, too, a combination of material incentives and popular demonstrations finally persuaded the old guard to retire and allowed the shift to an electoral system, albeit tainted heavily by money politics. But experts on Taiwan affairs pointed out that the mainland had barely begun to enter the lengthy period of transformation that only recently began to produce an electoral process on the island.[25] What type of system emerged next in China most likely would be yet another form of Chinese authoritarianism, embodying many of the features and dynamics discussed in this book. We would do well to pay close attention to the constant elements beneath the surface of elite-level political turnover and rhetoric in the coming years.[26]

Notes

1. The lack of consensus results partly from too little information, especially about decision-making at the apex of the system, and disparate types of information; in the 1980s both foreign and Chinese scholars began to apply the methods of disciplines other than political science to the avalanche of information newly available through both published sources and field research. The result was confusion stemming from the use of different paradigms, terminology, and methodologies, and from the difficulty of generalizing from the snapshots taken from different sectors and levels of the Chinese system.

2. New York: Columbia University Press, 1967.

3. Berkeley: University of California Press, 1992. See the discussion in Lieberthal's introduction, p. 7, of earlier academic work focused on either structure or culture and values, as well as the concluding chapter of this volume.

4. This means, of course, that the interests of extra-bureaucratic social groups are poorly represented, if not completely repressed. For illustration, electoral outcomes are determined by party decision-makers; legislation is drafted by party or government executives, depending on content. The content of policy programs determines the formal criteria for senior personnel choices.

5. "Bureaucratic authoritarianism" is borrowed from Guillermo A. O'Donnell's conceptualization of South American politics in the 1970s. O'Donnell uses the term *bureaucratic* to suggest the crucial features that are specific to authoritarian systems of high modernization: the growth of organizational strength of many social sectors, the governmental attempts at control by "encapsulation," the career patterns and power bases of most incumbents of technocratic roles, and the pivotal role played by large bureaucracies. See O'Donnell, *Modernization and Bureaucratic-Authoritarianism: Studies in South American Politics* (Berkeley: Institute of International Studies, University of California, 1979).

6. Andrew Walder, *Communist Neo-traditionalism: Work and Authority in Chinese Industry* (Berkeley: University of California Press, 1987), 1–27, was the first, and now classic, adaptation to the Chinese context of theories developed by Kenneth Jowitt in the Romanian and Soviet contexts.

7. See Kenneth G. Lieberthal and Michel Oksenberg, *Policy Making in China* (Princeton: Princeton University Press, 1988); David M. Lampton, ed., *Policy Implementation in Post-Mao China* (Berkeley and Los Angeles: University of California

Press, 1987); and Lieberthal and Lampton, eds., *Bureaucracy, Politics, and Decision Making in Post-Mao China.*

8. Lieberthal, introduction to Lieberthal and Lampton, *Bureaucracy, Politics and Decision Making,* 21. He points out areas of explanatory weakness, including the emergence of corruption and rent-seeking behavior.

9. This definition was given in an article that prompted the most recent wave of literature on the subject, Philippe C. Schmitter, "Still a Century of Corporatism?" in *Social-Political Structures in the Iberian World,* ed. Frederick B. Pike and Thomas Stritch (Notre Dame: University of Notre Dame Press, 1974), cited in Anita Chan, "Revolution or Corporatism? Workers and Trade Unions in Post-Mao China," *Australian Journal of Chinese Affairs* (AJCA) 29 (January 1993): 35.

In a comparative sense, there emerge concentric circles of ever-widening comprehensiveness: China can be compared to other "fragmented authoritarian" Communist states with relatively small and inefficient bureaucracies; it can be compared to a larger set of states during the historical postrevolutionary "neotraditional" phase of communism; it can be compared to the larger set of Communist and noncommunist periods of state corporatism; and finally, to other types of corporatism.

10. The definitional refinement appeared in Leo Panitch, "The Development of Corporatism in Liberal Democracies," *Comparative Political Studies* 10, no. 66 (1977): 65, cited in Valerie Bunce and John M. Echols III, "Soviet Politics in the Brezhnev Era: 'Pluralism' or 'Corporatism?' " in *Soviet Politics in the Brezhnev Era,* ed. Donald R. Kelley (New York: Praeger Publishers, 1980), 19.

11. The important implications of this "irreversibility" of authority delegation are explored by Peter Nan-shong Lee, "The Chinese Industrial State in Historical Perspective: From Totalitarianism to Corporatism," in *Contemporary Chinese Politics in Historical Perspective,* ed. Brantly Womack (Cambridge: Cambridge University Press, 1991), 153–79.

12. Anita Chan in "Revolution or Corporatism?" suggests ways in which a new elite may emerge within the bureaucratic structure who ably use it to defend genuine societal interests against those of the state, thus bringing about an evolution to a "socialist societal corporatism," such as existed briefly when the Jaruzelski regime in Poland recognized the legal status of Solidarity. Similarly, Mayfair Mei-hui Yang, "Between State and Society: The Construction of Corporateness in a Chinese Socialist Factory," AJCA 22 (July 1989): 33–60, creatively suggests a similar process whereby "horizontal integration of civil society is enhanced in the economic sphere, and civil society begins to detach itself from the state." Neither, however, addresses adequately the problematic transfer of system authority from the state to society.

13. In her welcoming remarks at the workshop, Susan Shirk emphasized the importance of using generic analytical concepts like "political incentives," "political roles," and "patterns of accountability and authority," and challenged insiders of the system to make explicit the rules, norms, and parameters that drive and shape Chinese politics. She develops her ideas in *The Political Logic of Economic Reform in China* (Berkeley: University of California Press, 1993).

14. Lin Zixin's presentation at the project conference on "The State Council and Economic Development," October 1991.

15. Party veteran Wang Renzhong in the early 1980s wrote of the importance of Politburo review of and State Council involvement in all major Secretariat decisions, and of the principle that "decision is never made by an individual but is made only after group discussion." Veteran Hu Qiaomu spoke of efforts in 1987–88 to formalize more democratic discussion and more open voting procedures in the Politburo and Secretariat. These seemed intended to require participants to register rather than withhold opposition

views, and to encourage delays on decisions to allow for the building of consensus, although Hu admitted the opinion of the general secretary still counted most heavily. See Wang Renzhong, *Red Flag* (Hongqi), May 1982, and Hu Qiaomu, notes from H. Lyman Miller on an oral presentation at the Woodrow Wilson Center in Washington, D.C., 1991. See also Hong Kong's *Hsin Pao*, September 18, 1992, p. 27, for a report that Vice Premier Zhu Rongji indirectly was blamed for riots in Shenzhen when his colleagues on the State Council blamed him for "acting on his own" and elder Yao Yilin admonished, "The State Council is a collective leadership; although there is division of work, we still have to communicate with one another."

16. Yan Huai explained that in 1956, twelve rank levels were set according to revolutionary experience; these were used only for wages and benefits, not for determining jobs and power. (The latter was decided by one's personal relationship with Mao.) In the 1985 wage reform, personal ranks were abolished except those retained by elders. Job and faction remain most important in determining influence or power. Zhu Xiaoqun made the following remarks based on his experience in Beijing City: The lower-level structure is a "clone" of the center. Central leaders control the lower levels by considering each a unit; they set up local units that are answerable to the center rather than the locality. So local leaders look up, not across or down, for guidance. The lower you are, the less room you have to maneuver. The lower you get, the more controlled, homogenized, personalistic, and dictatorial is the system. The degree of autonomy may vary a lot, however, depending on specific circumstances and the locality in question.

17. This is the theme developed in Liu Binyan, *A Higher Kind of Loyalty* (New York: Alfred A. Knopf, 1990).

18. Wang viewed the new State Production Commission as more powerful than the former SEC because it also had power over foreign economic relations. He predicted the next step would be to abolish the SPC and set up a new commission with power over all these areas, a ploy Zhu Rongji later attempted without success.

19. Chen Yizi explained that leading groups are often created for running political campaigns or pushing new policy programs, and then tend to "hang on" in the system at all levels. Their functions include: coordination; implementation (e.g., the anti-bourgeois liberalism campaign or the anti-crime campaign), often through setting targets or quotas; and routine decision-making. They vary in status, which depends on the rank and job of the leader.

20. See Suisheng Zhao, "Deng Xiaoping's Southern Tour: Elite Politics in Post-Tiananmen China," *Asian Survey* 33, no. 8 (August 1993): 750–53. For details of types of central documents and related distribution and security systems, see Huai Yan and Suisheng Zhao, "Notes on China's Confidential Documents," *Journal of Contemporary China* 4 (Fall 1993): 75–92.

21. Chen Yizi emphasized how carefully organizers pick those to attend document discussion meetings: one must invite representatives of the functional "special interests" involved, but also will want more "neutral" people. To discuss a draft of Zhao's May 1987 speech, Bao Tong and Chen invited managers, entrepreneurs, and provincial leaders to balance the required propaganda personnel.

22. See Wei Li and Lucian W. Pye, "The Ubiquitous Role of the *Mishu* in Chinese Politics," *The China Quarterly*, no. 132 (December 1992): 913–36.

23. Kam Yiu-yu used Hong Kong policy to illustrate the importance of knowing the jurisdictional limits of any institution. There are divisions of responsibility in the State Council for Hong Kong policy; the MFA oversees negotiations with the United Kingdom and the Hong Kong–Macao Affairs Office oversees administrative issues. Regarding the Sino-Vietnamese conflict in 1979, as another example, the MFA's sole role was to estimate foreign reaction and suggest how to manage it.

24. These concepts are adapted from the ongoing research on China's system transformation of Professor Ding Xueliang of the Hong Kong University of Science and Technology.

25. Professor Hung-mao Tien of the University of Wisconsin (Madison) Law School, in his remarks at the project's first, comparative, conference in October 1991, insisted that the mainland would face difficulty in duplicating the Taiwan experience. He pointed out that from the very beginning, Taiwan had a strong and technically skilled civil government and much room for autonomous social and economic actors; the Kuomintang never exercised truly totalitarian control. In his view, the PRC is far from obtaining the prerequisites for an incipient democratic pluralism like that evident on the island, which is based on a middle class that is 40 percent of the populace with a democratic political culture based on years of experience in local elections.

26. Here, we are echoing the concluding remarks in Lieberthal's introduction to *Bureaucracy. . .*, 27. We would not be surprised to see a noncommunist but still bureaucratic state corporatism emerge through the granting of full legitimacy for limited autonomy to unofficial entities.

Part I
Central Leadership and Executive Systems

1

The Nature of Chinese Authoritarianism

Yan Jiaqi

The 1911 Revolution overthrew the imperial regime that had existed in China for several thousand years. In name, it established a "republic," but in reality, it did not eliminate the root of authoritarian politics. The governments that followed, namely, the Beiyang warlords, the Kuomintang regime, and the Communist regime all share, to a great extent, the same authoritarian decision-making process as the Qing regime. Contemporary mainland China has a beautiful name, "the People's Republic," and according to the state constitution, the National People's Congress (NPC) is the supreme organ of power. But in reality, the nation's highest power remains concentrated in the hands of a few people, even one person.

Party Domination

The constitutions of the Chinese Communist Party (CCP) and of the People's Republic of China define the powers of the party's general secretary, the state president, and the premier of the government, but without clarifying their relations. In name, the National People's Congress, the State Council, and the Supreme Court have the highest legislative, executive, and judicial power, respectively. In reality, however, above these "highest" powers there is an even higher power—the Politburo of the Central Committee. One cannot locate this actual, highest decision center in constitutional definitions.

The members of the Politburo consist of the top leaders of the party, the state, the civilian and military bureaucracies, and a few important localities. Similarly, at the provincial, municipal, and county levels, the members of each party committee are made up of the heads of the party, people's congress, government, and police. Here, too, the party organization is a government above the government, the real decision-making center of a province, municipality, or county.

The Standing Committee at each level exercises strong direction over decision-making in the Politburo or party committees at lower levels. Under the direction of the Politburo Standing Committee, the Central Secretariat is the operational center for daily affairs, while the vehicles for policy-making are various leading small groups (*lingdao xiaozu*) or commissions (*weiyuanhui*), which supervise the important functional systems.[1] The major functional leadership organs are headed by a Standing Committee member and include the Central Foreign Affairs Leading Group, Finance and Economic Leading Group, Propaganda Leading Group, Political-Legal Leading Group (at times, Commission), and the Central Military Commission.

Members of the foreign affairs group usually include the president, the general secretary, the premier, the vice premier in charge of foreign affairs, the foreign minister, the minister of the international liaison department, and the minister of foreign economic relations and trade. Usually, the group leader is the general secretary or president; sometimes, however, it is the premier. Foreign visits of key figures in the party, government, military, National People's Congress (NPC) and Chinese People's Political Consultative Conference (CPPCC), as well as major foreign policies are decided within this small group. The power of the foreign minister is very limited.

The finance and economics group is usually headed by the premier. Members include the vice premier in charge of the economy, the heads of the State Planning and Economic Reform Commissions, and the Ministry of Finance.

The political-legal group is headed by the Politburo or Politburo Standing Committee member in charge of police, judicial, and state security affairs. Normally, he is concurrently chairman of the NPC. Members include the ministers of state and public security, chief of the People's Armed Police Force, chief justice of the Supreme Court, chief procurator, NPC executive vice chairman, and the ministers of supervision and justice. For ordinary legal cases at most levels, the police, procuratorate, and court all work together to reach a decision. But for major political cases such as those of Mao's widow [Jiang Qing], dissident Wei Jingsheng, or Zhao Ziyang's secretary, Bao Tong, the Central Political-Legal Leading Group makes the decisions and hands them over to the judiciary apparatus for implementation.

The propaganda group includes Politburo and Secretariat members with supervisory duties, and the heads of the Central Propaganda Department, Foreign Propaganda Group, Film and Broadcasting Ministry, Xinhua News Agency, and the *People's Daily*.

The Central Military Commission (CMC), usually headed by the party general secretary, has the highest decision-making power in military affairs and is higher in status and more powerful than the above-mentioned groups. The party and state CMC are "two organizations, one staff."

Dictatorship to Oligarchy and Back Again

In a Communist country, the death of a strong leader is always followed by a period of oligarchy, usually called "collective leadership," which is the legitimate norm in a Leninist system. After repeated power struggles, a personal dictatorship again emerges from the collective leadership. This cycle is the basic model for political change in all Communist systems.

In the early 1980s, Deng Xiaoping, Chen Yun, and Li Xiannian formed a collective leadership, which evolved into dictatorship by Deng. After the June Fourth massacre, Deng's power was severely weakened, however, and after Chen Yun's power increased, an oligarchy of political elders reemerged.

A given inadequate decision or failed policy will weaken and threaten a dictator's power and trigger a change in the cycle. For example, Deng's decisions to denounce Hu Yaobang in 1987, to launch radical price reform in 1988, and to implement martial law and the massacre in 1989 all weakened his power.

Human history contains countless examples of dictators who made decisions arbitrarily and eventually lost their power. But the dictators normally depended on at least a few advisers to make decisions. In Communist China, whether Mao Zedong or Deng Xiaoping controlled the highest power, even he needed to listen to different opinions. Sometimes they paid much attention to advice from their peers or aides, but in many other important instances, they made decisions themselves in order to protect their own personal interests.

In China the dictator would normally be the first-ranking member of the Politburo, as Mao was. Temporarily in the post-Mao era, political elders such as Deng Xiaoping and Chen Yun stood outside the Politburo, with greater power than the formal power organs of the Politburo and its Standing Committee. Deng's every word, in particular, must be obeyed by the Politburo. These elders now are old and suffer from poor health, however; because they are unable to make decisions on a frequent basis, their time is passing.

The Mao era was characterized primarily by dictatorship; the Great Leap Forward was a prime example. In May 1958, the second session of the eighth party congress was held in Beijing and passed the general guidelines on constructing socialism, as proposed by Mao. The whole country initiated a movement called the Great Leap Forward, establishing the people's communes. The guideline, the leap, and the communes became known as "three red flags," which turned into a disaster for China's economy.

In July 1959, at a leadership work conference at Lushan, Politburo member and Defense Minister Peng Dehuai openly criticized the 1958 decision. Mao treated Peng's criticism as a threat to his personal power, and at the eighth plenum in August that year, launched an "anti-rightist" campaign targeted against Peng and his followers. This allowed economic conditions to continue to deteriorate, culminating in a three-year nationwide famine in the early 1960s.

The Deng era generally was more of an oligarchy, with Deng Xiaoping's dictatorial power restricted to greater or lesser degree by Chen Yun's faction. This has been especially true since Deng's reputation and influence were reduced by the June Fourth Incident. Before his trip to South China in February 1992, which he used to provide evidence of provincial and popular opinion in favor of resuming rapid reform, the political climate was very unstable. The purpose of his southern trip was to change that, and the power of reformers generally increased thereafter. As a result, Deng Liqun and a number of his leftist supporters in the propaganda system, as well as many leaders' children in the "princes' party," were not chosen as delegates to the Fourteenth Central Committee. Deng's trip also laid the foundation for the congress's political report and choice of Central Committee members.

Nevertheless, evidence exists of Deng's continuing inability to solely dictate events. For example, in deciding whom to appoint as president and premier at the Eighth NPC in March 1993, Deng had to test the opinions of others. In the summer of 1992, therefore, when he inspected Beijing's Capital Steel Plant, he talked about vice premiers Zhu Rongji and Tian Jiyun, saying, "From the central to the local leaders, there are not many who know economics. I myself don't know economics, but I can understand it. Zhu Rongji knows economics, but unfortunately I found him too late. Tian Jiyun doesn't know economics, but he can understand it." In Deng's mind, clearly Zhu was the best candidate for the premiership. However, if Chen Yun's strong opposition were to require a concession from Deng, then Tian would be his alternate choice. The actual result—Li Peng's continuation as premier—was an indicator of the weakness of Deng's power.

Hierarchy and the "Following Imperative"

The power of the dictator rests on two means of exercising power: ultimate power over the choice of candidates for Politburo and Central Committee membership and unlimited right of intervention in decision-making. He determines the specific duties of Politburo Standing Committee members. This power is buttressed by the chief characteristic of the Chinese political system: strict hierarchy.

There exists a power sequence from the top down, in which officials at each level can interfere at any time and in any way in the decision-making process at lower levels. In this power sequence, the dictator stands at the top. He (alone) has complete freedom of speech and the highest decision-making power. For example, only Deng Xiaoping could insist on the need to uphold socialism, but then tell visiting African leaders that "I can't tell you what socialism is exactly; don't practice so-called socialism in your country." Similarly, regarding the Hong Kong issue, Deng said at one point, "The 'one country, two systems' policy should remain unchanged for fifty years." Later, however, he said that if the policy produced good results, it should remain unchanged for one hundred years.

Power of Appointment

The elders as a group control the nomination of Central Committee and Politburo members, and this is the source of their ability to intimidate even members of the Politburo Standing Committee, as well as all other high-ranking officials. For example, in the early 1980s, Hu Yaobang nominated Xiang Nan to head the Central Party School, but his plan failed because Chen Yun opposed it. Another example occurred in late 1986, when just before a meeting, NPC Vice Chairman Peng Chong mentioned that an article published in the Shenzhen youth newspaper proposed Deng Xiaoping's retirement. Upon hearing this, the elderly Bo Yibo became very angry and ordered an investigation. Turning to Politburo Standing Committee member Hu Qili sitting beside him, Bo said, "You all hope we die early, don't you?!" Immediately, Hu answered him reverentially, "We hope you all enjoy a very long life."

Policy-Making

Whatever Deng Xiaoping says must be carried out, unless it is not feasible. For example, in late 1986, when student unrest erupted in Hefei, Shanghai, and Beijing, Deng insisted that three prominent intellectuals be expelled from the party and a name list be drawn up of other liberals to be criticized. All this was accomplished by the spring of 1987. By contrast, however, Deng's statement in 1986 that the problem of the price system must be solved did not come to fruition because it was practically unworkable.[2]

The "speech space" and "decision space" are limited for leaders at every other level beneath the supreme leader. Even the decision-making sphere of Politburo Standing Committee members—whether the general secretary, president, or premier—is restricted. They are not allowed to speak differently from Deng Xiaoping. For example, regarding China's reunification, once Deng had declared that Taiwan could maintain its own defensive armed forces, even Yang Shangkun, as president and head of the Central Taiwan Affairs Leading Group, could not state the opposite. When Zhao Ziyang was in charge of formulating a blueprint for political reform, the first thing he had to do was summarize what Deng Xiaoping had said on the topic, and then act accordingly.

A provincial party secretary's space is limited even more by that of the central leadership. The space of a county party secretary or county magistrate in turn is severely restricted by that of the provincial level officials. Under normal circumstances, each cannot express his own opinions if they differ from those of higher leaders. Thus, leaders at all levels have little room for independent decision-making. They must constantly report, ask for instructions, and wait for instructions from higher levels. If we say that Deng uses 100 percent of his brain, then Jiang Zemin can use only 70 percent of his, provincial leaders 50 percent of theirs, county leaders 30 percent or less.

The hierarchical system produces followers unable to take initiative. For U.S. senators and representatives, the major factor that determines their political behavior is the "electoral imperative."[3] Even though they belong to a certain political party, the party organization has little to do with their renomination and reelection; the politician thus always looks to the will of his constituents. In today's China, the factor determining political behavior, even of so-called elected officials of the National Party Congress or the National People's Congress, is the "following imperative." Congress representatives must first of all follow the party line, as interpreted by the party leaders of his department or unit. Otherwise, he will not be "reelected." There is no electorate, and the "selectorate" ultimately is a handful of top party leaders, or even the supreme leader.

Rules of the Game

In such a system, the informal rules for a lower-level leader become: Never exceed the "speech space" set by Deng Xiaoping. Do more and talk less: Work in silence to avoid problems. Use the power of superiors to enhance your own power. Within your own decision-making sphere, be as right-leaning or left-leaning as possible to please your personal patrons, those one or few persons who determine your chances of promotion or demotion.

As an example of the latter rule, Politburo member Li Ruihuan leaned to the right in supervising propaganda affairs, to please Deng Xiaoping. However, Minister of Propaganda Wang Renzhi tried to be as left-leaning as possible in order to please conservative elders like Chen Yun, Hu Qiaomu, and Deng Liqun; sometimes he even exceeded the "speech space" set by Deng Xiaoping.

An example of the use of a superior's power occurred after July 17, 1981, when Deng Xiaoping met with Hu Qiaomu and Deng Liqun to tell them that ideological education should be emphasized. This incident became a tool for Deng Liqun to display and enhance his power. In several of his later speeches, he repeatedly said that "in July 1981, Deng Xiaoping talked to Qiaomu and me" so that the audience would have the impression that he often sees Deng Xiaoping and receives his instructions. In this way, he could better convince people of his own ideas and persuade them to follow him.

Once, when Minister of Culture Wang Meng convened a forum, I was sitting beside another official. During the meeting, I was puzzled when I saw him studying Deng's selected works and wondered why he read that boring stuff. Later I understood when I heard his speech. He was speaking strictly according to Deng Xiaoping's ideas; his so-called personal opinions were only an elaboration of Deng's words.

After I became aware of these rules, I gained greater authority in my own speaking. For example, when I visited Hong Kong, the propaganda department of Xinhua News Agency there invited me to make a speech. I spoke before about sixty people about the issue of developing and maintaining the capitalist system in Hong Kong. I said we needed to restrict the development of mainland-financed organizations in Hong Kong. Otherwise, I said, the "one country, two systems" policy (of Deng Xiaoping) would be endangered. I said we should not classify personalities of all circles in Hong Kong into "left," "middle," or "right"; we should treat them equally for the sake of the "one country, two systems" policy. I had the strong feeling that Xinhua welcomed my words, primarily because when I spoke, first I quoted Deng Xiaoping, and second, I spoke in a very sure tone. (Unfortunately, at that time, I hadn't learned fully how to show off my authority. I did not know how to build myself up by claiming to have seen or talked to somebody important.)

Power Struggle and Legitimation:
The Role of the Central Committee

In imperial authoritarian politics, succession to the crown always entailed fierce power struggles. In contemporary China, the same power struggle prevails. Liu Shaoqi, Lin Biao, Jiang Qing, Hu Yaobang, and Zhao Ziyang were all victims of the succession struggle. The main distinction is that the crown could be inherited. The emperor had to watch for conspiracies from his aides, but he himself did not need to legitimize his power every few years. In China, even though Mao, Hua Guofeng, or Deng might control the highest power, this power needed to be legitimized by a national congress of the CCP, according to Leninist ideological norms of "democratic centralism."

Thus, the key issue in the Chinese political system is ensuring the symbolic support of the majority of Central Committee members for decisions of the oligarchy by carefully selecting both representatives to the congress and the candidates for Central Committee membership.

Unlike traditional authoritarianism, modern Chinese authoritarianism is decorated with the beautiful name of "democratic election." Theoretically, a congress assembles delegates every five years in the highest leadership organization, which directly elects members of the Central Committee, which in turn elects members of the Politburo and other organs. Thus, the power of the Politburo and its Standing Committee should come from and be responsible to all party members.

However, the reality is completely different. The highest power of the party is concentrated in the hands of the Politburo Standing Committee and those elders who control them. Before a congress, therefore, the Standing Committee sets up two or three work groups to select both representatives to attend the congress and the candidates for Central Committee membership and alternate membership. Meanwhile, the delegates to the congress are "elected" by local party congresses based on recommendations from the party's central or local organization departments. Ninety-five percent of elected delegates come from these prearranged lists.

In the past seven or eight years, CCP members and their representatives have increased awareness of their rights and have dared to vote against well-known bad people and extreme leftists. This was reflected in Deng Liqun's loss of Central Committee membership during the thirteenth party congress, and of his associates' losses at the fourteenth congress. Basically, however, nominating power remains with the organization departments.

This is even more true for representatives to the National People's Congress, 99 percent of whom are elected according to prearranged name lists; all members of the Chinese People's Political Consultative Conference are directly appointed by the party. Controlling nomination and appointment power is the central means of CCP control over these organizations, which are intended to symbolize popular, nonparty support for party domination. The means of control are the presidiums of these two congresses, whose members are all determined by the Politburo. In preparatory meetings before the congresses, no impromptu nomination of presidium members is allowed, only votes to agree or disagree with the slate. Under these conditions, a few members at most may be added.

A further control mechanism is the division of each congress into tens or even hundreds of small groups. Even though it may be called a "national" people's congress, in reality most of the time the representatives are scattered among several big hotels throughout Beijing holding small group meetings. The only major events in the full sessions are listening to reports, "elections," or "voting." Although representatives have the right to speak, 99.9 percent do not exercise that right. The exchange of information is strictly controlled. The delegations and small groups communicate with each other through bulletins. But speeches unfavorable to the leadership plans for the congress are not published, only reported to the presidium and the Politburo through other channels. Thus, it is very difficult for delegates to form any impromptu opposition majority on a given issue.

Factionalism

There are always factions within the CCP. After Mao's time, Deng Xiaoping and Chen Yun led the two main factions. The formation of factions is related to policy differences, but essentially it centers on the struggle for power.

The power struggle within the CCP is most often revealed in the period of preparation for each party congress, since controlling the majority of the Central Committee members is the key to power. Before a congress, if a leader believes his position is threatened, he uses every possible means to eliminate his opposition. Extreme examples were Stalin's personality cult and purge in the 1930s and Mao's launching of the Cultural Revolution in the late 1960s, when he sought to prevail over Liu Shaoqi before the selection of the Ninth Central Committee.

Political campaigns are a central part of the process, as leaders attempt to shape the political atmosphere in their favor. Factions collect information on their opponents and use the press, speeches, and documents to attack one another, in terms of both person and policy. For example, criticism of Wu Han's play, "Hai Rui Is Dismissed from Office," was the starting point of Mao's attack on Peng Zhen. In the Deng era, during the 1987 campaign against "bourgeois liberalism" aimed at Hu Yaobang's supporters, the press in Beijing continuously published lengthy denunciatory articles, commentary, and editorials. The major purpose was to form a nationwide anti-liberal political climate that would make it impossible for someone accused or suspected of liberalism to be elected as a delegate to the thirteenth party congress, or to be chosen at the congress for any important position.

Even though the political campaign may not be at all true or convincing, it is still necessary in order to create a certain "political climate." During the Cultural Revolution, such false or distorted "black materials" labeling someone could kill a person politically. After the Cultural Revolution, collection of black materials was not allowed. But during the anti-liberalism campaign, Deng Liqun used this political trick once again to attack leading intellectuals including Zhao Ziyang's secretary, Bao Tong.

Manipulating the agenda of the congress itself is another part of the factional competition. Before the twelfth plenum of the Eighth Central Committee in October 1968, for example, 71 percent of the members and alternates of the Eighth Central Committee were labeled "traitors," "spies," and "counterrevolutionaries" by Mao's aides who organized the meeting. As a result, only forty of the original ninety-seven members were allowed to attend. Because this did not provide a quorum, ten alternates who supported the Cultural Revolution (most were heads of provincial cultural revolutionary committees) were then added.

According to the CCP constitution, those Central Committee members being criticized should have had the right to attend and speak freely. But if that had happened, Mao and his followers would have been in the minority. However, either those members did not realize they still had the right to speak so long as they had not yet been expelled from the party, or none of them dared to complain when deprived of their rights. As soon as the plenum began, Mao launched a fierce criticism of those party veterans who had protested against the Cultural Revolution in the "February Countercurrent" incident earlier that year. The plenum, sufficiently intimidated, passed a resolution expelling President Liu Shaoqi from the party. Only one person had the courage to lean on the table and not to raise his hand while everyone else voted.

Information, Legitimation, and Decision-Making

CCP rule is a kind of modern "divine politics," requiring self-legitimation from above in the absence of electoral legitimation from below. No matter who gains power, he needs to legitimize himself by proving the coherence of his policies with Marxist-Leninist-Maoist ideology. Thus, those in intellectual circles in China who are engaged in education, social science research, and the humanities also must propagate Marxist ideology.

One important function theorists performed during the economic reform era of the 1980s was to decorate the Western system with the beautiful name of "socialism" and "Marxism" so that it could be accepted and used in China. For example, the CCP admitted that the socialist economy also needed to combine "planned adjustment" and "market adjustment." So Professor Li Yining at Beijing University proposed the idea of a "second adjustment" (market being the first, government being the second); he suggested that the second should be used only whenever the first failed. Under the name of "socialism," Li's theory was spread widely in China and greatly influenced the major economic reform policies. Other theoretical debates among economists, regarding the responsibility system in the countryside and the shareholding system in enterprises, greatly affected reform policies.

The media also have greatly affected CCP decision-making. The "insider information" function of the press is a very important resource for decision-makers.[4] Politburo members and elders read Xinhua's *Restricted Current Domestic Information* (Guonei dongtai qingyang) and its "additional" edition on a daily basis. For example, in December 1986, when the student movement broke out in Hefei and quickly spread, these two media vehicles published lengthy internal reports every day. The problem was that their reports were unfair and exaggerated, frightening the elders and giving them the impression that the student movement was about to overthrow the regime. For example, out of the hundreds of posters that appeared in Shanghai, only the one saying "Down with the Communists" would be reported.

It is also believed that distorted information led Deng Xiaoping to expel three prominent intellectuals (Fang Lizhi, Liu Binyan, and Wang Ruowang) from the party. A biased report came in on an article written by Fang, Liu, and Xu Yingliang calling for a conference to commemorate the thirtieth anniversary of the "anti-rightist movement" of 1957. Deng Xiaoping was led by the report to connect "liberals" with the student movement and later, when discussing the movement, proposed expelling Fang, Liu, and Wang Ruowang from the party. Why Wang and not Xu? Because Deng mixed up their names, and no one dared to correct him. He remembered Wang because he had repeatedly demanded Deng's retirement. Deng concluded that Hu Yaobang's tolerance of the liberals led to the student movement and thus indirectly, in turn, mistaken information led Deng to fire Hu.

The two most important decisions in the 1980s were first, the decision to remove Hu Yaobang from office in early 1987 and, second, to define the student mourning of Hu Yaobang's death as "counterrevolutionary rebellion" on April 24, 1989. Both were related to one-sided information given to Deng Xiaoping. In the period from April 16 to 24, the Beijing municipal party committee exaggerated the severity of the situation in its reports to the Politburo, and this had a great influence on Deng's decision, published as an editorial in *People's Daily* on April 26.

Notes

1. See Yan Huai's chapter in Part I of this volume, and Carol Lee Hamrin, "The Party Leadership System," in David M. Lampton and Kenneth G. Lieberthal, eds., *Bureaucracy, Politics, and Decision Making in Post-Mao China* (Berkeley: University of California Press, 1992).

2. See Cheng's chapter in this volume.

3. Susan Shirk's opening presentation at the University of California–San Diego workshop in August 1992 offered this concept as a starting point for a fruitful comparative discussion.

4. See the chapter by Hsiao and Cheek in this volume.

2

The Evolution of the Central Secretariat and Its Authority

Ruan Ming

The Evolution of the Central Secretariat

The reestablishment of the Secretariat in 1980 was part of an effort to separate power within the party-state structure, following the model of the 1956–66 Secretariat run by Deng Xiaoping.[1]

The Eighth National Party Congress (1956–66) had experimented with diluting the Chinese Communist Party's (CCP's) highly concentrated power structure; part of the effort was to divide power between the Politburo and the Secretariat. Mao Zedong labeled the Secretariat "the first front" and the Politburo "the second front." Mao Zedong became chairman of the CCP and of the Politburo, while Liu Shaoqi, Zhou Enlai, Zhu De, and Chen Yun became vice chairmen. The newly elected general secretary, Deng Xiaoping, joined them as the sixth member of the Standing Committee of the Politburo. (At the second plenary session of the Eighth Central Committee, Lin Biao was recruited as an additional vice chairman and Standing Committee member.) The Secretariat became the executive organization in charge of day-to-day operations under the leadership of the Standing Committee, the highest decision-making authority.

There were several historical reasons for this change. First, Mao realized that one cause of the instability of the Communist Party of the Soviet Union (CPSU) after Stalin's death was Stalin's refusal to allow his chosen successor, Malenkov, to actually exercise power. Second, although Mao was dissatisfied with Khrushchev's denunciation of Stalin's cult of personality at the Twentieth National Congress of the CPSU, nevertheless, he felt compelled also to denounce the cult of personality at the Eighth National Congress of the CCP. Third, Mao had already reached the peak of his power by the Eighth National Party Congress and was quite self-confident. Thus, his

15

motivation for separating power was to strengthen the legitimacy and efficacy of party rule, not any external pressure to share his own power.[2]

The party leadership structure experienced major transformation during the Cultural Revolution, with the changes lasting until 1980. In accordance with Mao's proposal to reform the central leadership organizations, at the eleventh plenary session of the Eighth Central Committee, the largest Politburo Standing Committee in history was elected, consisting of eleven members (Mao, Lin Biao, Zhou Enlai, Tao Zhu, Chen Boda, Deng Xiaoping, Kang Sheng, Liu Shaoqi, Zhu De, Li Fuchun, and Chen Yun). The reorganization not only abolished the Secretariat but virtually abolished the Standing Committee of the Politburo as well, since six of its eleven members (Liu, Deng, Zhu, Chen, Tao, and Li) were no longer allowed to participate in decision-making because they were denounced as capitalist-roaders. Thus, the remaining five members did not constitute even half the membership.

Mao's reshuffle set up a special form of power concentration with two characteristics. First, power was highly concentrated in Mao himself; this allowed him to do as he wished, disregarding the constitutions of the state and the party. The abolition of the Secretariat, the dismissal of four out of five vice chairmen (except Lin Biao), the arrest of State Chairman Liu Shaoqi and the denunciation of the other Standing Committee members were all examples of his exercise of personal authority. These decisions were all individually made by Mao himself without going through any legal processes. Second, there was a two-dimensional structure under one person's control. The State Council, headed by Zhou Enlai, and the Central Cultural Revolution Leading Group, headed by Jiang Qing, became the two power centers. Mao intended to stabilize his personal power through manipulating these centers against each other, although later this system led to political chaos.

After Mao's death and the arrest of the Gang of Four, Hua Guofeng sought to continue the highly concentrated system, occupying the positions of party chairman, chairman of the Central Military Commission, and the premier. Although by title Hua accumulated powers equal to Mao plus Zhou Enlai, his actions caused widespread dissatisfaction among many other leaders who desired the deconcentration of power. In response, the third plenary session of the Eleventh Central Committee reestablished the position of secretary general, to which Hu Yaobang was appointed; Zhao Ziyang became premier; and Deng Xiaoping gained the position of chairman of the Central Military Commission. The reestablishment of the Secretariat at the fifth plenary session of the Eleventh Central Committee in 1980 further dispersed power.

Very shortly thereafter, however, power was again reconcentrated. The Twelfth National Party Congress abolished the office of the chairman of the Central Committee and gave prominence to the office of the chairman of the Central Military Commission. The amended party constitution also stated that the new head of the party, the general secretary, had the power only to convene central meetings, but not to preside over them, thus weakening the potential of the Secretariat. In essence, the purpose of this amendment was to complete the transfer of the highest power from the legally established organizations to the hands of two elders, Deng Xiaoping and Chen Yun, who could now veto decisions of the Central Secretariat. Two examples demonstrate this.

The first occurred after the "anti–spiritual pollution" movement when Deng Liqun was criticized by Deng Xiaoping for his left-leaning mistakes. The Central Secretariat then decided that Deng Liqun would no longer hold the office of Propaganda Department director and the decision was approved by the Politburo. However, the Voice of America (VOA) leaked this news before the official documents were sent out. In response, Deng Xiaoping stated, "We cannot follow the VOA's command." As a result, Deng Liqun remained in this office until 1986.

The second example occurred in 1986, when the Central Secretariat decided that Deng Liqun would no longer hold his position as head of its Policy Research Office. This time, the official documents were sent out, and the new appointee, Wang Zhaoguo, began work. However, Chen Yun disagreed with the decision, and shortly thereafter, the position was turned back over to Deng Liqun.

The power of the Central Secretariat was further weakened when Zhao Ziyang officially became the general secretary at the Thirteenth National Party Congress. Zhao Ziyang intended to make the Secretariat a small, purely executive body serving the Politburo, playing a policy advisory role. Before the congress, Zhao nominated some relatively young people as secretaries. When Bo Yibo, who was in charge of the personnel nomination leading group for the congress, read the list of names, he said, "Who is Bao Tong? I've never heard of him!" Thus he vetoed the nominations. Because the political elders did not agree with Zhao Ziyang's nominations, three of the five secretaries elected at the congress were concurrently members of the Politburo Standing Committee (Zhao Ziyang, Hu Qili, and Qiao Shi), and only two, Rui Xingwen and Yan Mingfu, were full-time secretaries. After the June Fourth Incident, four of the five were driven out of Secretariat; only Qiao Shi remained in office.

The Central Secretariat during the Hu Yaobang Era

Although the efforts in the mid-1950s and early 1980s to increase inner-party democracy through establishing the Central Secretariat both failed, they nevertheless left a significant mark on Chinese politics.

I will use the example of the decision to establish Special Economic Zones (SEZs) during 1980–81 to illustrate both the Secretariat's function and the constraints in the decision-making process under Hu Yaobang.

The work system of the Secretariat established after the fifth plenary session of the Eleventh Central Committee included two weekly meetings. One was to discuss major decisions and the other was to deal with daily matters. Important policy decisions on issues such as Tibet, Xinjiang, and the SEZs were all made during the first type of meetings and were usually announced as the Secretariat's "Meeting Summary."

In early 1980, Guangdong and Fujian Provinces, which were experimenting with special economic policies, were under pressure from the State Planning Commission (SPC) and attack from ideological organizations; both were controlled by the Chen Yun faction. The SPC used administrative decrees to disapprove development projects in Guangdong and Fujian; and Deng Liqun and Hu Qiaomu attacked the SEZs with their own "dogma." Under these conditions the leaders of Guangdong and Fujian found their work difficult and asked for help from the center. In this situation, Hu decided that the Secretariat would hear reports from both provinces and convened the fifty-second meeting of the Secretariat on September 23 and 24 for this purpose. During the meeting, Hu instructed that the two provinces should not only continue the SEZ policies but also become models to serve the goals of Chinese external affairs (especially regarding the return of Hong Kong). Among the eleven secretaries at that time, four (Wan Li, Fang Yi, Gu Mu, and Hu Yaobang) supported the policy and five (Wang Renzhong, Song Renqiong, Yu Quili, Yang Dezhi, and Peng Chong) remained neutral on the issue. The only two critical of the policy were Hu Qiaomu and Yao Yilin. Two of the other three participants in the meeting, Feng Wenbin and Zhou Jie, supported Hu Yaobang, and Deng Liqun favored Hu Qiaomu. Because the September meetings of the Secretariat had coincided with those of the Politburo where Deng initially proposed reforming the party-state system, however, the opposition (Hu Qiaomu, Yao Yilin, and Deng Liqun) dared not openly attack the SEZ policy. Consequently, the SEZs had an opportunity to develop quickly for three months.

Later, however, the Chen Yun faction chose the central work conference of late December 1980 as an opportunity to launch a comprehensive attack on the reform program, with the SEZ issue being one of their major targets. Chen Yun and his opposition faction used China's financial deficits and the imposition of martial law in Poland as warnings to call for the slowdown of the SEZ policy. In response, Deng compromised. His position was: "The SEZ policies in Guangdong and Fujian should continue, although at a slower pace." Throughout the meeting, Hu kept silent. Afterward, he stated that more investigation was needed on the issue. In late December, Fan Ruoyu, Sun Changjiang, Wang Guixiu, and I (all from the Central Party School) traveled to Shenzhen to investigate. We were all greatly impressed by the city's development through utilization of foreign capital and concluded that when domestic capital is not sufficient, the economy should try to attract foreign capital. We immediately wrote a report based on this observation, entitled "The Pace of SEZ Development Must Quicken," which was implicitly directed against the decision made at the central work conference. Hu read and transmitted the report to Gu Mu, the member of the State Council in charge of SEZ affairs. Simultaneously, he also sent the report to Guangdong and Fujian. Wu Nansheng, a member of the Guangdong Party Committee in charge of SEZ work, and Xiang Nan, the first party secretary of Fujian, later told me that the report sent by Hu helped in addressing the dilemmas created by the work conference decision.

In April 1981, Sun Changjiang, Wu Mingyu (of the state Science and Technology Commission), and I went to Xiamen for further investigation. After speaking with Xiang Nan, we wrote a report called "The SEZ Issue in Xiamen, Fujian." This report proposed enlarging the SEZ from the 2.1 square kilometers in the Huli area to the entire territory of Xiamen island, which covers 123 square kilometers. Furthermore, we recommended implementing an "open door" policy similar to that of Singapore and Hong Kong in order to attract foreign capital and developing Xiamen as free trade port, gradually building it into an international economic and cultural center to compete with Singapore and Hong Kong. Along with the report, we compiled a research thesis entitled "To Stimulate Our Country's Modernization by Utilizing the Merits of Capitalism through the Form of State Capitalism." Hu was satisfied with both the report and the thesis. He transmitted the report to Gu Mu and asked me to proofread it before sending it to the Central Committee. His comment on the report dated May 25, 1981, was: "It appears to me that their opinions are reasonable. Please ask the comrades in charge of this matter to follow up on the issue."

His comment to me on the thesis on the same day was: "I have already sent the report to Gu Mu to follow up the issue. Regarding your thesis, please send me a final proof after correcting it. I wish to comment on it and send it to the comrades in the Politburo and Secretariat, and other relevant comrades. This thesis is very helpful."

A few days later, he commented a second time, "This thesis is relatively rich in content with valuable opinions. I suggest that you also send it to Deng Xiaoping, Chen Yun, [Li] Xiannian, [Zhao] Ziyang, the secretaries of the Secretariat, and the vice premiers to read."

I later sent the report and thesis along with Hu's comments to Xiang Nan. On June 2, he replied:

> I received your letters and materials and finished reading them both in one sitting. Regarding the SEZ policy that causes so much ideological debate, we need to continually keep up research and experiment on a practical and theoretical basis. We can say without exaggeration that these materials are more important than the investments themselves.
>
> Therefore, I have copied both materials. Sorry I didn't tell you in advance, but please understand that I don't mean to expose a "secret" or to show disrespect to the original author.
>
> And although I don't place much hope in the Beijing meeting, I do however believe that things will improve gradually. The people will not allow us to move backward. Do we wish to constantly trail behind Taiwan? Without a strong economy, we can't speak of many things, including superiority.
>
> Your efforts there will stimulate the development of the "newborn" things. I'm looking forward to having more information from you; it needn't be limited to the SEZ issue.

At that time, the State Council was holding an SEZ work conference (the Beijing meeting referred to by Xiang Nan) presided over by Gu Mu. Hu intended to use these materials to have a positive influence on the meeting. However, Gu did not respond actively because he knew that the Chen Yun faction was preparing to launch an attack on the SEZs, which is what Xiang meant when he said, "I don't have much hope."

As Hu was sending out the above materials, Hu Qiaomu and Deng Liqun were also preparing their own. They wrote an essay called "The Concessions in Chinese History," describing the SEZs as "concessions" and "traitorous activities." They also claimed that "a central leader [meaning Chen Yun] wishes to abolish the SEZs." On July 5, 1981, when the Secretariat held a meeting to discuss the "SEZ work meeting summary," the two men criticized the materials transmitted by Hu Yaobang, stating:

> Today, after we have practiced socialism for thirty years and after we have moved from the new democratic period to the socialist period, there are still some who talk of state capitalism. They improperly connect the adoption of special policies and flexible regulations with state capitalism. This will certainly lead to ideological chaos.

These words were added retroactively to the "summary."

In a later response to the Chen Yun faction's attack, on January 14, 1982, Hu Yaobang made a speech during a Secretariat meeting entitled "Regarding External Economic Relations." He pointed out the need to utilize two resources—domestic and foreign—and to open two markets—again, domestic and foreign. And finally, he called for mastering two skills: organizing domestic development and dealing with external economic relations. Unfortunately, however, he did not gain the support of Deng Xiaoping and Zhao Ziyang. Meanwhile, the State Planning Commission, controlled by Chen Yun, still frequently interfered with the SEZs. On May 17, 1982, Xiang Nan wrote to me:

> Recently we have received much guidance and regulation from the center. According to them, the special policies are to be virtually abolished. The guidance is not only completely different from what Hu spoke of in his speech, but is also different from the center's guidance two years before. This guidance will eliminate the minor progress which we have achieved since the third plenary session.

From this episode, we can see that although Chen Yun did not openly call for the abolition of SEZs, he did work behind the scenes for their abolition. This situation didn't change until the second half of 1983 when the "anti–spiritual pollution" movement caused the entire country and the rest of the world to have strong doubts about China's reforms. It was at that instance that Deng Xiaoping finally began to intervene. He embarked on a southern Spring Festival trip in January 1984, choosing the three SEZs in Guangdong and Fujian, and the Bao Gang Iron and Steel Factory in Shanghai as his destinations. While traveling, he praised the positive results of the "open door" policy and after returning to Beijing called for the increase of the number of "open" cities.

Consequently, in March 1984, the Secretariat and the State Council jointly held a conference to discuss the opening of fourteen coastal cities. Chen Yun refused to attend the conference, adding that he would not visit any SEZs either. But his boycott was in vain. The Secretariat provided Hu with a useful forum and resources for limiting and countering the power of elders, the Politburo, and the State Council, thereby defending reform from attack.

Reflections on the Problem of Inner-Party Democracy

From the history of the Secretariat, one can see the difficulties in establishing inner-party democracy in the CCP. The establishment of the Central Secretariat system in both the Mao Zedong and Deng Xiaoping eras was a political reform aimed at changing the Stalinist totalitarian system—but both efforts failed. The failures cannot be imputed merely to a certain leader's personal will because the leaders were constrained by other political forces. One must note that, within the CCP, conservative forces have always resisted reform.

When Mao established the Secretariat system in 1956, he also proposed the principles of the "double hundreds" (cultural liberalization) and "ten great relationships" (economic liberalization), all directed against the Stalinist political, economic, and cultural systems. When Mao first appealed to the local provinces with these principles, 90 percent of them did not support his ideas. But when Mao turned against the "rightists" in 1957, 90 percent of the localities immediately supported him.

In 1980 Deng reestablished the Secretariat and proposed political reforms for the party and government leadership structure. Specifically, he sought to systematize and legalize great democracy so as to reform the authoritarian tradition of the CCP. Yet all his reform proposals met with fierce resistance from the Chen Yun faction. Thus Deng was forced to give up political reform and turn against "bourgeois liberalism."

From 1980 to 1987, when Hu Yaobang was general secretary of Deng Xiaoping's "empire," he attempted to establish a system within the party to replace the traditional autocratic rule and "palace conspiracy-type politics." The establishment of the Secretariat was one of his experiments. And even though he eventually failed because of suppression by the two patriarchs (Deng and Chen) in support of the conspiracies of party elders Deng Liqun, Hu Qiaomu, and Wang Zhen, Hu's efforts were still significant.

Hu's attempts at reform indicate that this system under the Communist "empire" has the potential to evolve peacefully. Hu and Deng had shared common views during the early 1980s on this point. And the establishment of the Secretariat was a direct result of this commonality.

One difficulty is that the old system inherently resists any political or economic reforms. In China, the traditional influence of authoritarian elders such as Deng and Chen, coupled with "palace conspiracy" politics, is especially strong. Therefore, unlike in the former Soviet Union, political reform in China will face even stronger resistance than economic reform. Only if a relative balance is maintained among the top leaders can this resistance be overcome and peaceful evolution result.

One factor that played into the failure of political reform was the isolation of the party's reform forces from the masses, whereas the socioeconomic forces released by the implementation of household responsibility policies and the development of rural enterprises greatly contributed to the success of economic reform. The alignment between the economic reformers and the masses has forced the Chen Yun faction gradually to retreat, though the struggle still continues. However, on political reform, ever since the December 1980 central work conference when the movement against "bourgeois liberalism" was launched, a full and steady alignment between political reformers and the masses has been impossible. Hu's tragedy lay in the fact that he did not depend on the support of social forces during the second half of his tenure as general secretary. As a result, he became politically weak and vulnerable, eventually falling victim to political autocracy. The lesson of Hu's loss of power and the June Fourth upheaval is that the basis for Chinese political reform must be the social democratic forces, not only the social elites.

Notes

1. The Secretariat of the Seventh National Party Congress (1945–56) had been the highest power center of the Chinese Communist Party. Members were Mao Zedong, Liu Shaoqi, Zhou Enlai, Zhu De, and Ren Bishi (Chen Yun was recruited after Ren Bishi's death). However, there was no general secretary. Day-to-day business and routine meetings were administered by the chairman of the Central Committee and its Politburo, Mao Zedong. In reality, the Secretariat functioned as the Standing Committee of the Politburo, being the highest power center and enjoying the power of both decision-making and executive authority. This system lasted until 1956, when it experienced its first major change.

2. Although one school of thought in the United States believes that Liu Shaoqi and Deng Xiaoping began challenging Mao as early as the Eighth National Party Congress, this was not the case, in my opinion. The conflict between Mao and Liu actually began in 1962, not before then.

3

"Documentary Politics": Hypotheses, Process, and Case Studies

Guoguang Wu

This chapter explores the process of formulating a political document (*wenjian*) at the top level of the Chinese political system and offers the following hypotheses: (1) The Chinese Communist regime operates by directives from the top, which are mainly given expression in documents, in contrast to Western democracy, which operates through constitution and law; (2) Chinese politics in this sense is "documentary politics," in which a group of leaders—an oligarchy—builds consensus, formalizes personal preferences, and gains ideological legitimacy by means of formulating a political document; (3) The formulation of a document is a central part of the policy-making process;[1] (4) The formulation process technically consists of seven stages, including initiation, drafter selection, top-down directives, research and writing, revising, approval, and dissemination; (5) A document that passes through these seven stages enjoys, both symbolically and administratively, authority in Chinese politics.

Two cases are presented to test and illuminate these hypotheses. The first case is the speech given by Zhao Ziyang, then premier and acting general secretary of the Chinese Communist Party (CCP), on May 13, 1987. This speech signaled the end of the "anti–bourgeois liberalism" campaign, which was launched in January with the forced resignation of party chief Hu Yaobang. The second case is the work report of the Politburo to the second plenum of the Thirteenth Central Committee of the CCP in March 1988, also given by Zhao. The author of this chapter drafted, or took part in drafting, these documents.

Defining Concepts: "Document" and "Documentary Politics"

The term *document* used here is not ideal, since in Chinese politics, the concept of *wenjian* has a much broader meaning than the word that is its closest English counterpart. Politically, *wenjian* covers all kinds of official paperwork produced by the governing bodies, distinguished from personal papers, media publications, and other kinds of nongovernmental documents.[2]

Such documents in China can be roughly divided into three categories: political, administrative, and information documents. A given document may perform all three functions of setting political principles, guiding daily administration, and offering information, but the different categories can be subdivided conceptually. Essentially, a "political document," the focus of this chapter, differs from the other forms in two ways: 1) it always discusses principal issues in politics; and 2) it sets basic guidelines for administration.

An early study of political documents focused on a specific series of important political documents produced by the Party Central Committee (*zhonggong zhongyang wenjian*). The study described "central documents" and defined them thus:

> This is the series of documents through which the top Party leadership directly communicates with the rest of the political system. . . . The Central Documents is only one of a number of streams of documents that flow from Central to local authorities in China. The documents in each of these series are numbered *seriatim* starting with the number 1 each calendar year. They are also labeled with a *pien-hao* [*bien-hao,* serial number] that indicates the institution that issues them. *Chung-fa* [*Zhongfa*] is the Chinese label currently used for Central Documents.[3]

In this chapter, however, the concept of "central document" is not as limited. As long as paperwork is formally and substantially discussed and approved by a central decision-making body, it is considered a central document. Such a document may be publicized in different ways, depending mainly on the appropriate administrative body, although political considerations also may be involved. From this standpoint, the numbered series labeled "*Zhongfa*" represent only one means of dissemination, though usually it is the most authoritative means. Other methods include a top leader delivering a speech, a news announcement through official media, and circulating other numbered series with various labels.

Certainly, many speeches of leaders that are not discussed and officially approved by the center should not be seen as central documents. The very important distinction in Chinese politics between the personal opinions of top leaders and official documents indicates that the Chinese regime ideally is not an autocracy, but an oligarchy. In Chinese political terms, it is a "collective leadership" (*jiti lingdao*), not a personal dictatorship (*geren zhuanduan*).[4] Only the collective leadership is legitimate, and a personal dictatorship is likely to be challenged (though it is also likely to be produced) by the regime. So it is important even for a hegemonic leader to transfer his personal preferences into collectively endorsed documents. How powerful a leader is amounts to how often and to what extent he influences document formulation and is able to express his political viewpoints and policy preferences in documents.[5]

The Politburo and its Standing Committee usually is the de facto decision-making center—the "collective leadership"—in China, even though according to the CCP's constitution, the Central Committee is the superior power organ.[6]

The Politburo, however, has not always been the decision center in the PRC's political history. From the fifth plenum of the Eleventh Central Committee in February 1980 to the thirteenth party congress in October 1987, the de facto power center was the Secretariat of the Central Committee.[7] Although, in principle, a Leninist party requires "collective leadership," in practice, a Leninist party is likely to be dominated by one supreme leader such as CCP Chairman Mao Zedong from the 1940s to the late 1970s, and then Deng Xiaoping, despite his lack of official title as senior party leader. This situation, however, never means that autocracy is legitimate.

The only way leaders have to establish legitimacy, even such hegemonic leaders as Deng and Mao, remains the transfer of their own personal preferences into collective decisions, regardless of the methods they may use. A major symbol of collective approval is the formulation of a document. So the process of formulating a document becomes a process of politically legitimizing personal preferences of leaders. In the post-Mao period, Deng did not have such charisma as Mao enjoyed, so the autocracy of the Chinese regime became even more an oligarchy. This has been even more true for Deng's political successors than for Deng himself. Thus documents have become more and more prominent in politics than have personal directives. Correspondingly, the concept of "document" has become broader.

In this sense, we prefer to call Chinese politics "documentary politics," which means "rule by documents" in an oligarchy, compared to "rule by law" in a democracy and "rule by a single dictator" under an autocracy. Functionally, the central documents first convey information that is vital for operating the highly centralized Chinese Communist regime; it works like the nervous system to link all political bodies, especially between the brain—the decision-making organ—and the rest. Second, the documents function as a main bridge linking abstract ideology to daily politics.[8] Official ideology therefore provides the Chinese regime with legitimacy, and offers the basic value system for political judgments and a criterion for policy choices. Third, the political regime in China is a closed system; many functions of the mass media, which play an irreplaceable part in an open society, have to be performed by documents, which are usually classified and disseminated step by step through the ranks of the political hierarchy. The privilege of obtaining documents thus helps officials to control the masses.

Naturally, oligarchy, as a regime of rule by a small group, requires consensus-building within the group; the group itself also needs ideological legitimacy. To formulate a document combines the processes of consensus-building and legitimacy-building. It also formalizes the personal preferences of hegemonic leaders. In sum, a document symbolically and technically represents the collective directive of the ruling group, the existence of consensus among leaders, the application of "pure ideology" to a specific situation, and a policy outcome that has already been approved officially.

The Formulating Process: Seven Stages

The process of formulating a central document can be divided into seven steps: initiation, selection of drafters, top-down directives, research and drafting, revision, approval, and dissemination. These steps and their order are not necessary for every document; some steps may be omitted at times, and some additional stages may occur relatively independently from these seven. For example, there may be an elaborate and separate investigation stage. These stages may also overlap, crisscross, or occur in a different order. Furthermore, there is no set timing; the stages may all be completed in one day, although this is rare; they may occupy a year or more in some cases. The time spent on drafting a document does not necessarily relate to the importance of the document.

Initiation

The central issues at this stage are how the agenda is set and where the initial ideas come from. The formulation of a document may be viewed as a by-product of a political decision by political leaders; here we deliberately exclude the initiating step as a precondition for the process of documentary formulation.[9]

Selecting Drafters

Once there is a decision to formulate a document, the leader(s) who are given the responsibility for this specific job have to select drafters. For an "administrative document," the appropriate administrative department(s) of the party and the government usually take the role of drafting.[10] For a "political document," however, a specific writing group is often organized to do this job. The members of such a group are selected and "borrowed" from various organs, either of the party or of the government, sometimes even from local institutions; most are chosen from the regular policy-consulting institutions.

Each of the top policy-making bodies, the Politburo or the State Council, for instance, has its own permanent policy-consulting and documentary-writing institution(s). An institution of this kind usually has a very close relation with the head of its supervisory organ, and rises and declines in influence along with the head's political career. In the early 1980s, the Research Institute of the Central Secretariat (Zhongyang shujichu yanjiu shi) headed by Deng Liqun, was the top organ of this kind, and it became a castle of ideologues who were opposed to the market-oriented reform in the mid-1980s. Party head Hu Yaobang tried and failed several times in mid-decade to restructure this institute. Hu's camp then established a new institutional basis for policy-consulting and documentary-writing, the office of the Central Secretariat (Zhongyang shujichu bangong shi), later also called the [Research] Office of the Central General Office (Zhongyang bangong ting bangong shi), and restructured as the Investigation and Research Institute of the Central General Office (Zhongyang bangong ting diaoyan shi). It was directly led by Hu Qili, an executive secretary of the party and a close ally of Hu Yaobang.

Premier Zhao Ziyang also organized a large-scale network for policy consultation under the State Council, including the Research Center for Development, the Research Center for Rural Policy, and the Economic System Reform Commission and its well-known semi-independent affiliate, the Economic Reform Institute.[11] During Zhao's transition to becoming party chief, he first organized a team to do research on political reform, then established the Political Reform Institute, headed by Bao Tong, to play the central role in documentary drafting and policy consultation on a broader front.[12] In addition, Zhao downgraded the functions of the Central Secretariat and in the process abolished Deng Liqun's institute and restructured Hu Qili's group as the Investigation and Research Section of the Central General Office.

After Zhao stepped down in 1989, Bao Tong's institute in turn was dismissed and replaced by a new institute, the Central Institute for Policy Research (Zhonggong zhongyang zhengce yanjiu shi). Wang Weicheng was appointed as director; he had been the personal secretary of Li Xiannian, an old revolutionary who was believed to have helped the new party general secretary, Jiang Zemin, obtain his top position. In the State Council, Premier

Li Peng dismantled Zhao's network and organized his own team in the Research Institute of the State Council (Guowuyuan yanjiu shi), a newly established consulting group directed by Yuan Mu.

Such institutes often are the pool from which a drafting team is chosen whenever the political patron of the institute is in charge of a document's formulation. At any given time, however, there are always several such institutions, which have not only different political inclinations but also different ranks in the hierarchy. The political leader makes his own choice as to who from which institute will interpret his ideas.

Top-Down Directives

At this stage, information and instruction flows from the top leader in charge of the aide group. The usual channel for such communication is direct discussion between leaders and those senior associates who have been selected to be in charge of the drafting process. Phone calls, circulation of specific information documents, and aides' attendance at related meetings of leading organs, are also frequently used for communication of this kind.

Research and Drafting

Assistants do their writing work at this stage. Continued communication between the group and the responsible leader(s) may take place frequently, by various methods, to help drafters understand the preferences of the leaders. In addition, the group often conducts travel for the purpose of "investigation and research" (*diaocha yanjiu*) to get information from, and learn the policy preferences of, levels below the top.

Revision

The fifth stage is revising a document in the course of communication between the drafters and the leader(s) responsible for formulating this document. I distinguish two kinds of revising: one that happens before the draft is sent to the leader(s) and one after that. Here only the latter is regarded as the "revising" stage, and the former is included in the last stage of writing. In sum, the "drafting" stage is completed by the small group of assistants, and the "revision" stage takes place directly between the group and the top leader(s).

Approval

A draft is now brought under formal discussion and offered for official approval by the top policy-making body, usually the Politburo, but during a certain period, the Secretariat. Some revising work perhaps will be done, but such revisions should be seen as essentially different from the revision stage above. This is a crucial stage to build consensus or win compromise among leaders, as we will see in the following cases. Only by getting through this discussion and approval will a document gain authority.

Dissemination

Now the document becomes a policy "outcome" by being publicized internally or openly. Many ways of publicizing a document exist; they do not essentially affect the document's authority as long as it has been approved by the top decision-making body.

The Case of the May 13 Speech

In early 1987, China experienced a political shock with the forced resignation of Hu Yaobang, the reform-minded party chief, and with the political campaign against "bourgeois liberalism." Although Zhao Ziyang, the top leader of the party and government after Hu's fall, endeavored to modify the campaign, economic reform progress was blocked and the plan to launch political reform in the coming autumn became hopeless.

On the morning of April 28, Zhao visited Deng Xiaoping and told him that the campaign was negatively affecting the ongoing economic reform and the planned political reform. Zhao stressed that it was necessary to revitalize the reform by mobilizing opinion favorable to it. Deng endorsed Zhao's ideas, saying, "To temporarily constrain the liberalization is necessary, but the reform should be insisted upon and pushed forward rapidly." He suggested that Zhao call a meeting and prepare articles to encourage the reform.[13] This conversation led to the meeting at which Zhao gave his speech on May 13, 1987.

After leaving Deng's residence, Zhao immediately met with Bao Tong, his top aide; Bao then met with several key staff members of the Political Reform Office,[14] a group working under Bao's direction to design the political reform blueprint for the coming thirteenth party congress. Bao transferred the information from Deng and Zhao to the aides, and then assigned them to prepare a speech for Zhao, because Bao himself had to focus his attention on the first draft of the report of the Central Committee to the coming party congress, which Deng had also urged Zhao to circulate.

Bao outlined the speech by summarizing Zhao's recent related talks and by adding Bao's own interpretation. Bao said, "Two issues should be talked about in this speech: One is the anti–bourgeois liberalism campaign, another is propagandizing reforms." He transmitted Zhao's relevant points at the most recent meetings of the Central Secretariat, in which Zhao stressed the need for "positive education" instead of criticism in the campaign, and called for convincing articles that people would be receptive to "in their brains." Zhao criticized those ideologues who were "professionals in writing in the past but were no longer reliable in producing good articles."[15] Zhao also expressed his hope that those people who were criticized in the campaign would make self-criticisms. Bao required the drafters to stress the point of opposing bourgeois liberalization in the speech. By contrast, the statements propounding reform must be moderate and tenable. Bao concluded:

> Please consider carefully what should be mentioned and what should not, what would be meaningful and what could be meaningless. The materials used in the speech must be irrefutable. The draft must be tenable, acceptable, all-sided, and high-quality. To talk about the "anti-liberalism" campaign is a precondition (of the speech). We have to realize the fact that if the campaign cannot be pursued, the leadership of the party will not have an out. The comrades who made mistakes must make self-criticisms. This is a very serious problem. How does ideological and propaganda work relate to speeding up reform? The speech should come up with some convincing arguments. Why do we talk about the two basic points? We had socialism before the Cultural Revolution. It was the third plenum (of the Eleventh Central Committee) that raised the "Chinese characteristics," and these characteristics were reform and openness. They are neither socialist nor capitalist, both socialism and capitalism have to use them. The first point should be stressed toughly, and the second point may be talked about moderately. It will be a victory only if reform is set on the agenda.[16]

Zhao and Bao fully showed how the speech should be politically subtle and sensitive; they had to create a balance between the two issues and walk a fine line to get the reform revitalized. Now the problem was how to give expression to those points in drafting the speech. The group preferred dividing the speech into three sections; three people were appointed to offer separate drafts for each section. The author was given the responsibility of completing the draft and changed the three sections into two, rewriting them in the process. By the evening of the 29th, the draft was finished. Then Bao Tong chaired a group discussion of the draft, which was accepted.[17]

Then the draft was sent to Zhao Ziyang. Zhao approved the draft but required the deletion of the sentences indirectly criticizing Wang Renzhi, head of the Central Propaganda Department. Earlier that year Wang said in a speech at the Central Party School that between the "two basic points" (to insist on upholding socialism and to insist on the reforms and openness), the first was the key link (*gang*) and the second was a detail (*mu*). Wang explained that the campaign against bourgeois liberalism would "restore order from chaos and return things to normal" (*boluan fanzheng*)." Deng had used, "*boluan fanzheng*" as a political slogan to criticize the Cultural Revolution and stimulate the reform in the late 1970s. By using the expression, Wang inferred that China should revert from reforms to Cultural Revolution policies. This was an extreme example of how the campaign activists were eager to oppose reform. Zhao told Deng about this in their conversation, and Deng said that he agreed with Zhao's view on the "two basic points" and criticized Wang's slogan.[18] So the drafters criticized Wang's points seriously in the draft speech for Zhao, though they did not mention Wang's name. But Zhao seemed to want to avoid even indirect public criticism of a senior official; he preferred to criticize Wang in private, and he did so directly when he met Wang a few days later.

When Zhao thought the draft was ready, he presented it to the Central Secretariat, at that time the formal decision-making body. The Secretariat held two meetings per week, on Tuesday and Friday, respectively; the May 11 meeting was devoted to discussing this speech. Two key reformers in the Secretariat, Wan Li and Hu Qili, were called back to Beijing, interrupting their visit to the work site of the Dayaoshan Channel on the multiple track project of the Hengyang-Guangzhou railway in Guangdong Province.[19] This indicated how much Zhao needed supporters at the top level.

At the meeting, no essential criticisms were raised except that Deng Liqun suggested adding one word to the quotation from Deng Xiaoping's recent talk with a foreign leader, in which Deng Xiaoping explained why China had to reform. Deng Xiaoping had said that once China was developed and prosperous, it could be said that China practiced socialism (*cai neng shuo gao le shehuizhuyi*). Deng Liqun suggested using "it can be said that China has practiced socialism *well" (cai neng shuo gao* hao *le shehuizhuyi*). Zhao disagreed, insisting, "We should cite Comrade Xiaoping's original words or not cite him at all."[20]

After the discussion and approval by the Central Secretariat, the speech gained the authority to represent the collective will of the entire party leadership, not only Zhao's personal authority. On May 13, a meeting of selected ministerial-level officials of the central organs of the party and government was held in Huairen Hall, Zhongnanhai. This later was known as the "meeting of officials for theoretical, journalistic, propaganda, and party school work." Wan Li chaired the meeting, and Zhao Ziyang delivered his speech.[21] A few days later, *People's Daily* published two editorials based on Zhao's speech, thus relaying the information nationwide.[22] One month later, on June 15, *People's Daily* published the whole speech along with an editorial urging party members, officials, and the people to study it.[23] The delay between these two publications reflected the normal process of publicizing an important document. Dissemination had to follow step by step, using the rule "First supervisors, and then subordinates; first within the party, then outside; and first the officials, then the masses."[24] Following internal briefings on the speech, its open publication in the news media marked the final point of the document formulation process.

The Report to the Second Plenum of Thirteenth Central Committee

After the thirteenth party congress, the Central Committee began to exercise some new rules on "internal party democracy" (*dangnei minzhu*). A major new rule was to hold at least two plenary sessions of the Central Committee each year, so that the Central Committee as a whole, not only the leaders of the Politburo and its Standing Committee, would exercise its constitutional power.[25] Usually the first plenum of each new Central Committee, which is always held immediately after the party congress, is devoted to the personnel arrangements of the top leadership, not to other substantial policy issues. The second plenum of the Thirteenth Central Committee thus was the first opportunity for practicing the new rule. It was held in mid-March 1988, approximately four and a half months after the party congress. Zhao Ziyang, now the formal general secretary of the party, reported on work done during this period by the Politburo.[26]

Compared to the May 13 speech, the report to the plenum should have been routine work; the leaders involved mainly focused on what the specific contents of the report should be. But since the second plenum was the first session to practice the new rule, Zhao paid more attention. As early as mid-December 1987, Zhao began to consider how to prepare for the scheduled plenum, and he occasionally discussed this with his major aides. On December 14, Zhao clarified that the Politburo would present a work report to the Central Committee.[27]

At that time, Zhao did not have clear ideas as to what would be discussed in the report. Bao Tong was asked to take responsibility for organizing a drafting team and making a proposal on content. Unlike the case discussed previously, this time Bao was required by precedent to invite some professional document drafters from other institutions as well as his core associates. Bao choose eight people for the team from the Political Reform Institute, which Bao himself directed and which now had become the major institution to produce central documents for the center.[28] At the same time, he asked the Central Committee General Office, the Research Institute of the State Council, and other institutions to participate.

The senior leaders of these institutions also participated in recommending ideas for Bao's proposal on the report's contents. Wen Jiabao, director of the General Office, and three of his deputy directors, Zhou Jie, Zhang Yueqi, and Xu Ruixin, were invited to share the responsibility of composing the proposal (Zhang was also the director of Zhao Ziyang's office).[29] They met with Bao on January 6 both to discuss the proposal and to schedule a date for the plenum.[30] Later Zhou Jie, as well as Zheng Bijian, a vice president of CASS and former director of Hu Yaobang's office, were invited to help Bao coordinate the drafting process.[31]

Zhao suggested his own ideas for the contents of the report both before and after the proposal was presented. The proposed report covered various topics including personnel issues relating to organizing a new cabinet at the coming National People's Congress in March; issues regarding CCP organization, discipline, and institution-building; means of communication between the regime and the people, which was called "social consultation and dialogue"; reform of mass media; and the new situation party organizations faced as the enterprise law was put into practice.[32]

This time the content of the report was not decided by the top leaders alone before the drafting group was organized, but shaped in the process of drafting, which lasted for two months, as drafters and the leaders and officials in charge communicated with one another frequently. Moreover, the political and economic situation was changing rapidly, so the report had to be revised substantially along the way. For example, at the first meeting of the drafting group on January 13, the report was divided into five sections and the responsible drafters were correspondingly appointed.[33] Then the drafters concentrated on research, especially on studying records of the meetings of top decision-making bodies, including the Politburo and its Standing Committee, the Secretariat, and the Finance and Economics Leading Group, since the thirteenth party congress. They formulated detailed outlines for each section. When the group discussed these outlines on January 19, however, Bao Tong suggested that they add an important and sensitive topic: the problem of inflation.[34]

The revised sketch of the report then consisted of seven sections: government personnel reform, prices and inflation, the coastal development strategy, the reform of enterprises and the enterprise law, the reform of governmental organizations, reform and institutionalization in the party, and nongovernmental social organizations.[35] Some topics mentioned previously were dropped; some were separated out from the report to be addressed later in separate documents.[36] The new outline was sent to Zhao Ziyang again, and he signed his approval on February 1.[37] In this case, the stages of top-down communication, the organization of the drafting team, the formation of ideas, and even the drafting overlapped and were integrated.

By February 10, the first draft of the report had been completed and sent to Zhao, and the drafting process entered into the stages of revision and approval. Zhao offered his comments, and the drafting group did another revision; a smaller group was selected to finalize the report.[38] On March 4, the Politburo, now again the top party organ, discussed and approved the draft. On March 15, Zhao Ziyang delivered the report at the second plenum of the Thirteenth Central Committee of the CCP.[39]

Concluding Remarks

The term *documentary politics* can be useful in interpreting Chinese Communist oligarchical politics, to clarify some key characteristics, and to aid in understanding its nature, operation, and expression. It highlights differences compared to democratic politics, which is ruled by the people's preferences, at least ideally, in the form of law, and autocratic politics, in which usually the personal preferences of the dictator are in command. In "documentary politics," documents play a significant symbolic role in political life and function as a means by which the ruling group reaches consensus and compromise and enhances legitimacy.

In Chinese politics, a document works as a collective directive with organizational authority and offers the official interpretation of ideology as applied to a specific circumstance. It is the concrete outcome of policy-making in China. The process of document formulation opens a window for observing political conduct in policy formulation. At different stages, the participants in policy-making contribute at different levels, from the top leadership to their aides, to the party and governmental institutions, and sometimes to lower levels. Partly because of constraints by official ideology and party disciplinary rules, conflicts among proponents of different policy preferences often take the form of disputes on issues, such as who will be in charge of the document formulation, who can join in the drafting, and which format and what words are chosen. Since document formulation occupies the central stage in Chinese politics, as law-making does in the United States, further studies of this topic are needed.

Notes

The author thanks Suisheng Zhao for his contribution in many ways to this article, Carol Lee Hamrin and Timothy Cheek for their useful comments on an earlier draft, Lynn T. White, III, for his consistent help and encouragement, and Mary Ellen O'Brien for checking of grammar. The author, however, takes full responsibility for this article.
    1. It literally combines elements of political interaction and analytical rationalization together. For the meaning of "political interaction" and "analysis," see Charles E.

Lindblom, *The Policy-Making Process,* 2nd ed. (Englewood Cliffs, NJ: Prentice-Hall, 1980), especially ch. 4.

2. Personal and organizational-but-not-nongovernmental paperwork can also be called *wenjian* in Chinese. But in political life when people say *wenjian,* they are talking about official paperwork produced in governing activities under the Communist Chinese regime. Note the use of "governing bodies," not "government," because there is not a clear-cut line between the government and the party in China, and party institutions actually dominate government institutions in their combined ruling of the country.

3. Kenneth Lieberthal, with James Tong and Sai-cheung Yeung, *Central Documents and Politburo Politics in China,* Michigan Paper in Chinese Studies, No. 33 (Ann Arbor: Center for Chinese Studies, University of Michigan, 1978), 1, 5.

4. See *The Constitution of the Chinese Communist Party* (Zhongguo gongchandang dangzhang), revised and passed by the Fourteenth Congress of the CCP, ch. 2, *People's Daily* (Renmin ribao), Overseas Edition, October 22, 1992, 1–2.

5. A later example is how Deng Xiaoping's talks during his travel in South China were given authority by being printed as *Zhongfa* No. 2 in 1992.

6. The Politburo and its Standing Committee represent the Central Committee and exercise its power during the time that the Central Committee is not in session. Because the Central Committee usually has more than two or three hundred members and alternative members, it seldom holds plenary sessions to exercise de facto its legitimate power, which thus is maintained on paper only. In 1987, Zhao Ziyang suggested that the Central Committee hold at least two sessions each year to do more to exercise its power. [The author's work notebook when he worked for Zhao, vol. 3, p. 33. Zhao first raised this idea at the second meeting of Central Seminar Group on Political System Reform (Zhongyang zhengzhi tizhi gaige yantao xiaozu), March 28, 1987.] This is far from challenging the centralized power structure that is dominated by the Politburo. Even this endeavor, however, was given up after the June Fourth Incident in 1989. Between the thirteenth party congress and June 4, 1989, the Thirteenth Central Committee held plenums three times in one and a half years. From June 4, 1989, to August 1992, the Central Committee held two sessions in three and a half years.

7. This structure was shaped by the power struggle between Deng Xiaoping and Hua Guofeng, the official successor of Mao Zedong, in the late 1970s. Before removing Hua from chairmanship of the party, Deng suggested the reestablishment of the Secretariat to exercise the daily power managing the party, the state, and the army. Hu Yaobang, a client of Deng's, was appointed general secretary. Soon after, Hu replaced Hua as the party chief at the sixth plenum of the Eleventh Central Committee in June 1981, but the structure in which the Secretariat monopolized power was not changed until the thirteenth party congress. After the congress, the Secretariat became an administrative organ that only managed party affairs and the Politburo became the power center again. See *People's Daily,* March 1, 1980, p. 1, and Kenneth G. Lieberthal and Bruce J. Dickson, eds., *A Research Guide to Central Party and Government Meetings in China: 1949–1986,* rev. and expanded ed. (Armonk, NY: M. E. Sharpe, 1989), 267–68.

8. In Franz Schurmann's words, documents function to transfer "pure ideology" to "practical ideology." For these concepts and their differences, see Schurmann, *Ideology and Organization in Communist China,* 2nd ed. (Berkeley: University of California Press, 1968), 21–30.

9. Though interest groups, bureaucrats, or other possible factors influence the decision-making process to different degrees, scholars seem to agree that a few political leaders make the major decisions in a Communist system. When the top leaders make their decision, the need arises to produce a document to give the decision expression, and we enter into the process of documentary formulation at its first stage. Some scholars stress

the role of bureaucrats in policy-making; see, for example, Kenneth G. Lieberthal and Michel Oksenberg, *Policy-Making in China: Leaders, Structures, and Processes* (Princeton, NJ: Princeton University Press, 1989), and Kenneth G. Lieberthal and David M. Lampton, eds., *Bureaucracy, Politics, and Decision Making in Post-Mao China* (Berkeley: University of California Press, 1992). Others focus on the influence of interest groups on policy-making; see, for instance, David S. G. Goodman, ed., *Groups and Politics in the People's Republic of China* (Armonk, NY: M. E. Sharpe, 1984), and Victor C. Falkenheim, ed., *Citizens and Groups in Contemporary China* (Ann Arbor: Center for Chinese Studies, University of Michigan, 1987). Also see H. Gordon Skilling and Franklyn Griffith, eds., *Interest Groups in Soviet Politics* (Princeton, NJ: Princeton University Press, 1971), 19, for the conclusion that "decision-making in its final stage still remains in the hands of a relatively small group of leaders at the top of the party hierarchy."

10. Michel Oksenberg, "Methods of Communication within the Chinese Bureaucracy," *The China Quarterly*, no. 57 (January–March 1974): 17.

11. The Research Center for Development (Guowuyuan fazhan yanjiu zhongxin), headed by veteran economist Ma Hong, was organized by combining three similar research centers, the Center for Economic Research (Guowuyuan jingji yanjiu zhongxin), the Center for Technology and Economic Research (Guowuyuan jishu jingji yanjiu zhongxin), and the Center for Price Reform Research (Guowuyuan jiage yanjiu zhongxin), in early 1985. The Research Center for Rural Development (Guowuyuan nongcun fazhan yanjiu zhong) was the same as the Rural Policy Research Institute of the Central Secretariat (Zhongyang shujichu nongcun zhengce yanjiu shi, later the Central Research Institute for Rural Policy, Zhongyang nongcun zhengce yanjiu shi), headed by Du Runsheng. The Economic Reform Commission (Guojia jingji tizhi gaige weiyuanhui, abbreviated as Ti gai wei) was mainly an executive branch of the central government, but took on many policy-consulting jobs because economic reform produced many policy problems. This commission was established according to Zhao Ziyang's suggestion, and Zhao himself became its founding director. The Economic Reform Institute (Zhongguo jingji tizhi gaige yanjiu suo, well-known as Ti gai suo), was directed by Chen Yizi.

12. The broadly defined function of this institute was "to take charge of the comprehensive studies and coordination during the process of political system reform, and to undertake studying related issues and drafting documents that the Center assigns." See *People's Daily*, February 28, 1988, p. 1.

13. The author's work notebook, vol. 3, p. 61.

14. Zhengzhi tizhi gaige bangong shi, or known as Zheng gai ban. It was the predecessor of the Political Reform Institute. These aides were Chen Yizi, Chen Fujin, Wu Guoguang, Huang Hai, Wu Wei, Zhang Wei, and Chen Xiaoping.

15. The author's work notebook, vol. 3, p. 61.

16. Ibid., vol. 3, pp. 61–62.

17. Ibid., vol. 3, pp. 66–67.

18. Ibid., vol. 3, p. 62.

19. See *People's Daily* to check Wan Li and Hu Qili's activity at the work site, May 7, 1987, p. 1.

20. The author's work notebook, vol. 3, p. 68.

21. Ibid., vol. 3, p. 70.

22. *People's Daily*, May 16 and 17, 1987, p. 1.

23. *People's Daily*, June 15, 1987, p. 1.

24. "Xian shangji, hou xiaji; xian dangnei, hou dangwai; xian ganbu, hou quanzhong." To my knowledge, we do not have studies on the information transmission

(*chuanda*) system in Chinese politics, which regulates how information is delivered in various ways within the regime and in the society. This, it seems to me, is an important facet of Chinese political life.

25. See Zhao Ziyang's report at the thirteenth congress of the CCP, *People's Daily*, November 4, 1987, pp. 1–4.

26. *People's Daily*, March 20, 1988, p. 1.

27. The author's work notebook, vol. 4, pp. 1, 19.

28. They were Chen Qunlin, Chen Xiaolu, Gao Shan, He Jiacheng, Huang Hai, Li Yuan, Sun Fangming, and Wu Guoguang.

29. Zhang replaced Bao Tong at this position after the thirteenth party congress; he was formerly secretary general of the Guangdong Party Committee.

30. The author's work notebook, vol. 4, p. 19.

31. Ibid.

32. Ibid., vol. 4, pp. 1–2, 19.

33. Ibid., vol. 4, p. 19.

34. Ibid., vol. 4, pp. 21–22.

35. Ibid.

36. For example, the reform of mass media shaped the topic of an independent document.

37. The author's work notebook, vol. 4, p. 26.

38. They were Bao Tong, Zhou Jie, Zheng Bijian, Chen Jinyu, Wu Guoguang, Gao Shan, He Jiacheng, and Li Changjian. Ibid., vol. 4, p. 33.

39. See the report in *People's Daily*, March 21, 1988, pp. 1–2.

4

Organizational Hierarchy and the Cadre Management System

Yan Huai

The basic Chinese political system shares with other Communist systems the following features of totalitarianism: an official ideology; mass participation in a single political party led by a single individual; the use of terror by political police; party monopoly of the tools of mass propaganda; party control of the military; and centralized control of the economy.[1] Several key traits, however, have been even more apparent in Chinese-style totalitarianism than in other socialist states: one-party rule, centralized power over the economy and society, and bureaucratic hierarchy.

One-Party Rule

The formal structure of the Chinese regime consists of three major bureaucracies—party, government, and military—operating at five levels—central, provincial, prefectural, county, and township. Within this framework, a system of political organization operates, which is divided throughout society into functional spheres called *systems* (*xitong*). While the formal structure of the regime may be viewed as its skeleton, this system of political organization is its flesh and blood. Corresponding functional party organs and officials supervise and control these systems, which encompass the entire political and social leadership, at each level. The top leadership organs in these systems are not part of the formal, legal organizational structure, and their names are generally not publicized, but they play a crucial role in the real activities of the political system.

At times these functional systems have been called *fronts* (*zhanxian*), emphasizing their function of transforming the economy and society in periods of class struggle, or *channels* (*kou*), emphasizing their more regular role of command and control. The main component systems, each usually headed by a member of the Politburo Standing Committee, are as follows:

1. The military system, composed of all the armed forces.
2. The political and legal system, composed of the Ministries of State Security, Public Security, Justice, and Civil Affairs, the Supreme Court and Procuratorate, the National People's Congress, and People's Armed Police Force.
3. The administrative system, government administration divided into various smaller, secondary systems such as foreign affairs; science and technology; sports and public health; and finance and economy (further subdivided into industry and communications, agriculture and forestry, and finance and trade).
4. The propaganda system, composed of the State Council's Ministries of Education, Culture, Radio, Cinema, and Television, Press and Publication Administration, Chinese Academy of Social Sciences, and the Xinhua News Agency; as well as the Chinese Communist Party's official mouthpieces, the *People's Daily* and *Qiu shi* (Seek Truth) magazine.
5. The united front system, including the Chinese People's Political Consultative Conference (CPPCC), the eight "democratic" political parties, the All-China Federation of Industry and Commerce, various religious, minority nationality, and overseas Chinese groups, as well as the State Council's Commission for Nationalities Affairs, the Religious Affairs Bureau, and the Offices for Overseas Chinese, Taiwan, and Hong Kong and Macao Affairs.
6. The mass organization system, including the All-China Trade Union Federation, the Communist Youth League, the All-China Women's Federation, and various subordinate trade union, youth, and women's organizations.
7. The organization and personnel system, mainly party organization departments and the government personnel ministry or departments at each level. They manage cadre within all the organizations mentioned above, sometimes directly and sometimes in coordination with the other functional systems.

Centralized Autocracy

Within the system of political organization, the CCP may be likened to the nervous system and the Central Committee to the brain, which directs the behavior of the skeleton, flesh, and blood, and nervous system. In the management of daily affairs, local governments look for direction to the next higher level of government and to the party committee at its own administrative level. On any major issue, they take orders from the central authorities. Instructions are commonly transmitted in documents signed jointly by the Central Committee and the State Council. Dozens of Central Committee circulars are issued each year, written comments transmitted by facsimile from central leading cadre, and instructions conveyed by coded telegrams from the Secretariat; telephoned instructions are even more frequent.

The expansion of local authority in the era of reform is the result of deliberate delegation of authority; the central authorities still hold the right of initiative. More important, the authority delegated is economic; political authority is explicitly retained at the center.

Autocratic rule by the minority rests largely on the covert vertical appointment system. The supreme leader has the final say about everything, and since personnel appointments are important levers of power, he personally controls the most important appointments. So the leader, perhaps in consultation with other elders, chooses the members of the Politburo Standing Committee and determines their assigned duties. The general secretary as head of the Standing Committee, in turn, recommends for the leader's approval a slate of candidates for the Politburo, Secretariat, and State Council. Then the Secretariat decides, with the help of the Central Organization Department, on the slate of candidates for all key appointments of ministers/vice ministers and governors/deputy governors, which comprise the Central Committee membership. The leader's approval is required nevertheless.

The continuity of China's highly centralized power structure is best illustrated by the major turnover in provincial party and government leading groups four times in the reform era—with the twelfth party congress in 1982, the National Conference of Party Delegates in 1985, the thirteenth party congress in 1987, and the fourteenth congress in 1992.

Unified Bureaucratic Hierarchy

All social organizations in China are divided into six categories: party organs, government organs, military units, enterprises, institutions, and mass organizations (collectively abbreviated as "units.") The six million such units nationwide come in all different shapes and sizes, bear many different names, have diverse functions, and differ in character. But they all have one point in common: all units are a part of a unified ranking sequence that assigns to each a fixed administrative rank. In addition to national party, government, and military institutions that belong to national-level units, all "units" nationwide are categorized according to their status in the counterpart hierarchies of localities, government, and military. Thus, there are units at

- province/ministry/army level
- prefecture/bureau/division level
- county/department/regiment level and
- township/section/battalion level.

Including both primary and secondary levels for each, there are a total of eight organizational ranks.

A unit's cadre deployment, staffing, budget, authority, remuneration, allotment of buildings and vehicles, and even the size of its signs and official seals are tied to its rank. The rank level of a party, government, or military leading organ is determined by its placement in the arrangement of the "regime structure." For example, the departments and commissions of the Central Committee and the ministries and commissions of the State Council are classified at the primary ministerial level, and bureaus directly thereunder are ranked at the secondary ministerial level; provincially governed cities are ranked at the prefectural level; and county government agencies are ranked at the township/section level.

The ranking of an enterprise, institution, or mass organization is based on the level of the body to which it is subordinate and the scale of the operation concerned. For instance, a theatrical company under the auspices of the Ministry of Culture would be ranked at the bureau level, whereas a theatrical company under the Beijing Cultural Bureau would be ranked at the department level. National organs of the democratic political parties, trade unions, the All-China Women's Federation, and the Communist Youth League would be classified at the ministry level, whereas provincial branches of the same organizations would be classified at the bureau level. Major enterprises are assigned to the prefecture/bureau level, and intermediate-scale enterprises are assigned to the county/department level.

Once a unit has been ranked, it is very difficult to change its status. If a unit rises in rank, then all its subordinate organizations and leading cadre must also rise in rank like "a boat rising with the tide" so that everybody is satisfied. For example, when Hainan became a province and rose in rank from prefecture level to province level and when nine cities were raised from the prefecture level to the secondary province level for the purposes of economic planning, all local organizations and cadre concerned were also elevated one or two ranks. In 1983, during China's nationwide "organizational reform," in order to promote more new cadre and provide adequately for old cadre, many localities upgraded the rank of many organizations. Therefore, the Central Committee issued a special document prohibiting unauthorized upgrading of organizational status.

There are relatively few instances of depreciation in a unit's ranking.

One such example was the case of *Hongqi* (Red Flag)—previously a publication of the Central Committee—which, because of the persistent leftist slant of its doctrine, was downgraded by Zhao Ziyang in 1987, renamed *Qiu shi*, and placed under the sponsorship of the Central Party School. (This move was one of Zhao's errors.) In this kind of situation, the leading cadre of the unit seek transfers out, and those left behind seek to maintain or regain their original ranking. Thus the Central Organization Department has stipulated that when a unit declines in rank, the cadre are to be evaluated using a "dual track system." For example, what had been the Ministries of Labor and of Materials before the Cultural Revolution were lowered in rank, becoming the General Administration of Labor and the General Administration of Materials, respectively. Of the administrators involved, those who had been at the vice minister level before the change were kept at that level, but any new cadre promoted after the change were given a rank at the primary bureau level. That is, "the old workers keep the old rank, and the new workers get the new rank." This only added to the conflict.

Determination of Cadre Ranks

Until quite recently, China has been a public-owned, nationalized society. Aside from farmers and private entrepreneurs, all workers were employed by the state and called state workers. Workers were separated into physical laborers and administrative functionaries called cadre. China had a huge cadre force of approximately 30 million workers, as of 1991. (According to official statistics, there were 27 million cadre in 1986, and another 820,000 were added in 1987.) There are fixed strata into which cadre are divided based on their home unit and the position they hold. From 1956 to 1985, the wage system was based on thirty administrative grades. But one position might encompass several grades and grades might overlap between positions, so one's position was not necessarily a good indicator of one's rank.

On June 8, 1985, the Central Committee and State Council issued the "Standard Wage Scale for Employees of State Organs and Institutions." In July, a job wage system was instituted, and all state employees, from the president on down to office workers, were divided into twelve grades, with wages linked to the grade. This renewed and clarified all cadre ranks and intensified grade consciousness among employees. For example, a deputy director of a bureau directly subordinate to the State Council would be classed at the primary bureau level, a vice chairman in a provincial branch office of one of the democratic political parties would be classed at the secondary bureau level, and a deputy to the chief of a department-level enterprise, institution, or mass organization would be classed at the secondary department level. Specialized technicians also have corresponding administrative ranks; an associate professor is equivalent in rank to the primary department level, and even religious practitioners are ranked. A Buddhist abbot is ranked at the department level and a Buddhist monk at the section level.

All workers are bureaucrats, so the unchecked spread of bureaucratism throughout society is hardly surprising. Thirty million cadre have been born and developed in a unified, pyramidal, rigidly stratified national bureaucratic system. A cadre's political power, economic remuneration, social status, information access, food, clothing, shelter, transportation, marriage, children, old age, illness, and death are all affected by his rank. Whereas a capitalist society is a commercialized society, where money determines everything, a socialist society is a politicized society, where power determines everything—and rank is the source and symbol of power.

China officially is a classless society, but its ranking system nevertheless makes it a rigidly stratified society. In political life, rigid rank consciousness is in evidence everywhere. For example, the newspapers follow a "name order" stipulating that the names of leading cadre of different ranks can appear only in similarly ranked newspapers. Moreover, when cadre appointed to the same rank appear, the order of names is very specific and carefully determined. When each conference convenes, the order in which officials arrive, speak, and are seated is always dependent on rank order.

When party, government, and military cadre die, the room placement of their cinerary caskets in Babaoshan Cemetery, and in fact even the placement in front or in back of the same room, is strictly determined by their position in the ranked hierarchy. The families of the dead fight tooth and nail to receive a placement in front for the deceased. Recently, the Veteran Cadre Bureau of the Central Organization Department settled this chronic problem in a suitable fashion by deciding that placement of cinerary caskets would form an ellipse, so that there is no front or back.

No matter whether a cadre seeks prosperity for China and his family, or seeks to make the most of his ability and to benefit society, he can only plunge full force into the pyramid of bureaucratic ranking and use every stratagem to work his way up through the twenty steps on the pyramid. He really has no other choice. The requirements of life and growth produce an impetus to pursue rank and status, and the underlying intention of all cadre is to get to the top.

One-party rule, a high degree of centralization, and the bureaucratic appointment system all keep cadre from opposing the party and make them unafraid of opposition from the masses. A cadre only wishes to be appreciated by his superiors. The level-by-level personal dependence of the subordinate on his superiors means that cadre are completely superior-oriented. The only means and standard of behavior a cadre can use to gain and consolidate power is to be completely responsive to his superiors.

Highly Centralized Personnel Management

The most basic principle of personnel matters in China is that "the party supervises all cadre." All cadre are subject ultimately to the supervision of the Central Organization Department (COD), which itself is under the direct guidance of the Politburo and Secretariat. The organization departments of the party committees at all levels work under the principle of "supervising lower levels" to keep a close eye on all several million administrative personnel, from the central government to the township/section level. Each organization department creates its own work system to cultivate, examine, appoint, and dismiss cadre in accordance with the policies and regulations laid down by the COD. All procedures are conducted under extreme secrecy. All "elections" are based on much prior groundwork, and all candidates undergo a rigorous examination and multilevel approval system. At the thirteenth party congress, Zhao Ziyang said that the greatest defects in the personnel system are that supervision is overcentralized and uses outdated, uniform methods. This is an understatement.

The directors of organization departments at all levels are appointed or removed by the organization department two levels higher up. For example, the COD, which oversees ministers and provincial governors, also supervises the appointment or dismissal of directors and deputy directors of provincial party committee organization departments at the bureau level. When considering a selection for this position, the party committee solicits the opinion of the relevant bureau of the COD, and finally suggests a slate of names. It submits this slate of names to the COD itself for comment, and thus guarantees the vertical independence of the organization department system.

The director of an organization department at any given level is simultaneously a standing member of the party committee at that level, and thus is an important leading cadre. Many provincial party committee secretaries and deputy secretaries have stepped into those positions from the post of organization department director. For example, as of 1991 the provincial party committee secretaries in Shaanxi and Anhui, and the party committee deputy secretaries in Beijing, Shanghai, Heilongjiang, Fujian, Henan, Sichuan, Guizhou, and Shanxi had taken that route.

After the Cultural Revolution, Hu Yaobang, Song Renqiong, Qiao Shi, and Song Ping all served as directors of the COD, after which each one rose to the highest levels of leadership. One-third of the Politburo Standing Committee members of the Thirteenth Central Committee had served as COD director. Elder Chen Yun had served in this position in Yan'an in the 1940s, and after the Cultural Revolution he was very involved with cadre work, developing close relationships with the successive directors of the COD. He often offered specific direction in organization work and listened to reports. Chen took a special interest in the formation of the reserve list of younger, future leaders and even listened to reports from the directors and deputy directors of the Young Cadre Bureau of the COD.

The Central Organization Department

The COD manages the approximately three thousand central and provincial cadre at ministerial and vice ministerial levels. (The approximately one hundred "leaders" in the seven national-level organs are controlled by the Politburo Standing Committee.) The COD portfolio covers both party members and nonparty cadre, including those within the Central Propaganda and United Front Work Departments. Even though the latter may recommend people, and the UFWD puts forward slates of nonparty candidates, the COD will still investigate before approval.

The COD, like any other central department, has a general office, a political research office, an administrative bureau, and a party committee. There are also the following professional bureaus unique to the COD:

1. Organization Bureau, in charge of party organizations, with divisions responsible for party membership recruitment and discipline processes; for routine party organization activities; and for document drafting and research on party constitutions and regulations.
2. Party-State Cadre Bureau, managing cadre in the political and the political-legal sectors of the party-state regime, including the Central Committee, Discipline Inspection Commission, Central Advisory Commission, Central Military Commission, National People's Congress, CPPCC, and the State Council. Its divisions correspond to the usual functional systems (*xitong*) other than economic and propaganda.
3. Economic Cadre Bureau (including leaders of state enterprises).
4. Cadre Education Bureau, with a division for training that coordinates with the Central Party School and other party schools regarding curricular requirements and assignments of cadre; and a division for intellectual work. This functions as the staff office of the Central Intellectual Work Leading Group and supervises the UFWD's sixth

bureau and the Science and Technology Bureau in the Ministry of Personnel.

5. Local Cadre Bureau, managing provincial leading cadre.
6. Young Cadre Bureau, responsible for the reserve cadre of the "third echelon," mainly at the bureau level with a few at the vice ministerial level but already "in reserve" for much higher future promotion. For example, Li Peng, Li Tieying, and Li Ruihuan were in this reserve status while ministers/mayor.
7. Cadre Political Investigation Bureau, with divisions for historical problems of individual cadre, such as a record of arrest by the Kuomintang; the performance of cadre during the Cultural Revolution; and grievances and rehabilitations. This bureau is quite important. For example, if Zhu Rongji were to be recommended for the premiership, the COD would reinvestigate his background from the very beginning. Access to such background information obviously gives the department directors, past and present, leverage over other officials.
8. Old Cadre Bureau, for retirement, funerals, and so on.

As the COD pursues its mandate to manage China's nomenklatura, there is no "pro forma" approval even if top leaders personally recommended someone. For example, Hu Yaobang recommended a Beijing Normal University professor for a post, but the COD discovered problems during its investigation and disapproved the appointment.

Central leading small groups (*lingdao xiaozu*) normally focus on policy rather than personnel matters, although the leaders may occasionally seek a post for someone in the system. For example, Qiao Shi asked the COD to find a position for the deputy secretary general of the Political and Legal Commission's General Office, and he was appointed first vice minister of public security.

In general, COD operations are very strict and not factionalized. Staffers are screened very carefully, are highly disciplined, and normally are promoted upon leaving. As a result, their opinions are highly respected by COD leaders. For example, Deng Yingchao (Zhou Enlai's widow) recommended her secretary for a vice ministerial post, but he had only an elementary school education, so the COD would agree only to an appointment as deputy secretary general of the General Office of the CPPCC (which she headed at the time).

If a leader insists on a personal appointment over the objections of the COD, the department will approve but keep its dissenting opinion on record. An example of the tensions that arise was the recommendation in

1984 that Chen Yuan (son of Chen Yun) be promoted into the Beijing City leadership. This was supported by both Bo Yibo and Wang Zhen. The COD disagreed since Hu Yaobang had directed that children of current leaders should not be appointed to the vice ministerial level and above. After much debate, finally the Politburo decided that the Beijing City leadership would no longer be under the COD's supervision, but directly under the Politburo. (Later, however, Chen Yuan lost in the city "elections.")

Conclusion

One-party rule, central autocracy, and bureaucratic hierarchy are the three essential features of "Chinese-style socialism." More than ten years of economic reform and political relaxation have eroded these characteristics to some extent, but not fundamentally. There are several implications of these characteristics.

Although the CCP Is Incapable of Running the Economy Efficiently, It Is Highly Effective in Political Rule

It may lack effective measures for running the country, but it is exceptionally good at controlling its populace. Communist rule is based on ideals, discipline, and "law." When the ideals are completely shattered and ideology has lost its legitimacy, then discipline and legal sanctions are the last resort. Disciplinary measures function mainly within units. In China, where there are almost no other employers except the party-state, the unit (*danwei*) system combines permanent residence registration—files and personnel records—to produce effective control over the populace. While these systems have become somewhat more flexible, their essential nature has not changed. These controls still worked efficiently once the situation was normalized after June 4, 1989, and the seven million citizens of Beijing had to return to unit control.

Under the personnel system, people are compelled to conduct self-criticisms in order to keep their positions and salaries. The system of personnel files (*dang'an*) forces people to support the regime in order to keep a clean historical record in their files. The authorities can remove any unorthodox individual from the permanent residence system. Many *People's Daily* reporters were sent to the provinces after June 4, for example, and after release from prison dissident Liu Xiaobo was expelled from Beijing Normal University and his residence registration was transferred to Dalian, where his parents live. "Legal sanctions" are repressive tools used by the police and security system, which oversees social order and keeps close surveillance on suspect dissidents.

*The Vulnerability of Leaders Contrasts with
the Stability of Regime Power*

Contention at the top is characterized by severe power struggles and unpredictable change. Of the first generation of founders of the People's Republic
of China (PRC), only Deng Xiaoping and Chen Yun remain, each leading
one major faction within the party. The second generation of leaders, who
joined the party before or after the war with Japan, was subdivided into
three factions because of differences in ideology: Hua Guofeng and Wang
Dongxing belonged to Mao's faction; Hu Yaobang, Zhao Ziyang, and Wan
Li represented Deng's reform faction, which gained authority based on their
achievements rather than mere seniority; and Yao Yilin and Song Ping
represented Chen Yun's planned economy faction, which is on the wane.
This second generation suffered great losses at the end of the 1980s, because of the legacy of stagnation handed down by the first generation and
early replacement by the third. The third generation of leaders, who joined
the CCP on the eve of victory in 1949, is composed of technocrats who
have been rapidly promoted in the 1980s thanks to a selection system that
selects the worst and eliminates the best. For this group, power comes
before ideals and political attitude is determined by political interests.

In contrast to the vulnerability of leading officials, however, the Communist
regime itself is extraordinarily stable because the foundation of its rule lies in a
solid political base composed of the army, the party, and the bureaucratic
clique, as well as the working class and the peasantry. Currently, the CCP is
still the only organized political force in China. Despite bitter complaints about
the party, most of its members would prefer the party's improvement to its
replacement. The 30 million cadre in the bureaucratic system are the benefici-
aries of the regime, which ensures that the only way intellectuals can have a
share in political resources and put their talents to work is to join the party and
become officials. The system works the same way the imperial examination
system worked to attract educated people to administrative service, thus consolidating feudal rule. The workers and peasants, meanwhile, have no choice
but to accept the guarantee of a lower-middle standard of living. Without a
political organization to represent their interests directly, this silent, unorga-
nized majority still contributes to the solidarity of the regime.

*Volatility in the Political Atmosphere Contrasts with
Extremely Gradual Change in the System of Governance*

Since all the top leaders of totalitarian regimes enjoy lifelong tenure, power
struggles and deaths are the main occasions for change, which comes with a

combination of volatility and swift resolution. Examples include the "blood-less coup" ousting the Gang of Four, and the dismissals of Chairman Hua Guofeng and the next two general secretaries. Opposition factions that could seriously upset order rarely arise in the system, since no faction wants to be responsible for splitting the party. The defeated party in a given power struggle swiftly loses its legitimacy, as it is denounced as ideologically flawed.

Thus, none of the precipitous political changes in China at the top have led to a fundamental change in its political organization; such change can be achieved only gradually and only within the party. No independent political forces or democratic forces within the party itself can consolidate and initi-ate substantial reforms, to say nothing of fundamental change. Autocracy puts the fate of both the party and the country in the hands of the very top leadership whose status, power, and interests derive from the status quo. They may make modifications, but are naturally most reluctant to bring about fundamental change. Only after the deaths of the elders will it be possible for pro-reform forces to gradually dominate the political situation and even then the negative impact of the chaos in the former Soviet camp will postpone the process of democratization in China. The whole bureau-cratic stratum naturally believes in gradual change, and democratization will be a long and arduous historical process.

Notes

This chapter is a shorter, revised version of "A Survey of Political Organization in Mainland China," prepared for the SAIS conference on "The Chinese Political Process in Comparative Perspective," October 7, 1991, and published in *China Report* 2, no. 4 (August 1991). It is included here with the kind permission of the editor, Jia Hao.

1. C. Friedrich and Z. Brzezinski, *Totalitarian Dictatorship and Autocracy,* 2nd ed. (Cambridge: Harvard University Press, 1965), 10.

5

Bulwark of the Planned Economy: The Structure and Role of the State Planning Commission

Wang Lixin and Joseph Fewsmith

More than most organizations in China, the State Planning Commission (SPC) combined institutional interest with political patronage to form the single most important force upholding China's planned economy and defending the "conservative" position.[1] From the fall of 1980 when the so-called petroleum faction was ousted from its control of the SPC until the spring of 1993, the commission was consistently headed by people loyal to Chen Yun, the conservative party elder who had long been in charge of economic work.[2]

As the organization charged with overall control of the planned economy, the SPC had a strong institutional interest in resisting, deflecting, and enervating the market-oriented reform policies put forth by reform-minded leaders such as Hu Yaobang (general secretary of the party until his ouster in January 1987) and Zhao Ziyang (who was premier from 1980 until 1987 and then replaced Hu Yaobang as general secretary until his own ouster during the June Fourth upheaval). At the same time, the SPC both reflected and supported the political power of Chen Yun. This combination of institutional interest and personal political power made the smooth implementation of reform impossible.

In order to better understand the role of the SPC in the reform decade, this chapter looks at its internal organization and its relationship with other major economic organizations, the linkage between politics and the formulation of the economic plan, and the role the SPC played in the economic reform process.

The Authority and Structure of the SPC

The SPC was established in November 1952, according to the Soviet model of the centrally planned economy. Planning theory, planning methods, planning content, and planning organizations were all copied; even the planning tables (*jihua biaoge*) were imported from the Soviet Union.

The SPC is the largest, most powerful, and most comprehensive Chinese economic policy-making organ, referred to informally as the "little State Council." In its capacity as the overseer of the planned economy, the SPC leads the work of the subordinate planning commissions in the provinces, municipalities, and autonomous regions throughout the country. Thus, the SPC forms the hinge that controls the network (*wangluo*) of the entire nation's economic operation.

The scope of the SPC's functional authority (*zhiquan*) remained very broad throughout the reform period, though efforts were made at various times to reduce its power. Before the reform era no formal restrictions were placed on its power. In the early 1980s, as a result of the retrenchment policy adopted in December 1980, the authority of the SPC was even enhanced. In the spring of 1983, as a new wave of reform began to build, the State Council drew up a document specifying fourteen functions for the SPC. Although this was an effort to define and limit the power of the SPC, one can see from the list of its responsibilities that it remained an extremely large and powerful instrument of state planning.

The most important duties are:

- formulating long-term (ten years or longer), medium-term (five years), and short-term (one year) national economic and social development plans;
- determining the target rate of growth of the national economy;
- setting major economic and technological policies;
- regulating state finances, credit, materials, import and export trade;
- maintaining a balance between the amount of commodities and the size of the labor force;
- determining the volume of currency to be issued and the scale of capital construction investment;
- approving and evaluating major capital construction projects;
- overseeing the construction and distribution of national defense industries;
- determining development plans for industry, agriculture, communications, transportation, science and technology, culture and education, sports and sanitation, commercial foreign trade, import of technology, use of foreign funds, population, and so forth;

- formulating price policy;
- distributing the state's fiscal funds and materials;
- participating in the work of economic structural reform;
- managing overall distribution of the nation's personnel, material resources, and fiscal resources.

The functions of the SPC manifest the concentrated, unified character of China's planned economy.

The most important decision-making forum within the SPC is the Chairman's Conference (*zhuren bangong huiyi*). Participants include: the chairman, vice chairmen, division chiefs, and related economic and technical specialists. These conferences are called to: (1) discuss and decide on important problems in the formulation and implementation of the plan; (2) discuss and approve draft reports and documents for the party's Central Finance and Economics Leading Group and the State Council; (3) discuss and approve investment for the state's important capital construction projects (such as Shanghai's Baogang Iron and Steel Factory); and (4) transmit downward the directives of the highest leaders and formulate ways of implementing them.

The SPC is an important organ for administering the planned economy and for doing research on various economic problems. Altogether the SPC employs about 7,000 people, who are engaged in three different types of work. First, about 1,350 people are directly engaged in planning work. These people are organized into 26 divisions (*si*) with over 140 sections (*chu*). Second, some 4,000 people are engaged in policy research that serves planning, such as gathering information, making forecasts, doing calculations, giving advice, drawing up designs, and so forth. Some of the most important organizations in this category are the Planned Economy Research Center, Planned Economy Research Institute, Capital Construction Research Institute, Communication and Transport Research Institute, Wage Research Institute, State Information Center, State Economic Forecasting Center, State Computing Center, International Construction and Consulting Corporation, National Planning Society, National Enterprise Association, and the publication offices of such periodicals as *Jihuajingii* (Planned Economy) and *Jibenjianshe* (Capital Construction).

Finally about 1,600 people are involved in administering other organs on behalf of the State Council. These organs, which are subordinate to the State Council but entrusted to the SPC to manage, include the State Statistical Bureau and the six national-level investment corporations established by the State Council.[3]

The most important research group is the Planned Economy Research

Center. When Song Ping headed the SPC, he was concurrently chairman of this center. Under the center is an office responsible for organizing the day-to-day work in accordance with the needs of the SPC. The research undertaken by this office always reflects major problems in the economy—such as the relationship between accumulation and consumption, the scale and efficiency of capital construction, the strategy for developing agriculture, and the relationship between construction in the interior and along the coast. The research reports generated by the office are sent to the minister and vice ministers, as well as the heads of the various divisions, and are frequently the topic of discussion at the Chairman's Conference.

The Planned Economy Research Center brings together some of the best and most famous economists in the country. Professor Li Yining of Beijing University, Professor Wu Naiwu of Chinese People's University, and more than thirty other professors have been special research fellows.

Leadership of Ministries

The SPC oversees the work of the various economic ministries with which it has a "professional leadership relationship" (*yewu lingdao guangxi*). Thus, each specialized section (*zhuanye chu*) in the SPC directly interacts with a counterpart (*duikou*) specialized ministry or subordinate bureau (*zhi shu ju*) of the State Council. For instance, the Education Section (jiaoyu chu) of the Social Affairs Division (shehui shiye si) of the SPC interacts with the State Education Commission; the Agricultural Section of the Agriculture, Forestry, and Irrigation Division (nonglin shuili si) with the Ministry of Agriculture; the Financial Section of the Financial and Monetary Division (caizheng jinrong si) with the Ministry of Finance; and the National Defense Industry Division with the National Defense Industry Office (guofang gongye bangongshi) of the State Council and the National Defense Science Commission.

The SPC and the Central Finance and
Economics Leading Group (FELG)

This group (Zhongyang caijing lingdao xiaozu) is the highest economic policy organ. It is a joint organ of the Politburo and State Council, and generally has between five and seven members. Because the group has only a small staff, its main responsibilities are entrusted to the SPC.

The Central FELG was established in 1954, with Chen Yun as the head.[4] During the Cultural Revolution the group was suspended; responsibility for economic work was undertaken by Zhou Enlai and Yu Qiuli. In 1979 Chen

Yun again became head of the FELG; this demonstrated the particularly broad influence over economic work Chen exerted at that time. After 1980, although Premier Zhao Ziyang became head of the group, his influence in the economic arena remained far smaller than that of Chen Yun. In economics, over a long period of time, only Mao Zedong could challenge Chen Yun's special authority in economic policy-making. Even today Deng Xiaoping must give quarter to Chen Yun.

Over the past forty years, the successive heads of the SPC have always been important members of the Central FELG, and struggles over the leadership of the SPC have always reflected struggles over the political line within the party. The first SPC chairman was Gao Gang, who was quickly labeled head of an "antiparty clique." The second chairman was Li Fuchun, a close associate of Liu Shaoqi and Zhou Enlai. Yu Qiuli replaced Li Fuchun in 1965, marking a political victory for Mao Zedong over Liu Shaoqi. In the early 1980s, Chen Yun placed his most trusted ally, Yao Yilin, in charge of the SPC; their supporter, Song Ping, later became the fifth chairman. The sixth chairman, Zou Jiahua, who was Li Peng's fellow student and close associate in the Soviet Union, also obtained the support of Chen Yun, Yao Yilin, and Song Ping.

The political importance of the SPC, particularly in the period after the crackdown of June Fourth, 1989, can be seen in the fact that of the six members of the Politburo Standing Committee, two (Yao Yilin and Song Ping) were former heads of the SPC. All three vice premiers at that time—Yao Yilin, Zou Jiahua, and Zhu Rongji—came out of the SPC. Moreover, "alumni" of the SPC have been promoted to important positions throughout the central and provincial governments. For instance, Wang Renzhi was promoted from head of the SPC's Policy Research Office to become head of the Chinese Communist Party's (CCP's) Propaganda Department. Both deputy directors of the State Council's Research Office, Wang Mengkui and Gui Shiyong, come from the SPC. Altogether, more than twenty ministers and vice ministers have been promoted out of the SPC,[5] as well as several dozen party secretaries and governors of the various provinces, municipalities, and autonomous regions.[6]

Politics, Policies, and the Formulation and Implementation of the State Economic Plan

The process of formulating and implementing the long-term, medium-term, and short-term national plans for economic and social development plans are closely linked with both policy-making and political competition, as follows.

Process of Formulating the State Economic Plan

On the basis of the general economic development orientation and policies decided by the Central FELG, the SPC first formulates the parameters for the state economic plan on the basis of forecasts and estimates for maintaining a preliminary balance. This outline is then transmitted to the provinces, municipalities, autonomous regions, and ministries as a basis for their draft plans.

Second, the draft plans of the provinces, municipalities, autonomous regions, and ministries are reported to the SPC, which then compiles and adjusts them to draw up a draft plan for the nation. After this is approved by the Central FELG, a National Planning Conference is convened by the State Council, usually in November. The head of the SPC presides, and the premier and vice premiers participate. The provinces are represented by the party secretary in charge of the economy (who is usually the governor) as well as by the heads of important economic organs, particularly the heads of provincial planning organs. The ministers and vice ministers of the various ministries of the State Council also participate in the conference as delegates. In addition, the division chiefs and some section chiefs of the SPC also participate. Altogether, about three hundred people attend.

The National Planning Conference is always an opportunity for the localities and ministries to lobby for greater investment, capital construction, labor power, and material, and they are always very active. Although the SPC always has the final word, the general trend throughout the 1980s was for the localities to be increasingly successful in wresting concessions from the center. This reflected the growing strength of the localities, the reduced influence of the SPC, and the growth of market forces in the economy. This trend also contributed to the expansion of investment and inflation in the late 1980s.

Third, on the basis of discussion and adjustments made in the draft plan at the national planning conference, the SPC draws up a revised draft of the national economic plan and refers it to the Central FELG for approval.

Fourth, on behalf of the State Council, the head of the SPC reports on the planning work to the National People's Congress (NPC) or its Standing Committee, which approves the plan. This approval process is a mere formality; the NPC has absolutely no decision-making authority in this regard.

Fifth, the State Council transmits the national economic plan as an internal document to the provinces, municipalities, autonomous regions, separately listed municipalities, and ministries of the State Council for implementation. The localities and ministries then subdivide the plan and transmit it to their subordinate units, whether counties or enterprises, for implementation.

For long-term and medium-term plans, this process—from the time research is begun to the time the plan is formulated and approved—takes about two years. For instance, the formulation of the eighth five-year plan and the ten-year plan (1990–2000) began in early 1989. Annual plans require about half a year, with the formulation of the following year's annual plan generally starting around May. For instance, research and formulation of the 1989 plan began in May 1988.

Implementation of the Plan

After the national economic plan is issued, the SPC is responsible for the thorough implementation of the plan. In the past, the State Economic Commission (SEC) was responsible for the implementation of the production plan and the State Capital Construction Commission was responsible for implementing the capital construction plan. Later, both organs were abolished and absorbed by the SPC (though in 1990 the SEC was resurrected as the State Planning Office, which in 1993 evolved into the State Economic and Trade Commission).

The SPC oversees implementation of the plan through the monitoring of statistics and inspections. Subordinate units are required to make frequent reports on the progress and circumstances of plan implementation, which are sent through the State Statistical Bureau to the SPC, which then collates the information and analyzes the situation, immediately handling any problems that arise. In addition, the various divisions of the SPC organize personnel from the various ministries to investigate the implementation of the plan and solve problems in the large and medium-size construction projects and key mines and enterprises. A responsible official from the SPC might spend four to five months a year traveling throughout the country, solving problems and compiling statistics and background materials.

Relationship between the Plan and Policy

The state economic plan and economic policy are closely related, and they are always formulated at the same time. For instance, in 1979 the state plan emphasized developing agriculture, planning that agriculture would develop between 5 and 6 percent (it normally grows around 4 percent). In order to attain this goal, as the SPC was drawing up the plan it also formulated four economic policies that were essential to its realization. These were to: (1) raise the procurement prices of sixteen agricultural products, including grain, cotton, oilseed plants, and pork, in order to stimulate the peasants' enthusiasm; (2) grant subsidies to offset the losses caused by not raising the corresponding selling prices of grain, cotton, and so forth; (3) give a subsidy of five yuan per month to every worker to subsidize nonstaple foods (such as fish, meat, eggs, and vegetables); and (4) give 40 percent of the workers an average wage increase of one grade.

Planning and Political Conflict

Formulating and revising the plan is inextricably linked with political conflict. An extreme example occurred in 1965, when Mao Zedong totally negated the state economic plan with one speech. In 1963–64, the SPC, led by Li Fuchun, formulated the third five-year plan (1966–70) according to the Central Committee's policy of "readjustment, consolidation, filling out, and raising" in order to continue to mitigate the results of the economic disaster brought about by the Great Leap Forward. The plan placed primary emphasis on developing agriculture, light industry, and the standard of living, while relegating national defense to a secondary position. This plan was passed by the National Planning Conference and the party's Central Work Conference in 1964.

In 1965, at the Hangzhou Conference, however, Mao Zedong, after listening to a report from Yu Qiuli, declared that it was necessary to prepare to fight a war and that factories along the coast and in large cities should be moved to the "Third Front" areas of the Southwest and Northwest. Newly established factories should be primarily constructed in "Third Front" areas. It was necessary to scatter them, place them in mountains, and place them in caves. It was necessary first of all to strengthen national defense and to subordinate agricultural investment to the construction of the "Third Front" in the interior.

Mao decided to have Yu Qiuli organize the "little planning commission" (*xiao jiwei*) to replace the SPC and to formulate a new third five-year plan that would put the priority on preparing for war, the development of national defense industries, and accelerating the construction of the "third front" (an interior industrial base). A comprehensive movement to move industries and transportation and communication lines inland, which began in 1966, caused tremendous waste in production and chaos in distribution. In 1977 and 1978, the SPC undertook an investigation of the losses caused by the Third Front and determined that direct losses (referring to ineffective investment) exceeded 150 billion yuan (more than US $50 billion). Indirect losses were two to three times as great.[7]

A less extreme example of political pressure on the SPC came in the winter of 1975. That year, the destruction wrought by the Cultural Revolution caused the economy to contract. The annual New Year's editorial in

Renmin ribao (People's Daily), however, had to proclaim that economic progress had been made. On the evening of December 31, members of the SPC were at Qianmen Restaurant, where the National Planning Conference was still in session. At 10:00 P.M., as people were preparing to celebrate the New Year, Politburo members Wang Hongwen and Zhang Chunqiao called the responsible officials of the SPC and demanded that their report of negative growth be changed within the hour to one of positive growth. Under such political pressure, the SPC revised its report to state that the economy had grown 0.056 percent, and thus the editorial in the next day's *Renmin ribao* could state that the rate of growth of the national economy was somewhat greater than it had been the previous year. Such falsification of statistics continues to the present. The needs of the political leadership dictate whether the economic growth rate figures are routinely adjusted up or down by 1–2 percentage points.

The SPC and the Reform of the Economic Structure

The essence of economic structural reform is precisely to reduce the concentration of authority at the center, that is, to weaken the planning system and the authority of the SPC. Because reform was the main trend of the 1980s and economic changes were taking place throughout society, the SPC could not adopt an obstructionist position and directly oppose reform. Thus, at times it had to yield to economic developments and political pressures and compromise with reform, but at other times it was able to distort various reforms to maintain its own position or to oppose reform in the name of restoring economic order. Particularly when economic reform had an adverse affect on the planned economy, the SPC clung to Chen Yun's line that the "planned economy is primary, the market economy is supplementary," allowing reform to operate only within a limited scope.

With regard to rural reform in the late 1970s, the SPC played both a positive and a negative role. The SPC took an active role in criticizing the Gang of Four, including the agricultural policies that had been implemented in the 1960s and 1970s. Starting in 1978, the Agricultural, Forestry, and Irrigation Bureau (*ju*) carried out in-depth investigations of the conditions in rural areas. It soon discovered that the state's low procurement prices for grain, cotton, and oilseed plants undermined the peasants' willingness to carry out agricultural production and in fact affected the stability of the rural areas. SPC chief Yu Qiuli subsequently accepted a recommendation that the procurement prices of primary agricultural products like grain and cotton be raised. Thus, the state decided that, after 1979, the procurement price of grain would be raised 20 percent, that of cotton 15 percent, that of oilseed plants 25 percent, and that of live pigs 26 percent. The prices of primary agricultural prices were raised again in the mid-1980s. At the same time, the mandatory quotas of grain, cotton, and other primary agricultural products to be sent to the center were reduced several times, thus giving localities and peasants greater autonomy.

These investigations into rural conditions were implicitly critical of the Dazhai model, which emphasized ideological mobilization and played down material rewards, and thus undermined the position of Politburo members Chen Yonggui and Ji Dengkui (who were then in charge of agriculture). The new policies of raising procurement prices and reducing mandatory quotas also helped push forward the rural economic structural reform and stimulate the development of the free markets in the countryside. This impact of the policies, however, was largely unintended. At the time, Yu Qiuli and the SPC favored developing agriculture through the rapid growth of fertilizer production and mechanization, not the implementation of the household responsibility contract system.

"Some Provisional Regulations on Improving the Planning System," issued by the State Council in October 1984, is an example of the SPC's being forced to yield ground to the political and economic situation. The economy was growing rapidly and 1984 marked a high tide for reform, as the Central Committee adopted the Decision on Economic Structural Reform. Under pressure from both Premier Zhao Ziyang and General Secretary Hu Yaobang, the SPC was forced to draw up these regulations, which gave greater freedom to extra-plan production.

A similar example occurred in 1986, when the SPC issued documents reducing mandatory quotas in the state plan from over one hundred to around sixty. Reducing the mandatory quotas gave localities and enterprises greater autonomy, benefited the overall economic structural reform, and helped open up and enliven the national economy.

At this same time, the SPC organized a small group to carry out research on the reform of investment in capital construction, which Zhao Ziyang supported at the 1987 Beidaihe meeting. Under pressure, the SPC produced the "Program for the Short-Term Reform of the Investment Management Structure." After receiving the approval of the Central FELG and the State Council, this plan was finally implemented beginning in July 1988.

The formulation of this investment reform plan illustrates both the SPC's yielding to pressure for reform and its ability to shape reform measures so that they do not fundamentally undermine the authority of the SPC. According to this plan, four investment corporations were set up for agriculture, transportation, energy, and raw materials. Each of these corporations drew personnel from the SPC and remained under its control. These investment corporations proved very successful and soon made money. Thus, housing conditions and compensation were better for their employees than for those of the SPC, prompting the SPC to require that some of their profits be transferred to it.

The attitude of the SPC toward reform is suggested by its long-term refusal to establish a division as counterpart (*duikou*) to the state Economic Reform Commission. For years, the SPC had only an economic structural reform section (*chu*) in the General Office (*zonghe ju*) to coordinate problems of structural reform. It was not until 1987 that the SPC finally upgraded this office by establishing a System Reform Division (tizhi gaige si).

While yielding reluctantly to pressure for reform at times, the SPC managed to continue to exert great control over the economy throughout the 1980s. Those primary planned quotas that affected the essentials of the national economy continued to be implemented through mandatory planning and were accompanied by direct administrative interference in the economy. The power to distribute natural resources, electric power, steel, lumber, cement, nonferrous metal, grain, cotton, and other essential products remained in the hands of the SPC. The market mechanism was thus restricted.

Moreover, central finances, central capital construction investment, and credit and monetary powers continued to be under the control of the SPC. Nearly one thousand major construction projects in every sector of the economy continued to be directly controlled by the SPC (via the state investment corporations described above); the economic operation of several thousand large and medium-size backbone enterprises continued to be overseen by the SPC. The continued public ownership of the means of production restricted the autonomy of enterprises.

The SPC was also able to take advantage of periods of economic overheating to reassert its control over the economy. In the 1980s, there were two periods of economic overheating, the first from the latter part of 1984 through 1986 and the second from 1988 to mid-1989. In the first period, the scale of capital construction greatly exceeded the investment scale that had been set by the state plan. Localities and enterprises used the increased revenues they derived from the devolution of authority and granting of benefits (*fangquan rangli*) in the area of finance (that is, more control over their own funds) to construct a number of "extra-plan investment projects." Some even used bank loans to invest in these. This brought about the "investment hunger disease" and shortages in materials. Accordingly, the prices of major materials were increased greatly, and the higher costs of "upstream products" inevitably caused the costs of inputs of "midstream products" and "downstream products" to increase.

At the same time that the cost of important materials was rising, the phenomenon of "premature consumption" was appearing throughout the country. Particularly in 1986, consumers went on a buying binge, causing aggregate consumption to exceed greatly aggregate supply. Commodity shortages (especially of food products such as meat, vegetables, and oil) and "panic buying" (in which consumers rush to purchase durable goods to prevent the erosion of the value of their money) became widespread. In state finance, this was manifested as the increase in fiscal revenues lagging behind the increase in national income.

In order to deal with these difficulties, the nation began to carry out readjustment policies (though the politically sensitive term *readjustment* [*tiaozheng*] was not used). Beginning in late 1985 the central authorities tightened the money supply, cut back investment, and restricted credit. By 1986 more than two hundred large and medium-size investment projects and several thousand small and medium-scale investment projects had been stopped. These measures, on the one hand, cooled down the economy, but, on the other hand, a number of capital construction projects were stopped in midcourse, wasting manpower, material, and funds, and the resulting shortage of circulating capital gravely affected the normal production of enterprises.

This period of economic overheating and subsequent retrenchment sharply exacerbated power struggles at the highest level of the CCP and contributed to Hu Yaobang's fall from power in early 1987. In reporting to the Central Committee and the State Council, the SPC would blame the "loss of control" over the economy on reform going too far. Hu Yaobang was singled out for criticism. Even though Hu was not directly in charge of the economy and in fact was not even a member of the Finance and Economics Leading Group, he intervened in the economy in ways that angered the SPC. Because of the CCP principle that the party is in charge of everything and Hu Yaobang was in charge of the party, Hu had the authority to intervene in economic affairs. He did so primarily through two channels. On the one hand, he regularly toured the provinces, giving instructions and approving projects. Frequently, Hu's instructions contravened the instructions of the SPC. On the other hand, Hu could exert pressure on the SPC through party channels. He would demand that party groups (*dangzu*) in the State Council give reports (*huibao*) to the Secretariat, which would then report to him. Thus Hu stirred up great resentment in the SPC. In late 1986, not long before Hu was forced out, Song Ping openly criticized him. Around the same time, rumors began to circulate in Beijing that Hu would not be general secretary much longer. Though there were many reasons for Hu's ouster, these pressures from the SPC certainly played a role.

Of course, Hu Yaobang's ouster in January 1987 did not resolve the problem of the economy being "out of control." In 1988, several meetings of provincial governors and mayors were held as well as national planning meetings. They adopted measures to tighten the economy, but the problems of "investment breakthrough" and "consumption breakthrough" became ever more serious. The result was the economic overheating of 1988 and 1989 and the great readjustment that followed.

The two episodes of economic overheating and the economic readjustments that followed from 1985 to 1989 were actually one large combined economic and political crisis. Just as the SPC had worked to undermine Hu Yaobang, so it then worked to weaken Zhao Ziyang. One effort in this regard was the decision in 1988 to abolish the SEC and merge its functions into the SPC. The SEC and the SPC had long been at loggerheads, with the SEC frequently representing the perspective of enterprises in government meetings. (Although within government councils, the SEC supported the expansion of enterprise authority and other reform measures, the SEC also had conflicts with enterprises, which at times resisted or distorted its orders regarding plan implementation.) The idea of abolishing the SEC was first proposed at an SPC Chairman's Conference in late 1987. It was later brought up at a meeting of the State Council, where it was approved. Abolishing the SEC deprived Zhao Ziyang of a natural bureaucratic ally and strengthened the position of the SPC. Approval of this move reflected Zhao's increasing weakness.

Moreover, just as Song Ping had criticized Hu Yaobang in late 1986, Vice Premier Yao Yilin criticized Zhao Ziyang in late 1988. At a high-level SPC meeting in December, Yao openly criticized Zhao for taking reform too far and causing the national economy to be chaotic. He said that Chen Yun was very angry about this; this situation could not continue. In early 1989, the rumor circulating at a State Council meeting was that Zhao would no longer be general secretary.

What made the SPC such an effective, if ultimately weakening, opponent of market-oriented reform was the particular combination of its commanding role in the planned economic system, its institutional interest, and the strong ties between its leadership and Chen Yun. As an institution that had enormous research capabilities, the SPC could gather data to show where reforms had misfired and thereby support the political positions of Chen Yun. Conversely, when Chen's political fortunes waxed favorably the SPC became a willing instrument for implementing his policies.

Over the course of the decade after the inauguration of reform, however, the SPC was fighting a rearguard action. Especially in the heady days around 1984, the SPC had to yield ground, though it did so grudgingly. As the reforms deepened and as the problems of the coexistence of a planned economic structure and market forces became more serious, the SPC made a major effort to reassert its role. When the third plenum of the Thirteenth Central Committee in 1988 called for a period of "readjustment and improvement" (zhili zhengdun) and especially following the June Fourth crackdown in 1989, the SPC made a major effort to restore the former prominence of the planned economy. The reforms, however, had already gone on too long and become too deep to be rolled back. Market forces continued to expand even as planners tried to halt them. The fourteenth party congress in 1992 and the first session of the Eighth National People's Congress in 1993 appear to mark a major setback for the SPC. It remains, however, a formidable bureaucratic organization. Whether its organizational mandate or ethos can be changed and its resistance to marketization overcome remain to be seen.

Notes

1. The literature on contemporary China generally speaks in terms of *conservatives* and *reformers,* terms that are not ideal but nonetheless point to important conceptual differences among leaders throughout the Dengist period. The term *conservative* refers to those who upheld the essential features of the planned economy, seeking to improve and strengthen planning (including by making the planning system less all-encompassing) rather than introduce market forces throughout the economy. In contrast, reformers sought a market-oriented reform that would redefine planning in terms of making long-range development plans, forecasting, and exercising macroeconomic control. In the early years of the Dengist period, reformers accused conservatives of seeking a "board and plank integration" (*bankuai jiehe*) of plan and market (meaning that market forces would be allowed to exist but only outside the purview of the planned economy) while reformers sought an "organic integration" (*youji jiehe*) of plan and market in which plans would be based on market forces. In turn, conservatives accused reformers of destroying the "essential characteristics" (*benzhi tezheng*) of the socialist economy. See Joseph Fewsmith, *Dilemmas of Reform in China* (Armonk, NY: M.E. Sharpe, 1994), ch. 3.

2. Yu Qiuli was replaced by Yao Yilin in 1980. Yao headed the SPC until 1983, when he was replaced by Song Ping. Yao then took charge of the SPC again in 1988. In 1990 Yao was replaced by Zou Jiahua. In the spring of 1993, the hold of this Chen Yun group over the SPC was finally broken with the appointment of Chen Jinhua at the first session of the Eighth National People's Congress.

3. These are the National Energy Investment Corporation, National Raw Material Investment Corporation, National Agricultural Investment Corporation, National Electronics Corporation, National Light Industry and Textile Investment Corporation, and the National Forestry Investment Corporation.

4. The deputy head was Li Fuchun, head of the SPC, and members included Li Xiannian, who was deputy head of the SPC and minister of finance, and Bo Yibo, who was head of the State Economic Commission.

5. These include Huang Yicheng, minister of energy; Liu Suinian, former minister of the Material Ministry; Gu Xiulian, minister of the chemical industry; He Guanghui, first

deputy head of the State Economic Reform Commission; and An Zhiwen, secretary of the commission's party branch.

6. These include Jilin provincial party secretary He Zhukang and Fujian provincial party secretary Chen Guang. Li Hao, formerly mayor and then party secretary of the Shenzhen Special Economic Zone, was formerly a cadre in the SPC's Agriculture, Forestry, and Irrigation Division. Those in charge of managing the economy and planning work in national minority areas such as Tibet, Xinjiang, and Inner Mongolia have always been dispatched from the SPC. The economic counselor in the Chinese embassy in the United States is also from the SPC.

7. On the development of the Third Front, see Barry Naughton, "The Third Front: Defence Industrialization in the Chinese Interior," *The China Quarterly*, no. 115 (September 1988): 351–86.

6

The United Front Work System and the Nonparty Elite

Tong Zhan

The Central United Front Work Department (UFWD) is the main organization responsible for managing the nonparty elite—the "social elite" as
distinct from the political elite—to ensure that it is both supportive of
and useful to the ruling party. The social elite refers to individuals who
are (1) "representative" of key interest groups outside the party; (2) socially
influential, whether in politics, the economy, or in academic research; and
(3) willing to cooperate with the Communist-dominated system. Specifically, this includes the 300–400,000 leaders and members of the eight noncommunist "democratic" parties left over from the pre-1949 period; the
well-educated intellectuals and former aristocracy of the national minority
groups; leaders and professionals in the five officially recognized religious
groups; influential persons in Hong Kong, Macao, and Taiwan; former
Kuomintang personnel who stayed on the mainland or subsequently de-
fected; former capitalists; and key independent intellectuals. Relations between the Chinese Communist Party (CCP) and noncommunist parties is by
far the most important work of the UFWD.

Cooperation has a strong historical basis—the alliance against the
Kuomintang (KMT) in the 1940s and the skillful use of nonparty economic
professionals in the 1950s (when most of the members of the Chinese
Academy of Sciences were members of the noncommunist Jiusan Society
and China Democratic League). The CCP has also had a continuing political need to find ways of cooperating with the nonparty elite. The CCP never
could enforce an absolute monopoly of power as the Communist Party of
the Soviet Union (CPSU) did, given the proletariat's social weakness and
the CCP's rural base.

United front work has been a perennial "puzzle" for the leadership, even
before 1949, and success has come only with difficulty; a UFWD director

could expect to come to a bad end, with an average time in office of four and a half years. Current trends driven by the opening of China to the outside world pose especially serious problems for the CCP's united front methods of controlling society. Marketization weakens the CCP's interlocking political, economic, and security control mechanisms. The UFWD had a bad reputation and had considered changing its name from the militant "*tongyi zhanxian*" (united battlefront) to the more peaceable "*lianhe zhenxian*" (unity federation).

Nevertheless, united front work remained effective, even in the wake of June Fourth, 1989. For example, Democratic League Chairman Fei Xiaotong had been severely persecuted at times by the CCP, yet after his rehabilitation still cooperated with it, most recently by proposing that Shanghai be used as the engine of future economic growth. The CCP still manages to retain control over society through control of the social elite for several reasons:

1. The social force of the party is strong compared to other forces, especially of religious groups and minorities. Since the latter are not the mainstream of Chinese culture, they have no true mass appeal and remain largely rural and isolated in the small and medium-size towns.
2. In the state structure, power has always resided in the UFWD system, which is flexible and well-organized, with especially tight control in the urban areas, compared to the disorganization and scattered power of religious and minority groups, especially in urban areas. The frontier regions have traditionally not been of much concern to the CCP.
3. Regime policy is to "divide and rule," for example, using the Panchen Lama against the Dalai Lama and preventing different sects within the religions or the various democratic parties from uniting against the party.
4. Control over information is critical. Whether or not the CCP has been able to infiltrate these groups, it still has very good intelligence and thus a good understanding of these groups.
5. From a historical perspective, these groups have never successfully challenged state power in China (compared to the European situation).

Given these advantages, the party still can meet its strategic goal; to open up limited nonparty activity, relax restrictions, and eliminate "extreme leftism" in party behavior, but to attack if the "extreme right" (the nonparty groups) gets out of line in pursuing its own strategic aim to revive and reassert its own culture and interests.

Moreover, united front work should not be viewed in isolation. It is only one of three interlinked "magic weapons" of the CCP: armed struggle (the People's Liberation Army), united front work ("alliance" with nonparty), and party building. Problems in any one of these alone cannot damage the whole; the CCP still would have two legs to stand on and can use the other two legs to address the one problem area or compensate for it. A good example is June 1989. Despite demonstrations by many social groups, which would suggest that the united front had collapsed, the regime still survived because the PLA and the CCP stood firm and later the UFW system was revived. In fact, political and military stability is primary—more important than social stability.

United Front Work and Mass "Work"

The UFWD does not oversee party organizations for youth, workers, and women, only for democratic party members, minorities, and religious believers, even though all are of a "mass" nature (large-scale, grass-roots social groups) and their leaders might well be part of the "nonparty social elite." However, the same leaders at the Secretariat or Politburo level would often oversee united front and mass work, as Yan Mingfu did in the late 1980s.

Reasons for this division of labor may include the following: (1) historically, the CCP was heavily involved in youth and labor organizing; (2) the CCP places much greater importance on controlling youth and labor, and therefore these (along with the women's organization) are on the same hierarchical level as the UFWD, and therefore at a higher level than counterpart social organizations for minorities, religions, or democratic parties; and (3) it is considered "legitimate" for the CCP to overtly and directly control youth, labor, and women, but "illegitimate" for the CCP to run ostensibly noncommunist organizations like religious groups (minorities are largely identified with religions) or other political parties, so they are run in an "underground" or clandestine fashion through the highly secretive united front work system.[1]

Function and Structure of the UFWD

The director of the UFWD is head of the party committee, a very powerful component as in all party organs (whereas in state organs, the party core group has more power than the committee). He is "head of the nonparty clan"; the UFWD is assigned by the CCP to "represent" its constituencies' interests via other "clans" (*xitong*) within the bureaucratic system/extended family, but also to be responsible for their behavior. For example, National

People's Congress Vice Chairman Xu Deheng's granddaughter was involved in a crime and was sentenced in court, but the UFWD intervened to get her out of prison. Actually, there is a second constituency of the UFWD, besides the social elite; the department's own cadre, with their own special interests. Both types of constituencies are organized and mobilized by the UFWD through its control over personnel selection and the granting of special privileges.

The UFWD is relatively small, but still quite important, compared to other central party and government organs. Cadre are very carefully screened for party loyalty (a high percentage of leaders' children, including Hu Yaobang's son, work there), given good training and strict discipline, are rarely moved elsewhere in the system, and enjoy more or better privileges, such as housing, than other cadre. They tend to be very hardworking, even workaholic.

The first bureau, for democratic party affairs, is responsible for what is considered the most important work of the department—overseeing the eight noncommunist parties and recommending appointments of their members to the National People's Congress (NPC) and the Chinese People's Political Consultative Conference (CPPCC). The latter is purely a "front"; it has no offices or staff, and its work is done entirely within the UFWD. The position of CPPCC chairman is purely honorary, although its standing committee has tried to gain influence over personnel appointments within the unit.

The second bureau, for nationalities and religious affairs, gives directives to the State Nationalities Affairs Commission and the State Religious Affairs Bureau, which originated as a bureau of the UFWD and whose staff therefore all came from the UFWD. They maintain a close department-bureau working relationship. The bureau, in turn, oversees the five "patriotic" religious organizations.

The third bureau, the "Taiwan Bureau," ostensibly supervises the State Council's Overseas Chinese Affairs Office, Taiwan Affairs Office (TAO), and Hong Kong–Macao Affairs Office. The working relations with the latter two are not so close and hierarchical, however, but amount to coordination between nearly equal-ranking bodies. This is because the TAO and its superior, the Central Taiwan Affairs Leading Group, were set up before the simultaneous creation of the UFWD third bureau and the State Council's Hong Kong and Macao Affairs Office.

The fourth bureau, the Personnel Bureau, is responsible for compiling personnel recommendations from the other bureaus and forwarding the department's overall recommendations for candidates for all nonparty elite posts in the political system (especially the NPC and the CPPCC), organizing political education for those appointees, and taking care of such matters as rehabilitating former KMT members.

The fifth bureau, the Economic Bureau, oversees nonparty economic organizations, primarily those affiliated with the National Association of Commerce and Industry, but including other recent efforts in the 1980s to organize private entrepreneurs. The UFWD has tried to encourage new entrepreneurs to join the old associations rather than start new ones, but not being entirely successful, they have also tried to control the new ones.

The sixth bureau, for nonparty (*dangwai*) intellectuals (prominent "personages" belonging to neither the CCP nor the "democratic parties"), is a new bureau broken off from the first bureau in 1987 in an effort to focus on this group, given the many chronic problems in implementing intellectual policy. It may well be defunct at this point, however, since Yan Mingfu and the bureau were blamed for mishandling Tiananmen. As the Secretariat member responsible for united front (including nonparty intellectuals) and mass work (students), Yan was assigned by the leadership to negotiate with those in the square. Given the emergency situation, he used the existing sixth bureau facilities and personnel.

The General Office is the combined clerical staff, assistants used by all bureaus.

The Political Research Office is in charge of studying policy issues, drafting policy documents, and supervising the Institute of Scientific Socialism (used to educate "democratic" party or nonparty officials). Other bureaus forward policy recommendations to this office.

Implementation of Policy

In the mid-1980s, the nonparty elite raised the issue of "saving the middle-aged intellectuals" (from meager pay, poor housing and working conditions, and heavy workloads). The CCP reformers wanted to implement a pro-intellectual policy to gain allies against entrenched bureaucrats, who were dragging their heels against giving out higher wages, hiring and promoting intellectuals, and so on. Since the UFWD directly controlled only the democratic party apparatus, it had to rely on local party and government departments and enterprises to actually carry out pro-intellectual policies in other units.

The UFWD's role and capability are subject to priorities and limits, as exemplified in this arena of intellectual policy. Its main task is to be the party's "eyes and ears" in finding out information relevant to policy-making, given its wide access throughout society. It had several ways of checking up on implementation of intellectual policy, for example. Intellectuals would write letters to or reports for the department; its staff would conduct local inspections; local UFWDs would report back or help inspect.

Its means of enforcing policy implementation include requiring localities to report on implementation of specific documents, and reporting noncompliance and problems to the Secretariat for further action. Its "sticks" included getting provincial party secretaries to discipline noncompliant individuals or groups. "Carrots" included extra funds to the compliant, obtained either from the fairly large special annual account set aside by the Central Committee for united front work or from the department's own "slush fund."

An example of implementation occurred when a major problem emerged in a county in Sichuan during Hu Yaobang's term of office. The local police took a dissident intellectual (a muckraking journalist) to the criminal execution grounds to observe an execution, just to intimidate him. Someone from the higher level UFWD on inspection tour informed the central UFWD; they, in turn, informed Hu Yaobang. On his orders, they talked to Sichuan Party Secretary Yang Rudai, who then removed the county secretary in charge of the local police.

Selection of the Nonparty Elite

After 1949, the NPC was originally intended to replace the CPPCC, but instead the CCP decided to maintain both. The CPPCC essentially became an adjunct of the UFWD, which decides its appointments. Given the lack of historical link between the NPC and the UFWD, however, whenever new NPC appointments are decided, a block of positions for the nonparty elite is set aside for UFWD recommendation.

During the process of NPC and CPPCC "elections," the first step is for CCP leaders to clarify the criteria for choosing nonparty members. In Mao's time, the emphasis was on those with historical influence; in Deng's time, the emphasis was on diversity in order to incorporate all social groups, which has allowed more controversial figures into the select elite.

The second step is "operation and verification," whereby a special working group in the UFWD puts together a name list, and the Organization Department reviews it for approval. The third and last step is "selection behind the scenes for appointment on the stage." The name list is discussed and approved at a meeting of the Secretariat or Politburo and then sent to the NPC and CPPCC for formal appointment. On rare occasions a CCP elder goes outside this process to appoint an old friend, but normally regular procedures are observed.

Political Participation by the Nonparty Elite

The nonparty elite accounts for 20–30 percent of NPC members and 60 percent of CPPCC members, with many in nominal government posts at various levels. Only a very small number have posts with real power, at the deputy governor, deputy mayor, or deputy minister level, reflecting continuing suspicion by the CCP that they may form an opposition if given too much authority. The UFWD and some intellectuals have proposed raising the nonparty quota, but significant change is unlikely. Since democratic party members are so few in society, it is unlikely they would be elected on their own.

Ambivalence toward the nonparty elite has always prevailed in the minds of top leaders, leading to inevitable problems. This ambivalence is evident in "dialectical" united front work policies, such as:

1. Respect ("unite") and use control ("struggle"). For example, Hu Yaobang ordered CCP liaisons to withdraw from the democratic parties and demanded more government posts for their members, but also signed documents strengthening CCP control over the parties.
2. Compromise (on minor issues) and firmness (on major issues). For example, Mao ordered military action to put down the Tibetan uprising in 1959, but purposely allowed the Dalai Lama to escape to avoid his martyrdom at the hands of Chinese, which would have been an unprecedented historical crime.
3. Dictatorship and (a show of) democracy. For example, the CCP monopolizes key government posts, with only nominal posts given to nonparty officials.

As a result of CCP distrust, which severely limits opportunities for official political participation by nonparty figures, they participate mainly through many unofficial channels. These include professional societies, bimonthly forums between nonparty figures and provincial leaders to discuss policy issues, CCP-sponsored meetings before important events such as a party congress to hear outside views, small-scale (three to five person) seminars held by leaders to get advice, individual contact with leaders in a private meeting of some kind, and secret contacts such as with the Dalai Lama, dissidents overseas, and both the KMT and the opposition on Taiwan.

The roles the nonparty elite play at times have included:

1. Political struggle, launching an attack on the enemy of an ally. In the late 1970s, nonparty figures formally proposed that Deng Xiaoping replace Hua Guofeng.

2. Social analysis, giving advice based on independent analysis. One nonparty official predicted the 1986 student movement several months in advance.
3. Influence on personnel decisions. Nonparty influentials gave Zhao Ziyang important support to retain his position in 1988 when he was criticized by elders for the 1987 price reform.
4. Economic decisions. Many economic reform policies were proposed by nonparty people.[2]
5. Maintaining stability. The nonparty elite backed off their appeal in early 1989 for the release of political prisoners when conservatives attacked reformers.
6. Liaison. In 1989, members of the social elite kept CCP leaders and dissidents informed of each other's views.
7. Mediation. Nonparty people acted as go-betweens between the government and students in 1989 and may be critical for future CCP-KMT negotiations.
8. Reflecting public opinion. In the wake of the post–June Fourth crackdown on intellectuals, nonparty influentials proposed several policy adjustments to ease the tension.
9. Budgetary lobbying. Nonparty people are often effective in getting some of the government's "flexible account" assigned to projects or sectors they favor.
10. "Pacifying the frontier." The CCP has made a significant investment over the years in the nonparty elite from border areas, with considerable payoff in stability; very few former aristocrats have taken part in various Tibetan independence movements.

Reform in United Front Work

There was no overall plan for reforming united front work in the 1980s, but there was definitely a reform tendency in operational ideas. Yan Mingfu personally wanted to make improvements, especially in relations with intellectuals, by placing less emphasis on class struggle, although more "struggle" than "unity" prevailed regarding religious believers. Yan also was tasked with creating better plans for reunification policy. But while debates on policy, in which Yan was involved, took place within the leadership and within the department the debates didn't reflect differing opinion so much as shared ambivalence. When confident, the CCP became more liberal; when it felt threatened, it tightened up.

The general cycles in China in the 1980s of loosening and tightening were evident in policy toward recruitment of new members for the democratic parties, with periodic recruitment drives or moratoria. Under Hu Yaobang, recruitment into democratic parties grew quickly and they expanded, especially those parties for intellectuals. People joined for different reasons: Those who had been persecuted by the CCP and therefore had no future there joined in order to enter the political elite. Some simply sought the economic advantages, such as housing and cars for VIPs (democratic personages), preferential access to quotas for wage increases or UFWD assistance in negotiating additional subsidies or expanded quotas, or help with getting jobs for their children or going abroad.

Others who knew they were too independent-minded to be selected by, or at least to succeed in, the CCP, would join another party for the political protection. (Once you are kicked out of the CCP, you can't join another party.) For example, many June Fourth demonstrators were democratic party members, but were not disciplined and purged, or even criticized, unlike the CCP members involved. They were merely forced to conduct self-criticisms and undergo reeducation.

Tensions in Party-Nonparty Relations

Since the Cultural Revolution and Mao's death, the nonparty elite has been rehabilitated and has had increasing political influence for several reasons. First, the CCP found it could not deal alone with the many and complex problems that emerged after the Cultural Revolution. Second, given the persistent political struggle within the CCP between reformers and conservatives, politicians have sought allies outside the party. Third, most recently, the collapse of the Soviet camp shocked the CCP into strengthening control over the nonparty elite, but at the same time recognizing the need for good relations in order to consolidate regime rule.

The nonparty elite have gone through several stages of reawakening. (1) First, they demanded rehabilitation through the review of the political movements of the past, beginning with the Cultural Revolution and then the anti-rightist movement, with some even questioning the legitimacy of the 1955–56 socialist transformation. (2) In discussions of political reform, they requested consideration of a formal checks and balances system, but Deng Xiaoping banned consideration of this. (3) They carried out passive resistance during periodic political campaigns. (4) They demanded comprehensive economic reform, including of property ownership. (5) Finally, they revived the classical ideas of liberal democracy, launching the petition campaign of 1989.

In the wake of 1989, the party has made policy adjustments to get better control over these groups, but also maintain their support: using the Institute of Scientific Socialism to strengthen political education; tightening control over the screening of candidates; cracking down on secret democracy groups; tightening up regulations for "multiparty cooperation"; increasing investment in border areas and funds to religious groups; and expanding the open door economic policy to gain more support from overseas business groups, especially overseas Chinese.

Over time, the need of reformers for support from the social elite is likely to increase and allow growing mutual influence, even bargaining. Even during the 1980s, the UFWD debated whether CCP members, especially cadre from minority nationalities, should be allowed to be religious believers. The possibility exists that "Chinese-style socialism" could expand to allow for religious adherents within the party. The future holds the possibility of greater independence for, even opposition from, the nonparty elite.

Notes

1. This view was offered in workshop discussion by Ruan Ming, who worked in the Communist Youth League leadership with Hu Yaobang.

2. Zhao Ziyang attempted to enlist the help of nonparty economists during the price panic of 1988. He asked Yan Mingfu to organize ten famous economists to give advice on how to better implement price reform. At the workshop, Cheng Xiaonong pointed out some of the weaknesses of this tactic for dealing with the bureaucracy. According to him, Zhao didn't consult this group until Yao Yilin's retrenchment plan was nearly complete. The State Council was supposed to hold an advisory meeting in mid-September 1988, for which the UFWD was to contribute alternative plans from the nonparty group. But actually, while that meeting was under way, provincial officials were already on their way to Beijing for another meeting to announce the end of price reform.

7

Open and Closed Media: External and Internal Newspapers in the Propaganda System

Ching-chang Hsiao and Timothy Cheek

On the face of it, the function of the Chinese media is totally different from that of Western media. Whereas media in the West seek to act as watchdogs, Chinese media are required to serve as the "mouthpiece" and "tool" of the Chinese Communist Party (CCP) and the government, both of which stress "uniformity in public opinion" and "speaking along the same lines." In particular, this means that media must mainly applaud the "virtues" of the current administration. In public, journalists are permitted only to report good news and must withhold unpleasant information.

In fact, however, Chinese journalists are allowed to write about bad news, but only in secret, in controlled party channels. Generally speaking, these internal periodicals are called *Neibu cankao* (Internal Reference material) or *Neibu qingkuang* (Internal Situation). The public never sees these internal media. Therefore the Chinese media have two faces: open and closed. One publishes "large newspapers" (*gongkai,* or open publications); the other publishes "small newspapers" (*neibu,* or internal publications). The latter serves as the "eyes and ears" of the CCP and is closer to, although not the same as, the watchdog function to which Western media aspire.

The heads of propaganda organizations at each level repeatedly stress that reporters have two jobs, one to write public reportage, the other to write internal reports. Internal reports are more important than the public ones because some of the important "internal situations" provide the basis for government policy formation. So a good reporter has to be "a farsighted person" and "a well-informed" person. During a career as a reporter in China for over thirty years, one of the authors of this chapter was deeply impressed with this rule, which was stressed by the propaganda authorities.

The Propaganda System

The "propaganda state" in the People's Republic of China is firmly based in the ideology and organization of the CCP.[1] While the data in this book, and this chapter, demonstrate the current crisis of the CCP political system in general, and its propaganda system in particular, both systems are highly articulated and grounded in the historical experience of twentieth-century China. The system is in trouble, but it is still operating, so it is foolish to dismiss it as a dead horse. At the very least, whatever emerges in the future will be constructed from the remnants of the current system.

The propaganda system in China is a two-way process based on Mao Zedong's famous description of mass line politics as "from the masses, to the masses." The CCP gave its most clear definition of the role of propaganda and the media in 1942 during the famous Yan'an rectification campaign:

> Newspapers are the most useful tools for party propaganda and agitation work, every day reaching hundreds of thousands of the masses and influencing them. Because of this, successful handling of newspapers is a central task of the party. . . . The most important responsibility of newspapers is to propagandize party policies, link up party policies, reflect party work, [and] reflect the lives of the masses.[2]

This model has dominated society under the CCP ever since. In 1985 even the reformist general secretary of the CCP, Hu Yaobang, insisted that the press must be "the mouthpiece of the party" and that all exposés must be approved by higher party committees.[3] Since the crackdown in 1989 the CCP has reiterated this approach even more strongly.

The open (*gongkai*) system of positive propaganda in the media is well known, but this is only half the system. Material in the open press is intended to *mobilize* readers to act on party policy. The ideological basis for this mobilizational role for the media can be found in the classic Maoist formulation; people are to internalize the refined version of their own needs (per kind favor of the efforts of Communist cadre working with Mao Zedong Thought) as systematized and popularized by the party. This, however, requires the propaganda system to have another, internal, side: the solicitation and reportage of what the masses are up to and what their problems seem to be. Journalists who produce public propaganda in the open media also make reports in limited circulation periodicals (some generally available to officials, some quite secretly) that inform the CCP leadership about social conditions so it can "refine and systematize" solutions to current problems. In short, the broader propaganda system not only seeks to mobilize the public to effect policy implementation but also serves the function of *political feedback* on the results of policy and needs for policy change.

This institutionalizing of the mass line in the bureaucracy of state media in China is founded on basic tenets of Marxist-Leninist ideology. As Professor Su Shaozhi has noted, ideology is central to both the legitimacy and the historical (socially transformative) mission of the party. The propaganda system is justified by Marxist concepts of ideology and is designed to "actualize" that ideology in practice. Marx defined ideology—that is, the system of ideas, beliefs, and practices—as the "second side" of the superstructure. Along with the formal aspects of state power (the legal and institutional aspects), ideology is thus one of the key tools of ruling a society.[4] The Leninist version of Marxism, on which the CCP is based, posits the need for a Bolshevik-style party to grasp these tools and monopolize their functions "in the service of the people." This in turn requires dictatorial powers and "strict and unified ideas." In order to liberate the working masses from "bourgeois dictatorship" the party must create a "new socialist man" by enforcing "theoretical education, direction, and control from above." That is, the party must control the public sphere.[5]

This control of public discourse is rigidly institutionalized in the PRC. Chapter 4 by Yan Huai in this volume gives an excellent outline of the political system in present-day China. Within the three bureaucracies of the party, state, and military, and the five levels and channels of state administration, the propaganda system is one of the key functional "systems" (*xitong*) along which decision-making authority travels. The task of the propaganda system is to manage ideological work on behalf of the party.

Nominally under the supervision of the State Council, the propaganda system includes the Ministry of Culture, the Ministry of Broadcasting, Television, and Film, the State Media Publication Office, the Academy of Social Sciences, and the Xinhua News Agency; under the party Secretariat, it includes the *People's Daily,* the leading media outlet of the CCP Central Committee, and the party's theory journal, *Qiu shi* (Seek Truth), as well as the mass media and cultural establishments around the country.[6]

Actually, it is the Central Propaganda Department of the CCP that really manages these elements of the ideology and propaganda system in China. At the pinnacle of real decision-making power in China is the Standing Committee of the Politburo of the Central Committee of the CCP. The *xitong* report to individual leaders at that level in the form of "leading small groups" (*lingdao xiaozu*). The Central Propaganda and Ideological Work Leading Group since 1980 has provided this function. It is made up of roughly half a dozen senior officials, including a Politburo member, a leading aide or secretary at the central level, and representatives of the leading propaganda organs, such as the Propaganda Department, *People's Daily*, the Central Leading Group for External Propaganda, and so on.

The Propaganda Department is the key implementer of instructions from the leading group. The Propaganda Department not only directly leads the propaganda system mentioned above but also works through the propaganda departments of party committees (*dangwei*) at different levels to control all newspapers, journals, books, broadcasting, television, film, literature and arts publications—indeed, all mass media—as well as cultural establishments such as writer's unions, universities and schools, and research institutions. This should not strike us as strange, given the fundamental role ascribed to ideological work, that is, propaganda, in CCP political philosophy.

Of course, one central institution, the Propaganda Department of the CCP, cannot by itself directly administer control of public information in a huge country like China—not to mention the proper control of "internal" reports on actual conditions. The network of control exercised by the CCP in the propaganda system is actually even broader and more sophisticated. It includes a ramified network of controlling institutions and powerful incentives for individuals to cooperate. The network of institutions includes the professional propaganda system of the party at all five levels of administration from the center to the village. Propaganda control in the educational system, for example, is exercised through the propaganda departments of the Education and Health Work Departments of the local party committees; similar specialized supervisory systems oversee the party committees of scientific and cultural research institutions, such as the Chinese Academy of Sciences and the Chinese Academy of Social Sciences, the formal mass media institutions (periodicals, book publishers, broadcast media), and the united front (nonparty elite) and mass (social) organizations. In all, the propaganda division of the respective unit's party committee enforces the will of the central authorities in all ideological work. In addition, the Propaganda Department of the General Political Department of the People's Liberation Army handles the control of ideology and public information in the vast military system. The party school system, from the Central Party School in Beijing to schools in the provinces, localities (municipalities), and counties, controls the political training of cadre and government leaders. Both the military system and the party school system are not subject to administrative control of the Propaganda Department—they are coequals reporting to other top level institutions. This serves as a check *within* the CCP system against monopoly by the Propaganda Department, but also paves the way for trouble whenever there is a lack of unity at the top level of the party as different leaders can control parts of the propaganda system to push their own ideas and attack rivals.

Control relies not only on institutional authority and the monopoly—forcible exclusion of alternative media institutions outside this system of control—but on ideological persuasion, or at least compliance. Before the Cultural Revolution this system was empowered with a persuasive sense of mission such that even in the face of overwhelming factual contradictions, many participants chose to believe the line coming down the propaganda system over their own observations and common sense. Indeed, they tried not to let their common sense "run wild." Sidney Rittenberg has reported with admirable honesty his experiences in just this form of "autosuppression" of conflicting thoughts while he was a CCP member in the 1950s and 1960s.[7] He was not alone: it made no sense to *think* thoughts in contradiction to party ideology because if you thought them, as Rittenberg notes, you would sooner or later say them and that would bring upon your head heaps of criticism or worse.

In a period when the party has great prestige, this conformity is a form of discipline based on trust; when the party does not have prestige, as is the case now, it is a form of intimidation that, while still working most of the time, generates a reservoir of resentment and alienation from officialdom. Furthermore, increasingly, as this chapter shows, the "internalized controls" of the propaganda system do not always work.[8]

Internal Publications in the Propaganda System

Public propaganda has long been studied by scholars in China and abroad. However, studies of the internal reporting side of the propaganda system have been fewer and hampered by the lack of material available to outsiders. The same system described above that handles "open propaganda"—the downward flow of finished policy to be mobilized—also handles the "internal propaganda"—the upward flow of factual information to inform the leadership of social conditions and the current results of previous policy. Since internal publications mainly carry unpleasant news, most of them reveal the negative side of the system, including social problems, illegal activities, and all kind of conflicts among government officials. Internal publications are marked with the warning "guard carefully" or "return after reading," and sometimes bear the words *confidential, secret,* or *top secret.* This "news" is precisely the most accurate and newsworthy; it is a real mirror of the essence of society, and therefore has considerable value to political leaders. It has been said that "the news in China does not appear in the public newspapers; it is in the internal publications."[9] Nicholas Kristof wrote an article in the *New York Times* called "The Real News in China Is in Limited Periodicals"—something Chinese correspondents have always known.

Because various internal publications carry different contents, they circulate among different readers. Some of them are restricted to members of the Politburo and the Secretariat; some are restricted to members of the Central Committee and those at the ministerial level (*bu*); some are distributed to the sectional level (*si*) and to the bureau level (*ju*). All the local media have their own internal publications, some of which are submitted to Beijing or to provincial authorities according to their different contents. The internal publications of *Wenhui Daily* and *Liberation Daily,* the two largest newspapers in Shanghai, are sent to the central government directly. The semi-independent *Shijie jingji daobao* (World Economic Herald), established in the early 1980s, was also ordered to send its internal publication to the Central government. The print shop, the composition room, and the proofreaders of the internal publications are supervised by a specific "reliable person" in order to prevent leaks.

The most secret internal publications are called Red Headline Reference Material (*hongtou cankao*) and Restricted Current Domestic Information (*guonei dongtai qingyang*). The titles indicate that these publications are extremely important and urgent. Xinhua News Agency and all the major newspapers in each city have this kind of internal publication, but Xinhua's is the most authoritative. Some editions are handwritten and restricted strictly to a very few persons because they contain information on highly sensitive and crucial issues or incidents. These editions are marked "top secret" and circulate only among members of the Politburo or Central Committee. Material from these internal periodicals is not allowed to be published in the open newspapers. Examples of news in this category include the current developments of the student demonstrations in many cities at the end of 1986 and the massive popular protests in the spring of 1989.

All newspapers are required to produce such internal publications and reports. Usually a deputy editor, who is, of course, a party member, is in charge of such situation reports and publications. In some cases, such as the *Hainan Daily* in the 1980s, the editor, in this case Cheng Kai, personally supervised the internal reporting. His reporters spent 70 percent of their time on public reporting and 30 percent on internal reports. The special editions his paper produced included both a more generally available internal paper and a more restricted set of notes sent to Beijing.[10] Major papers, like *Wenhui Daily* and *People's Daily,* especially produce the very secretive reports directed to the Politburo.

The system for delivering such reports is quite developed. The classified channel for internal reports includes a system of couriers—in Beijing they once included a corps of motorcyclists in black uniforms with special vehicle number plates that allowed them to drive directly from the *People's Daily* office into the Zhongnanhai government compound.[11] In Shanghai, a special vehicle carried a sealed box of internal reports daily from *Wenhui Daily* to the airport; in Beijing the plane was met by a similar set of couriers, who drove the materials direct to Politburo offices.[12] These reports are delivered to a special classified communications office within the Central Committee's General Office.[13] Like the secret palace memorials (*zouzhe*), which provided similarly classified reports from the provinces to the Qing dynasty emperors, the internal reporting system of the CCP seems largely factual rather than analytical in nature. Nevertheless, the amount of accurate information this system delivers to top leaders is impressive. For example, according to Mao's private doctor, Mao had a very clear idea of the adverse economic impact of the Great Leap in 1958 despite the fake reporting by local officials.[14]

Another example is a Xinhua Red Headline Reference Material I [Chingchang Hsiao] read in March 1980, concerning the persecution of Liu Shaoqi. I was then a resident correspondent of *Wenhui Daily* in Beijing, and I interviewed Liu's widow, Wang Guangmei. One of the Xinhua News Agency reporters showed me this edition. The communiqué of the fifth plenum of the Eleventh Central Committee officially had announced the rehabilitation of Liu Shaoqi in late February 1980. Mao Zedong's name was not mentioned in this communiqué, which, along with all the public news and commentary on the subject, stressed that Liu was persecuted by Lin Biao and the Gang of Four. This gave the impression that Mao was unaware of this persecution. However, the Xinhua edition, which stemmed from different news sources, reported that when Liu was confined in his residence in Zhongnanhai during the early part of the Cultural Revolution, Mao's bodyguard Wang Dongxing observed Liu every day by peeping through a specially made window. Then, in the afternoon, Wang wrote "a report about Liu's daily condition" and submitted it to Mao, who then read and wrote instructions or comments on the report. Thus Mao not only knew everything about Liu's situation but also instructed subordinates on how to manage Liu.

Even though this kind of "internal publication" was accurate, we could not write this in our public articles, for two reasons. First, we were instructed to absolve Mao from blame for the Cultural Revolution. Second,

Wang Dongxing was then vice president of the Central Committee of the CCP. If we had published these facts in the open press, they would have caused a public outcry. But the internal report was useful to some leaders who were trying to weaken Wang politically.

In addition to the two most restricted Xinhua editions, there are many other categories of news reports that classify the different contents of various internal publications. Some of the "internal publications" are allowed to be reedited, and do ultimately appear in the public press after receiving higher-level official approval. The CCP classified "internal reports" into several categories, according to their contents:

Disclosures of the negative side of society. This category of news report, including coverage of government officials' and their sons' or daughters' privileges, corruption, or abuse of power for personal profit, is generally sent to central government and local high-level officials; very few of them appear in the public press. Yet sometimes journalists take a stand against governmental control and try to report a few exceptional stories in the public newspapers.

An example of this category is a very interesting story that happened in Shanghai in 1979. A high school graduate who had been assigned to live and work in the countryside for a long time became very frustrated. He then pretended to be a son of a high-ranking general from Beijing and proceeded to extort money as well as partake in the privileges only high-ranking officials can enjoy. He was a con man, but reporting on his case exposed the privileges of high-level cadre and the pervasive decadent abuse of personal connections (*guanxi*) among such elites all over the country. The vast majority of people felt really disgusted. When the reporter wrote this story in an "internal publication," he thought it ought to be disclosed in the public newspapers in order to halt the degeneration of society. But because a vice secretary of the municipal CCP secretariat and a famous opera actress were involved in the swindle, the municipal secretariat did not allow the story to appear in the newspaper to preserve these people's reputations.

Finally, Sha Yexin, a playwright, wrote a satirical comedy based on this case, *Jiaru wo shi zhende* (If I Really Were), which caused a sensation throughout the country, even though it was restricted to "internal performances" for fellow artists (and high cadre). For two years the Shanghai Propaganda Department continued to prevent the story from being printed in the public newspapers until the swindler was brought to trial and was sentenced to prison. Then, the editor-in-chief of the *Wenhui Daily* sent this article to its Beijing bureau and asked the bureau chief to submit it to the central Propaganda Department for approval. Finally, Deng Liqun, then head of the Propaganda Department, deleted many details and approved the story for publication in the *Wenhui Daily* first. The next day, other newspapers in Shanghai published it as well.

Exposing units for not seriously carrying out party policy. An example in this category would be a unit that did not implement the policy on intellectuals or other party policies, so that government work suffered or the unit had a negative impact on society. This category of news report, although only concerning government work, has always been taken seriously by the authorities. They usually select a model case to circulate as a cautionary example for officials in different ranks, or assign the editor responsible for publishing the case in the open press to write a commentary for the public. Thus to some extent the media serves as a watchdog of the government.

A reporter at the *Wenhui Daily* wrote an "internal publication" article in 1982 concerning a refrigeration expert at the Research Institute of the Shanghai Municipal Commercial Department. In his early years, this expert was an overseas graduate student in Germany, and he returned to contribute his expertise to his country. Nonetheless, he was long despised by the head of the Commercial Department. He became so frustrated that he finally resigned and emigrated to the United States. This occurred just when a new policy on intellectuals was sent down by the central government, which asked the heads of all work units to give full play to intellectuals' professional knowledge and skills. When the Shanghai authorities read this "internal publication" report, they saw it as a model case of disregarding the new policy on intellectuals. They immediately gave instructions to *Wenhui Daily* to write a report. Its purpose was to promote the implementation of the new intellectual policy in other units. The article had wide repercussions after it was published. All units in Shanghai and other cities felt the pressure to examine their own problems in this regard. This was a shining example of the party utilizing the "internal publication" system in a positive way.[15]

Reflections of ideological trends, or some prominent person's perspective on sensitive issues. The heads of all units, especially those in charge of ideological matters, are very attuned to this category of news report. To prevent negative trends from becoming pervasive they usually take some measures immediately, including criticism of the negative trend or positive education.

For example, in early 1989 after he had investigated the current thinking of university students, a reporter at *Wenhui Daily* wrote an "internal publication" report. It said that university students generally had lost confidence in the leadership of the CCP, that they did not want to study hard or do difficult work; some of them only wished to go abroad, make money, smoke, drink, play mahjong, and gamble. The atmosphere at the universities was degenerating. Certainly, this "internal publication" report was not allowed to be published but it provided an important basis for government leaders to attempt to reeducate young people. As the events of 1989 show, the authorities singularly failed to avail themselves of this opportunity. Naturally, positive education alone, in the absence of a crackdown on the corruption that had so demoralized the students, would not have been particularly effective.

Launching a criticism movement stemming from an "internal publication" report. One of the present authors had a personal experience relevant to this category—the "Débussy Criticism" of 1963 and 1964. In September 1965, Mao Zedong called on party members to "never forget class struggle." At an ideology conference in Beijing shortly afterward, the issues of anti-revisionism, preventing revisionism, and anti-bourgeois ideology were all raised. Yao Wenyuan (later named as one of the Gang of Four), then recognized as "the most sensitive and keen rising star in ideological circles," attended this conference. After Yao returned to Shanghai, he wrote an article for the *Wenhui Daily* with the headline "Please Look at the 'New and Unique' Perspective." Yao criticized the book *Mr. Kruss*, written by French impressionist musician Claude Débussy and published in translation by the Beijing Music Publishing House. The editor of the publishing house wrote in the preface to the translation that Débussy's many perceptions were new and unique. To Yao, Débussy was an impressionist musician, and impressionism was a kin of "decadent ideology," so how could the editor say Débussy had "new and unique" views? This was proof, to Yao, of typical bourgeois ideas as well as revisionist ideas, so it ought to be criticized.

The ridiculous aspect of this trumped-up criticism was that Yao had failed to follow Débussy's meaning in his book. Yao took Débussy's humorous and sarcastic words at face value; therefore his criticism was riddled with errors. He Luding, the president of the Shanghai Conservatory, greatly resented Yao's unreasonable and ignorant attack on Débussy. President He called me on the phone and told me his views on Yao's article. He then wrote a commentary for *Wenhui Daily* indicating Yao's errors. In the meantime, I wrote an internal publication report concerning He Luding's perspective on how we should regard European musicians of the late nineteenth and early twentieth centuries.

Essentially, this was an academic matter. Nevertheless, when Ke Qingshi, first party secretary of the Shanghai Municipal CCP as well as member of the CCP Central Committee Politburo, read my report, his immediate response was "this is a new trend of class struggle," and "it's an attack on the proletariat by the bourgeoisie; we should orchestrate people to strike back." He Luding was then labeled a "bourgeois element within the party" and "a representative of bourgeois ideology in literary circles." Yao, in turn, was praised as a distinguished proletarian writer. Since He Luding had come out to attack Yao, Ke Qingshi said that we should grab this opportunity to counterattack. Thus, a large-scale movement, the so-called Débussy discussion, began in the summer of 1963 and lasted until the spring of 1964. Actually, it was a campaign to criticize "bourgeois ideology" in literary circles in Shanghai (here represented by He Luding), Beijing, and other cities.[16] Later, Jiang Qing said the criticism movement was great; it was part of the media preparation for the Great Proletarian Cultural Revolution.

Conclusion

Internal publications and public newspapers are twin pillars of the broader propaganda and political system of China. Sometimes we would have the internal report of an item first, then we would report the news later in the public newspapers. Sometimes we would have to collect the reactions from people of all social strata after an article had been published in the open newspaper and write an article for the internal press focusing on people's reactions. But all the important reporting published in the public newspapers was first written for the internal press. This remains the regular pattern in the Chinese print media.

Notes

This chapter stems from a presentation on November 21, 1991, in Washington, D.C., as part of the "China's Political System" project coordinated by Carol Lee Hamrin and H. Lyman Miller at the Johns Hopkins University School of Advanced International Studies. It is based on the personal experiences of Ching-chang Hsiao as a Chinese journalist and the research of Timothy Cheek on the Chinese propaganda system; it includes discussion and examples from the participants of "The Changing Propaganda System" conference of November 21–22, 1991, held as part of the broader "China's Political System" project.

  1. The CCP, naturally, borrowed the basic concepts of the "propaganda state" from the Soviet Union. See Peter Kenez, *The Birth of the Propaganda State: Soviet Methods of Mass Mobilization, 1917–1929* (Cambridge: Cambridge University Press, 1985).

  2. March 16, 1942, Directive of the CCP Central Propaganda Bureau, reprinted in *Mao Zedong xinwen gongzuo wenxuan* (Selected writings by Mao Zedong on journalism) (Beijing: Xinhua chubanshe, 1983), 91.

  3. Hu Yaobang, "On the Party's Journalism Work," given February 8, 1985, and printed in *Renmin ribao,* April 14, 1986; translated in Foreign Broadcast Information Service, *China Daily Report,* April 15, 1985, K1-K15.

4. Su Shaozhi, "The Control of Ideology in China" (paper presented at "The Changing Propaganda System" conference, SAIS, Washington, D.C., November 21, 1991).

5. Ibid., p. 4.

6. This information is taken from chapter 4 by Yan Huai in this volume and Su Shaozhi, ibid., pp. 9 ff.

7. Sidney Rittenberg, comments at "The Changing Propaganda System" conference, SAIS, Washington, D.C., November 22, 1991; his stories are beautifully recounted in his recent book with Amanda Bennett, *The Man Who Stayed Behind* (New York: Simon and Schuster, 1993).

8. See Meirong Yang's chapter in this volume for a case study of the *World Economic Herald*, and Timothy Cheek, "Redefining Propaganda: Debates on the Role of Journalism in Post-Mao China," *Issues & Studies* 25, no. 2 (February 1989): 47–74.

9. H. Lyman Miller, at the November 1991 conference on "The Changing Propaganda System," remarked when comparing *gongkai* and *neibu* publications before the 1980s: "There was no news in the open press, and no mistakes" —everything is for the purpose of mobilizing the public readership.

10. Cheng Kai, comments at "The Changing Propaganda System" conference, November 22, 1991.

11. Anne Thurston, comments at "The Changing Propaganda System" conference, November 21, 1991, based on the book of reminiscences from Mao's personal doctor, Li Zhisui, *The Private Life of Chairman Mao* (New York: Random House, 1994), for which she was editorial assistant.

12. Hsiao, comments at "The Changing Propaganda System" conference, November 21, 1991.

13. Xu Yamin, comments at "The Changing Propaganda System" conference, November 21, 1991, reporting on research he and Anne Thurston have undertaken on this topic.

14. Anne Thurston, comments at "The Changing Propaganda System" conference, November 21, 1991, from *The Private Life of Chairman Mao*.

15. Of course, the Party has been less enthusiastic when individual reporters and writers, such as Liu Binyan or Wang Ruowang, have offered similarly well-intentioned social criticism of current abuses without going through all the official channels this case went through to become public.

16. For the broader context of the academic debates leading into the Cultural Revolution, see Merle Goldman, *Advise and Dissent* (Cambridge: Harvard University Press, 1981).

Part II
Bureaucratic Structure, Process, and Politics

8

Mechanisms of Foreign Policy-Making and Implementation in the Ministry of Foreign Affairs

George Yang

China's Foreign Policy-Making

Authority over foreign policy matters is highly centralized in China. Zhou Enlai, the late premier who was in direct charge of China's foreign policy-making and implementation for twenty-seven years, repeatedly stressed that "there is no small matter in foreign affairs" and "the authority of foreign policy decision rests with [the highest executive body of] the Central Committee of the Chinese Communist Party (CCP) with very limited power delegated [to other 'central' party and government organs or local authorities]." This arrangement mostly still holds true. Major issues are decided at the very top by party leaders or the elders who command the real power behind the scene, like Deng Xiaoping.

The Ministry of Foreign Affairs is the main body for foreign policy recommendations and implementation. The Foreign Affairs Office of the State Council, unlike its predecessor before the Cultural Revolution, is a purely administrative setup with no policy discretion; its function is to coordinate mostly routine matters for the top leaders. Meanwhile, the National People's Congress has no foreign policy-making power. The competence of the International Liaison Department of the CCP and the Ministry of National Security has been narrowly confined; the Chinese media make virtually no public commentary on foreign policy issues.

Although the Foreign Ministry's authority over foreign policy issues increased in the 1980s, the structural reform of the economy and the decentralization of international trade and economic relations diversified central institutional interests and raised demand for a say in foreign economic affairs at the local level. This, in turn, required a redefinition of the concepts of foreign policy and "economic diplomacy" as well as more effective coordination on policy matters among institutions at the central level.

There is a large degree of continuity in the general guidelines and principles of China's foreign policy. While Deng Xiaoping has completely abandoned Mao Zedong's "theory of continuing revolution," which focused on fostering insurgencies, he has inherited the substance of the foreign policy formulated before and after the Cultural Revolution by Mao Zedong and Zhou Enlai almost in its totality. So far, foreign policy issues have not yet been central to inner-party factional struggles. The contrast between drastically changing domestic policies and a fairly stable foreign policy owes to the fact that China's foreign policy is based on practical rather than ideological considerations, though its enunciation may be coated with ideological jargon. The most basic concern in the foreign policy of China is national security and national interest. There is a high degree of consensus in the top leadership on that basic concern, though there may be different interpretations and tactics. One reason for consensus is that China's means for extending its purposes abroad are still very much constrained, and so its approach and stand on international issues remain "strategic" and generalized. Most of its involvement in international affairs, especially in "crisis situations" or "hot spots," is indirect.

As long as China is not in a position to seek regional or world hegemony and does not venture to use its military force outside its borders, its security goals are relatively simple and can be clearly defined, and its foreign policy is less vulnerable to internal disputes. The special features of Chinese foreign policy and diplomatic practice lie more in the expressions of the Chinese way of thinking and behavior that are nurtured by the cultural tradition rather than in manifestations of political inclination.

Organization of the Foreign Ministry

The Foreign Ministry can be divided into three main components.

- *Missions abroad*: embassies and consulates general.
- *Institutions* affiliated with the ministry: Chinese People's Association for Friendship with Foreign Countries, Chinese People's Institute of Foreign Affairs, Institute of International Studies, Foreign Affairs College, and World Knowledge Publishing House.
- *Ministry* proper (excluding political work, personnel and logistics de-

partments, etc.): regional departments such as Asian, West Asian and North African, African, East European and Central Asian (former Soviet and East European), West European, and American and Oceanic affairs, where the staffs are divided into political analysts for situation evaluation and policy recommendation, and general practitioners for diplomatic case operations; functional departments such as protocol, information, consular, international organizations, and international laws and treaties; special departments such as Taiwan affairs, Hong Kong–Macao affairs, and affairs of the provincial and local foreign affairs offices.

The ministry proper has three tiers: division (or section), department, and ministry. The division is the basic working unit, while most policy or operational recommendations are coordinated at the department level before submission for endorsement to a higher organ.

Division of labor in the ministry is on the whole well defined. Duplication of functions is rare. Negligence of duties can be easily traced. Internal squabbles over material issues such as investment and enterprises are by and large nonexistent, as the ministry handles only paper entities. But interpersonal struggle for higher position is constant, since the only ladder to more power and personal benefits is promotion in the hierarchy.

Foreign Ministry Personnel

Professionalism has become the hallmark of the Foreign Ministry, as the makeup of its personnel has undergone a marked change. There are no "political appointees" and no military or security officers of a CIA-KGB type in the ministry as was common in the 1960s. Sizable transfers of middle-ranked officials from other ministries or provincial governments to the Ministry of Foreign Affairs has not taken place since 1963–64. The new recruits are mostly college graduates majoring in a foreign language or international relations. Those who are currently holding high posts in the ministry have worked their way up in the profession for more than twenty-five years. It has become the pattern that the retired foreign minister is promoted to the position of a Politburo member and vice premier for overall foreign relations. The power base of foreign affairs officials thus created is vertical, contained in the area of foreign affairs, rather than horizontal, embracing a variety of fields such as the power base the veteran revolutionaries used to enjoy. Professionalization has grown stronger with the practitioners having an increasing say at the top.

Sources of Information for Foreign Policy-Making

Sources of information for the purpose of foreign-policy making loosely fall into two categories: public and "internal," or classified. Public sources of information include "political" news dispatches, with an emphasis on news releases of the prominent world news agencies, newspapers and magazines from nearly every country and region in the world, analyses and comments in the influential Western journals, and research papers by the relevant institutes of the Chinese Academy of Social Sciences.

Xinhua News Agency, which is by far the largest disseminator of public international information, translates the messages gathered from foreign news media and provides the following "internal" publications: *Daily News Digest*, a daily condensation of top world news; *Reference Materials*, detailed translations of information from the foreign press, probably the most important public source for top leaders; *Reference Materials Leaflets*, translations of detailed summaries of the most significant international events or developments for prompt consumption; *Special Edition of Reference Materials*, the translated texts of important speeches and documents by foreign leaders and governments or lengthy backgrounders by Chinese reporters assigned to foreign countries; and *Xinhua News Release*, for domestic information. Special attention is given to analytical articles of international affairs by the Chinese press in Hong Kong, Taiwan, Singapore, Malaysia, and Thailand, and by the Japanese news media, because of the common approach to international issues rooted in Asian cultural similarities.

So far as "internal" sources of information are concerned, the most important are perhaps the coded telegraphic dispatches between the ministry and its missions abroad, which by custom are broadly categorized into background evaluations and operational cases requiring action. Most of this data is collected through diplomatic channels and personal contacts. Written materials include transcripts or summaries of top leaders' talks with foreign dignitaries; minutes of in-house foreign policy speeches; examinations of work; current analyses of specific situations and issues; internal surveys by the ministry's Institute of International Studies with an emphasis on background and long-term perspective; memoranda of policy recommendations for approval from above; records of the views and activities of significant foreign visitors; a semiannual pamphlet on Chinese foreign policy edited by the Information Department for the consumption of other ministries and local governments; information from other ministries, such as the Ministry of State Security and the Second Department of the headquarters of the People's Liberation Army General Staff; and sensitive materials from intelligence channels and monitoring-decoding units, which are highly classified with limited circulation.

Mechanisms of Foreign Policy-Making

The mechanism of policy-making in the Ministry of Foreign Affairs is perhaps an archetype of a professional bureaucracy in the Chinese government. A vigorous system of strict discipline and hierarchic grading is applied to the diplomats. There are clear channels and procedures for policy consultation and decision in most instances, especially on major issues. An individual's weight of influence in the policy-making process is determined by his "line of business" and his position in the "line of command," which in the first place determines his access to the necessary materials and classified information. Situation evaluations, policy proposals, and operational directives are submitted for ratification from above in the name of the institution, such as the department or the ministry, instead of the individual. This requires consensus among the participants on the basis of frequent discussions and consultations. The consensus thus reached takes the form of a formal report or a memorandum for approval that offers the unanimous recommendation with no options offered.

For issues of policy or operation that are in the sole functional jurisdiction of the Foreign Ministry, the process starts with the person in the responsible division who is in immediate charge of the matter. He forms his own opinion first and discusses it with the division chiefs for an agreement. Selected other people or the whole division may join the discussion if necessary. A consensus draft is worked out at this level before the issue goes to the department directors. The pooling of wisdom guarantees that in most cases the suggestions of the division are accepted. The directors of the department then sign the document with some technical amendments or alterations and hand it over to the minister or vice ministers.

If the issue is of a routine or less important nature that is in the competence of the Foreign Ministry to ratify, the proposal enters the implementation stage when the green light is turned on by the minister. Otherwise, it travels to the top leadership for final decision. At any given level from the department up, the cosignature of at least two leading persons in charge is required for most cases before the issue advances further. When a significant difference of opinion occurs, the matter is handed back down with the views of the higher body for reconsideration. On such occasions or on critical and urgent issues, a top leader or a minister may directly consult his subordinates or call a meeting of relevant persons in the hierarchy.

If matters involving other countries are in the primary jurisdiction of a governmental, military, or party organ other than the Foreign Ministry, they are dealt with independently by that organization so long as these matters are of a nonsensitive nature and there are guidelines to follow without evoking consideration of a new foreign policy or breaking with an existing one. If neither of these occurs, then the institution has the duty to consult the Foreign Ministry at the departmental and ministerial level, and this proposal must be cosigned at the Foreign Ministry before being brought to the top. However, such distinctions are often obscure in practice.

When an issue falls into the jurisdiction of more than one department in the Foreign Ministry or more than one ministry, the department or the ministry that is primarily responsible for the case is obliged to initiate interdepartmental or interministerial consultations and take up the drafting of the proposal. The process also starts at the division level and goes up step by step basically following the same procedure as described above. Counterpart consultations are conducted among the corresponding divisions or departments when necessary. The document must be cosigned by all the departments or ministries involved before it is delivered to the proper authority for final ruling. Disagreement by any party indicates inadequate consultation among the participants, and renegotiation is required until a consensus is reached.

Consultations are on the whole democratic and sincere, albeit sometimes not thorough if pressed for time. The highest official in the group listens to the views and suggestions of others attentively and tries to draw in the opinions thought to be reasonable. The official sums up the discussions using his own judgment; this conclusion often serves as the basis for consensus. A junior may occasionally best his senior in such discussions. But ample evidence and convincing argument must be provided, and only through the proper channels. A child or an intimate friend of a top leader may arrange to have a rejected recommendation referred directly to the top leader for a reverse decision. But it should normally be in the sphere of their official business and is usually a minor issue or an individual case. In most instances, a discrepancy between stated policy and actual practice will be the product of just such a "jump start" procedure.

The policy-making mechanism is also greatly influenced by the personal work style. For example, using metaphors from traditional Chinese painting, one might say that Zhou Enlai used a fine and detailed brushwork style while Deng Xiaoping employs a broad and freehand style. This determines the general approach subordinates may take and the relative room in which they have to maneuver.

Policy-Making Mechanisms at Work

The bureaucratic procedure may sound complicated, but anyone who is in the system for some time will know his or her power and limits, the rules of the game to observe, and the techniques to adopt to exert utmost influence. The following cases were selected as typical to illustrate how the mechanisms for foreign policy-making function in real circumstances.

Year-End Review of Situation and Work

This ministry-wide project requires the simultaneous and parallel review by all the departments and missions abroad of the political-economic situation in the past year and its possible development in the coming year for each and every region or country for which the unit is responsible, as well as an assessment of the effectiveness of the unit's past work, and suggestions for future actions. This normally lasts about two weeks, and nearly everyone is involved. Discussions are extensive, and there are often interesting arguments between those with different views. In the end, the director of the department or the ambassador makes a summary speech; and the results are put into a polished report by the unit. An embassy's report is evaluated and responded to by the corresponding regional department. The Ministry works out a condensed report of its own by using the departmental reports as the basis, presenting it to the relevant central body for review. This report often serves as the framework for the foreign policy part of the report on government work at the annual plenary session of the National People's Congress. This practice is not intended for troubleshooting or issue solution, but for supervision and control and for setting the direction and focus for the next year's work in foreign affairs.

Evaluation of Ronald Reagan's
Strategic Defense Initiative (SDI)

"Strategic" issues of great magnitude that concern the international balance of power require the joint effort of all related departments and embassies and are coordinated at the ministerial level. Regarding SDI, the first step was to scrutinize information from both the public and "internal" sources, including reports from the relevant embassies. Studies were carried out from different angles: the U.S. Division of the American and Oceanic Affairs Department covered the background, extent, and aim of the program; the West European Affairs Department analyzed the diversified reactions of the countries in their region; and the Information Department and the Institute of International Studies provided the overall and long-term perspectives. Respective analysis papers were presented at discussion sessions presided over by a deputy minister. Assessments were sent to the top leaders and other organizations involved in the project. The Ministry of State Security and the Second Department of the headquarters of the PLA General Staff also made their independent evaluations. Direct results included the review and revision of China's stand on military competition in space; by-products included the stimulation of China's space program, and perhaps a later high-tech development proposal by thirty prominent Chinese scientists.

Suggestions on the Enhancement of Economic Relations with West European Countries

This was a six-month-long attempt by a single department to explore the new sphere of "economic diplomacy," with data gathering from and some consultations with the Ministry of Foreign Economic Relations and Trade (MOFERT). Departmental discussions were conducted on proposals put forward by the divisions, and department-ministry exchanges of views were frequent.

There were debates on the exact meaning of "economic diplomacy" and on how the Department of West European Affairs and the Foreign Ministry could become involved without stepping on MOFERT's toes. Several redraftings and revisions were made before the final proposals were submitted for affirmation by the ministry and above.

The core suggestion was to promote the concurrent and balanced development of economic relations with Japan, the Untied States, and Western Europe, with each being given a third of the China pie. Its aim was to further political cooperation with Western Europe, reduce China's dependence on any particular source of trade, and counteract Taiwan's economic diplomacy in Europe. This suggestion was well received by the top leadership, but implementation has not been satisfactory because of the high prices of European merchandise and economic structural problems in China.

An African Country's Request for a Medical Team and Some Agricultural Experts from China

This case fell under the jurisdiction of several ministries, but MOFERT had the primary responsibility. MOFERT first consulted the Ministry of Foreign Affairs on the "political" aspect of the issue, that is, whether the request ought to be considered in view of the state of bilateral relations. MOFERT then consulted the Ministry of Public Health and the Ministry of Agriculture, respectively, on the "technical" aspects, that is, which province or provinces had the capability and should take up the job, and finally when and how the Chinese team should to be sent. The recommendations were drafted by MOFERT and cosigned by the other three ministries. They were dispatched to the local authorities for implementation after the endorsement from above was given.

Practical Problems Caused by
the Sudden Death of a President

This is in essence a case of crisis management. The president of a southern African country was diagnosed as having pancreatic cancer. But since nobody expected his illness to deteriorate rapidly, he maintained that his vice president should embark on a planned trip to China, in his capacity as the national chairman of the ruling party. But the president fell critically ill only a few days after the vice president's departure, and the government asked China to facilitate the vice president's immediate return. The Chinese ambassador happened to have been recalled for new assignment, and telecommunications between the embassy and the ministry were extremely difficult. Making matters more complicated, the vice president's visit was sponsored by the party's International Liaison Department, while such crises were normally dealt with by the Foreign Ministry. Worse still, that country had no airport that could handle a large, long-distance airplane.

Fortunately, the ministry had coordinated the operation well and assisted the young chargé d'affaires by setting up a direct telephone link with the office of a high-powered official for foreign affairs in the State Council. A plan was worked out to get the vice president to Hong Kong by a chartered Boeing 707 for connection with the earliest commercial flight for the nearest neighboring country. The chargé's suggestion to have the message of condolence (the president had not yet died) and the message of congratulation for the vice president's succession ready for dispatch at his signal was promptly approved, but his proposal to have a ranking Chinese government representative sent for the funeral and inauguration was reluctantly accepted only after his repeated argument. The constant information exchange that the chargé established with the country's ministers and the U.S. embassy helped him to remain abreast of developments. Eventually everything went smoothly. In a crisis situation, improvisation is important; reliable information channels and direct access to the office with decision-making authority are absolutely necessary.

A Famous U.S. Columnist's Visit to China

This is a case in which a junior in the line of command changed the initial decision of a senior. Richard Nixon proposed a trip to China by a well-known columnist. He hoped that the columnist would help reduce the resistance to his China policy from the American right. The visit was in the official realm of duty of the Information Department. But for such a politically sensitive issue in the early years of contacts with the United States, the baton was placed in the hands of the American and Oceanic Affairs Department.

The division director in charge of U.S. affairs intended to decline the proposal on the grounds that for years the columnist had attacked China in his articles and there was no guarantee that he would do otherwise now. A junior official at the U.S. correspondents' desk of the Information Department, however, went through nearly every available writing of the columnist and worked out a long assessment paper that argued that the "facts" the columnist used in his attacks were not too far from reality even though his perspective was reactionary, and he also seemed to have a strong nostalgia for China, though his imperialistic attitude would likely not be altered in one trip. The junior first obtained the full backing of his division chiefs and department directors before presenting his implicitly dissenting view. Just as the U.S. affairs director was about to give in, Mao Zedong made a sweeping remark, not specifically addressed to this case, that Americans of all political persuasions from left to right should be welcomed in China, especially those from the right, for the unique role they could play. The director then was completely convinced.

The final report for instructions that recommended acceptance of the proposal was approved by Zhou Enlai with cosignatures of other top leaders. With this document as the "imperial sword," the information director went to the places the columnist was to visit for extensive advance preparation work, as many places were still in chaos because of factional fighting in the. Cultural Revolution. The columnist's important views and major activities while in China were reported to Zhou and others through a daily dispatch. The columnist was accurately quoted by Zhou on some of his remarks when the two met for a long interview. After the talk, Zhou joked with the information officers, laughingly suggesting that they acted like the bodyguard-lover of Catherine the Great, to whom the Russian empress said: try the visiting emissary out for three days before I offer him an audience. The visit turned out to be a success for both Nixon and for China and the subordinate's views were vindicated.

9

Decision-Making and Implementation of Policy toward Hong Kong

Kam Yiu-yu

Based on personal experience over forty years as a party worker in Hong Kong, receiving instructions from the Central Committee of the Chinese Communist Party (CCP), and doing my best to carry them out, I could not help but conclude that in the Chinese political system, there was no real "power structure," but rather personal power vested in Mao Zedong and a few other leaders in the uppermost strata of the party.

China's constitutional "proletarian dictatorship," mandating "the leadership of the CCP," is in essence a one-party dictatorship. The party constitution, in turn, stipulates that "an individual member should obey the party as a whole and the whole party should obey the Central Committee." The Central Committee should, then, obey whom? There is no definite answer. The constitution mentions only that Marxism-Leninism and Mao Zedong Thought should be the guiding ideology. Since Marx and Lenin have long been in heaven, the implication naturally is that it was Mao Zedong to whom the party should show its obedience. Hence, the essence of the "proletarian dictatorship" is a special kind of oligarchy, a one-person dictatorship. The power of decision-making on vital questions such as Hong Kong was vested in one person, Mao Zedong. On the basis or under the principle of decisions made by Mao, other leaders at the top level of the party power structure assumed the responsibilities of implementation. It was only at this stage that they could enjoy some right to speak—that is, to make some new interpretations or add some new ideas to Mao's decisions with no deviation from the main principles but made more suitable to the practical circumstances at that time.

At least this was true regarding major issues such as Hong Kong, during both the Mao and Deng eras. It was the view of the party that the Hong Kong question was very big and complex, left over by the history of Sino-British relations, a focal point of East-West struggle with extensive repercussions. Therefore, the main guidelines and policies on this question and its related policies toward Britain and the United States could be decided only by Mao Zedong and Zhou Enlai, with Foreign Affairs office director Chen Yi and deputy director Liao Chengzhi as executive officers. The names of Liu Shaoqi, Deng Xiaoping, and others were never mentioned in briefings on important decisions on the Hong Kong question in the Mao period to my knowledge.

The first such important decision was relayed after the People's Liberation Army (PLA) crossed the Yangtze River in April 1949. It was made clear that the Hong Kong question, a leftover from history, would have to be solved after historical conditions had matured. The PLA's crossing of the Yangtze was intended merely to overthrow Chiang Kai-shek's rule on the mainland. Hong Kong would keep its present shape. Our main anti-imperialist struggle was against the United States, not Britain, so Hong Kong was to be left in British hands. It was emphasized in the briefing that this decision was made by Chairman Mao, using Marxist historical dialectics applied to the practical conditions in Hong Kong and the prevailing international circumstances. Throughout my tenure in Hong Kong, it was clear that in making decisions on the Hong Kong policy, Mao Zedong and Zhou Enlai did not treat the Hong Kong question as an isolated one, but viewed it in the context of the global struggle between East and West and took into consideration the changing international situation, especially in Sino-British and Sino-American relations.

As a result of the Kuomintang's (KMT's) destruction of CCP organizations in Taiwan, in 1947 I was ordered by the party to leave the island, where I had been working as a member of the standing committee and Propaganda Department chief of the Taiwan Provincial Work Committee. I arrived in Hong Kong by early January 1948, to report for duty with the CCP's Southern Bureau. The next year, I was assigned to the Hong Kong Xinhua News Agency to assist Director Qiao Guanhua in policy research on the Hong Kong question and Sino-British and Sino-American relations. After 1950, I became party secretary of the Press and Publicity Division[1] of Xinhua–Hong Kong. Under my direction were newspapers and periodicals which took a political stand favoring the CCP, such as *Wen Wei Po, Ta Kung Pao, Xin Wan Pao* (New Evening News), *Shang Pao* (Commercial Daily), *Zhou Mu Pao* (The Weekend), and, later, *Jin Pao* (The Crystal Daily). My chief responsibilities were to relay to these institutions guidelines and policies for propaganda work in Hong Kong and overseas set by the party central authorities and to supervise their implementation. In 1955, because of political struggle against the British–Hong Kong authorities, I was assigned to *Wen Wei Po* as party representative and concurrently vice editor-in-chief.[2] I held this position until the 1980s, except during the Cultural Revolution, when I was sent back to the mainland and, like many other veteran cadre, had a very hard time for ten years.

Based on my forty years of experience working in Hong Kong, I would like to offer a concise review of policy-making and implementation regarding the Hong Kong question and relations with Great Britain and the United States.

The Nature and Function of Xinhua–Hong Kong

The party institution operating under the name of Xinhua–Hong Kong was established in 1946. Although it gave the appearance of a press organ dispatching news releases from the Xinhua Headquarters in Yan'an, Xinhua–Hong Kong was actually an office of the CCP's Southern Bureau stationed in Hong Kong for public relations and activities. Fang Fang, secretary of the Southern Bureau, had his office in Hong Kong.

After the liberation of Guangzhou in 1949, the Southern Bureau moved back to the provincial capital and was reorganized as the South China Branch of the Politburo. Xinhua–Hong Kong was accordingly reorganized as a work team of the South China Branch. Huang Zuomei was both the party secretary of the Work Team and director of Xinhua–Hong Kong. I myself was both a member of the work team and a staff member of Xinhua–Hong Kong.

As the leading organ of the CCP underground network in Hong Kong, the work team was responsible for various duties in Hong Kong, including publicity, publication, culture and education, and united front organizations in industrial and trade circles, in local CCP-led trade unions, and in financial and business institutions funded by the People's Republic of China (PRC). These institutions were professionally under the leadership of their respective superiors on the mainland while politically and ideologically under that of the work team.

The work team (officially, the Hong Kong–Macao Work Team) was the sole channel through which all instructions from the CCP regarding policies and guidelines on Hong Kong affairs were relayed to various "lines" (divisions), separately or together. These "lines" included the Press and Publicity Division, Culture and Publication Division, United Front among Industrial and Commercial Societies and Organization Division, and Trade Unions and Education Division. Among them, the Press and Publicity Division, for which I was responsible, enjoyed the first priority in receiving these instructions so that party policies could be made known as soon as possible to all cadre and compatriots in Hong Kong, to British–Hong Kong authorities, resident offices in Hong Kong of various countries, overseas Chinese, and the international community.

In implementing decisions and instructions of the party Central Committee, the work team served as the main sluice gate while the Press and Publicity Division was the largest, speediest, and most open channel. So the first thing for cadre to do every morning, especially leading cadre of Chinese institutions in Hong Kong, was to read *Wen Wei Po* and *Ta Kung Pao*, to have a day-to-day understanding of the party policy, attitude, and inclination through editorials, commentaries, headlines, and, sometimes, the layout itself.

In the mid-1950s, the Hong Kong–Macao Work Team again reorganized into the CCP Hong Kong–Macao Work Committee, a further promotion, organizationally and politically, for the institution, with an expanded setup and staff. Its responsibilities, however, remained the same.

By this time, the Politburo had closed down its regional branches, so the new Hong Kong–Macao Work Committee was put under the direct leadership of the Foreign Affairs Office (FAO) of the Central Committee headed by Chen Yi, concurrently vice premier and foreign minister, with Liao Chengzhi as first deputy head and Li Yimeng, Kong Yuan, and Zhang Yan as deputy heads. The FAO had a Hong Kong–Macao Department, which established direct connections with the Hong Kong–Macao Work Committee in Hong Kong. Above the FAO was the Central Foreign Affairs Leading Group, led by Premier Zhou Enlai, with Chen Yi as one of its members.

Henceforth, as the Hong Kong–Macao Work Committee was transformed into a party organ stationed in Hong Kong by the FAO, all policy instructions and briefings on international and domestic issues were handed down directly from the central (FAO) Working Committee, not going through the South China Bureau or the Guangdong Provincial Committee as before. The work committee also sent reports or requests for instructions on policy or practical questions directly to the FAO.

The Norms for Policy-Making and Implementation

The supreme responsible person on Hong Kong–Macao work then was none other than Zhou Enlai. Zhou was in charge of general policy and guiding principle, but it was Mao Zedong who had the final say. The duty of the FAO under Chen and Liao was to apply policy and principle in practical work and supervise the implementation by the Hong Kong–Macao

Work Committee, which also had the duty to report to the FAO on the local situation and existing problems for the latter's consideration and reference in mapping out new policies.

Much stress was laid on the work of the Work Committee Press and Publicity Division, whose responsible cadre, including party and nonparty personnel, were summoned by the FAO to attend meetings in Beijing, generally twice a year with one around May 1 (Labor Day) and another around October 1 (National Day), with each meeting lasting about three days.

As a rule, these meetings were presided over personally by FAO Head Chen Yi, or Deputy Heads Liao Chengzhi or Zhang Yan. They listened carefully to our reports on the present situation and our questions. The meetings would end with concluding remarks and instructions by Chen or Liao. They would always make it clear that these instructions were given with the approval of Zhou Enlai, to whom they had made reports about the meetings and asked for directives. This showed clearly that the work in Hong Kong and Macao was under the personal and direct guidance of Zhou Enlai. I remember that Chen Yi repeatedly told us Zhou's words: "In doing foreign affairs work, one shoulders very heavy responsibility with very limited warranty." In the eyes of foreigners, he would continue, as foreign minister I may appear quite sharp and resourceful, but in fact the principles I used in dealing with international relations were all provided by Chairman Mao, with interpretation and guidance from Premier Zhou.

Cultural Revolution Changes

During the Cultural Revolution, tremendous changes occurred in party work in Hong Kong, presenting a very abnormal situation. Briefly speaking, at the end of 1966, the "rebels" supporting the Cultural Revolution, led by Lin Biao and Jiang Qing, first seized control of the FAO and later had it dissolved. In fact, this was meant to deprive Zhou Enlai, Chen Yi, and Liao Chengzhi of their power in conducting foreign affairs, Hong Kong–Macao work included, and to vest it in the hands of Lin Biao and Jiang Qing.

As a result, the Hong Kong–Macao Work Committee was put under the command of the then all-powerful Central Cultural Revolution Leading Group. The "Anti-British, Anti-Atrocity Struggle" (Hong Kong's own "Proletarian Cultural Revolution"), staged in 1967, was under the direct command of Lin, Jiang, and their subordinates, including Wang Li and Yao Dengshan. Under Jiang's direction, Wang Li wrote an editorial for the *People's Daily,* calling openly for "sweeping the colonial rule of the empire of Great Britain in Hong Kong onto the dust heap of history." Jiang further called for "sending the Hong Kong–British (authorities) to hell if they refuse to bow to us." This was done unbeknownst to Zhou Enlai, who was not even in a position to check whether the new strategic line was initiated or approved by Mao Zedong.

In 1967, fully occupied with the crisis on the mainland, Zhou was unable to do anything about Hong Kong. In 1968, however, the situation on the mainland was more or less under control again. Zhou summoned the secretary and deputy of the Hong Kong–Macao Work Committee to Beijing to inquire into the Hong Kong situation. After listening to their reports on the yearlong struggle, Zhou told them: "I have asked Chairman Mao whether the situation in Hong Kong had changed and our Hong Kong–Macao policy had accordingly changed [meaning to take back Hong Kong]. Chairman Mao answered, 'The situation in Hong Kong? I don't see any change! Our Hong Kong policy has been set and practiced for several decades. I don't see any new conditions or new factors to have it changed.' "

Zhou went on: "It is now clear that the struggle you staged for a year, together with its slogans and targets, was not the view of Chairman Mao's party, and hence was erroneous. I order you to stop the struggle immediately, withdraw all the people deployed and reach a peaceful solution." Clearly, even Premier Zhou Enlai was not in a position to make decisions concerning the status of Hong Kong. That power rested only in the hands of Mao Zedong.

Post-Mao Return to the Norm

After the Cultural Revolution, a decision was made in 1978 not to restore the former FAO, but to set up a Hong Kong–Macao Office under the State Council, with Liao Chengzhi as its director as well as the leader of the Hong Kong–Macao Work Committee, which still functioned underground in Hong Kong.

With power restored to him, Liao immediately began to rehabilitate the work committee through a reshuffle of the leadership, an all-out effort to rectify the "ultra-leftist" line and "rebel" style of work. This was yet another change of power structure in Hong Kong–Macao work, brought about by the shift of central leadership and political line, rather than by a change in the political system. In China the change in power structure always follows the change of persons in power.

There was a return to pre–Cultural Revolution policy as well as structure. In the instructions given by Mao, Zhou, Chen Yi, and Liao Chengzhi, one could already find the roots of the "one country, two systems" concept, introduced by Deng Xiaoping in the 1980s. Premier Zhou very early established the guideline in Hong Kong work, that is, dealing with Hong Kong and overseas in their own context, not copying practices on the mainland. In a 1957 briefing, Liao had relayed Zhou's instructions at a meeting in Shanghai: Hong Kong is a capitalist society that could exist and develop only according to the capitalist system. Later, Premier Zhou instructed us through Liao: "Your task in Hong Kong is to spread patriotism and not socialism, to form an extensive patriotic united front and not a socialist united front in Hong Kong."

Liao Chengzhi died in the summer of 1983, when Sino-British negotiations on the solution of the Hong Kong question had just begun. Before the appointment of Ji Pengfei to succeed Liao as director of the Hong Kong–Macao Office, Deng Xiaoping and General Secretary Hu Yaobang decided to send Xu Jiatun, party secretary of Jiangsu Province, to Hong Kong to be the new secretary of the work committee. As a high-ranking ministerial-provincial level party leading cadre, Xu was directly appointed by and answerable to Deng and Hu, equal to rather than subordinate to the Hong Kong–Macao Office director. This reflected high-level attention at a time when Sino-British negotiations on the Hong Kong solution were in progress and Hong Kong was on the threshold of a historic transitional period. Throughout the negotiations, Deng was at the helm, rapping the gavel on every important issue. The Hong Kong–Macao Work Committee under Xu Jiatun often bypassed the State Council's Hong Kong–Macao Office and reported directly to the Central Secretariat under Hu Yaobang, and through it, reaching Deng Xiaoping's office. This naturally caused serious tensions between the work committee, the State Council's Hong Kong–Macao Office, and the Foreign Ministry.[3]

What I want to underscore here is not the bureaucratic quarrels but the fact that Sino-British negotiations were conducted from beginning to end under Deng's personal leadership. It was known that before the negotiations formally started, the British side proposed to separate Hong Kong's sovereignty from its administration, in order to hand over the former to China in principle while retaining the latter for Britain in reality. The question was referred to Deng, who was said to have replied: "Nonsense! Sovereignty and the power of administration are inseparable. What is sovereignty without the power of administration? Both have to be taken back. If they don't want to give them, we will take them back ourselves." The question was thus settled. As in the Mao era, one person had the final say.

Two more examples illustrate this. The first was the question of whether the PLA should send forces to be stationed in Hong Kong after 1997. Before Sino-British negotiations started, some top party leading cadre believed that since the principle of "one country, two systems" was to be practiced in Hong Kong, Beijing should not send a single soldier there; Liao Chengzhi said as much in 1983 before his death. In 1984, meeting with people from Hong Kong–Macao business circles, Huang Hua and Geng Biao, then vice chairmen of the Standing Committee of the National People's Congress (NPC), also said China would not send the PLA to Hong Kong. However, a little later, when asked to confirm this view in a meeting with NPC delegates and CCP members from Hong Kong, Deng Xiaoping flared up and insisted: "Huang and Geng are talking rot! If we don't sent the PLA there, how would we show our restoration of sovereignty?" Thus an impromptu remark by Deng settled an all-important question, with neither an exchange of views at the party's top level nor any discussion or decision by the Politburo. Even General Secretary Hu Yaobang and Premier Zhao Ziyang had no chance weigh in.

The second example concerns China's policy during Hong Kong's transitional period. In 1987, three years after the signing of the Sino-British Joint Declaration marking the beginning of Hong Kong's transitional period, the State Council's Hong Kong–Macao Office felt dissatisfied with or uneasy about some of the British–Hong Kong authorities' political and economic policies. This became known to Deng, and he told officials in the office, "We should try to take part in Hong Kong affairs during the transitional period to prevent the British from playing about with us, leaving endless troubles for the future."

Thus, since that time, Chinese leaders, from officials in the Hong Kong–Macao Office to the premier and even the general secretary, have interfered in Hong Kong's internal affairs repeatedly to influence such matters as the deficits in the Hong Kong government's annual budgets, inflation in Hong Kong, the construction of Hong Kong's new airport, and the election of members of the Legislative Council. Open criticism, censure, and even opposition have been aired by them publicly, bringing about a serious situation.

The often conflicting signals reflect confusion over Hong Kong policy among officials who must interpret and implement Deng's guidelines. Does Deng's term "to take part" mean "intervention" or "interference"? Is there any difference between the two alternative definitions of Deng's term? How should China go about "taking part" and what are the means to do so? Is it done indirectly through well-known persons in Hong Kong? These are questions Deng never answered, yet no official has dared to ask.

The previous two examples reveal how in present-day China there still exists primarily the personal power of the supreme leader, not an institutionalized power structure. As far as Hong Kong is concerned, this basic situation has not changed, even though Deng's personal involvement decreased after the Hong Kong solution in 1984, because fewer major issues demanded Deng's attention.

Other evidence of the importance of personalities over institutions can be seen at the level of decision-making on Hong Kong one level below Deng. Zhou Nan succeeded Xu Jiatun as secretary of the Hong Kong–Macao Work Committee and director of Xinhua–Hong Kong, upon the recommendation of party elder Li Xiannian (then PRC president) and Premier Li Peng. As Zhou could now bypass Lu Ping, chief of the Hong Kong–Macao Office (succeeding Ji Pengfei) and reach Li Peng directly, a Zhou-Lu struggle for power and favor arose. This struggle was aggravated by the agreement reached in 1991 between Beijing and London to the effect that Sino-British communications would be conducted thereafter at the two levels: that of chief of the Hong Kong–Macao Office on the Chinese side and the governor of Hong Kong on the British side, as well as between foreign ministers on both sides. This means that Zhou Nan, as director of Xinhua–Hong Kong, would not be in a position to conduct talks with the governor and hence would lose his importance (it was then reported that Zhou requested to be transferred from his post in Hong Kong, partly because of his conflict with Lu). The developments also demonstrate that the political setup has no well-defined mechanism, but changes from person to person.

In summary, my personal experience of more than four decades shows that in discussing policy-making regarding Hong Kong, the most important question is not the power structure but the person in power. No complete and highly institutionalized procedure of policy-making and implementation exists, but rather personal styles of top leaders in decision-making and then procedures used by institutions (the CCP's FAO and the State Council's Hong Kong–Macao Office) in implementation. Lower levels could only raise new ideas or views on practical questions within the limits of the overall policy set by the leader in conjunction with the changing international circumstances and Sino-British and Sino-American relations.

Such decision-making practices do not necessarily mean inefficency. On the contrary, sometimes efficiency was high. Because Mao's words were regarded as sacred truth, Zhou, Chen, and Liao would act promptly in accordance with Mao's overall policy under any circumstances. As a result, if a supreme leader made a serious erroneous decision, the whole nation could be plunged into disaster. The Cultural Revolution is typical in this respect. This is the real picture of China's autocracy: the one-party dictatorship, the oligarchy, the so-called "*ti yan tang*" ("what I say goes" system). Here exists no strongly established system, no well-defined structure.

Notes

1. The official Chinese term is "line" (*xian*).
2. Li Zisong, a member of the Central Committee of the Revolutionary Committee

of the KMT with headquarters in Beijing, was its editor-in-chief. Note that romanization for Hong Kong journals follows local practice, not *pinyin*.

3. So long as Liao Chengzhi headed both the party and government organs responsible for Hong Kong–Macao affairs, there was no bureaucratic conflict. Conflict emerged when Ji and Xu headed two coequal organs using different channels of communicating with the center. Hong Kong University Professor John Burns, citing an unspecified internal source, writes, "According to what was probably the Hong Kong–Macao office's 1987 submission to the State Organization and Establishment Committee in preparation for the 1980–1990 reorganization of the State Council: relations between the Hong Kong and Macao Affairs Office and the Work Committee are not smooth. The Work Committee is a provincial-level organization that comes directly under the General Office of the Central Committee. The General Office also has given the Hong Kong and Macao Affairs Office [certain tasks] to manage, [which results in] informally beating around the bush (*raole gewan*). The Work Committee is dispatched to Hong Kong by the Central Committee (*paichu jigou*) while the Hong Kong and Macao Affairs Office is an organ of the State Council. Much of the work of the Work Committee depends on government departments to be accomplished. [Of course], the major policies on Hong Kong questions are determined by the center [Politburo]. This is a problem of relations between party and government" (unpublished manuscript, 1993).

10

The Structure of the Chinese Academy of Social Sciences and Two Decisions to Abolish Its Marxism-Leninism-Mao Zedong Thought Institute

Su Shaozhi

The Chinese political system entails many institutional and legal regulations. De facto operation of the system, however, is quite different from these stipulations. The relationship between the Chinese Academy of Social Sciences (CASS) and the Marxism-Leninism-Mao Zedong Thought Institute can be used to illustrate de facto operation—the nonprocedural characteristics of the Chinese political system.

The Administrative and Party Structures of CASS

According to administrative regulations, CASS is a national-level organ under the State Council. As such, its president and vice presidents must be appointed by the State Council. Because they are of ministerial rank, these appointments must be approved by the National People's Congress (NPC).

In terms of party structure, CASS has dual leadership (see figure 10.1). First, CASS has a party group (*dangzu*), which is subordinate to the party group of the State Council (which is normally headed by the premier). There is also a party group in each institute.

Second, CASS has a party committee (*dangwei*), which is subordinate to the Party Committee for Organs Directly Subordinate to (Zhong zhiji guan dangwei) the Central Committee. There is also a party committee in each institute, and, below that, Party branches (*zhibu*) and cells (*xiaozu*). This structure is shown in figure 10.1.

Figure 10.1. **Administrative and Party Structure of the Chinese Academy of Social Sciences**

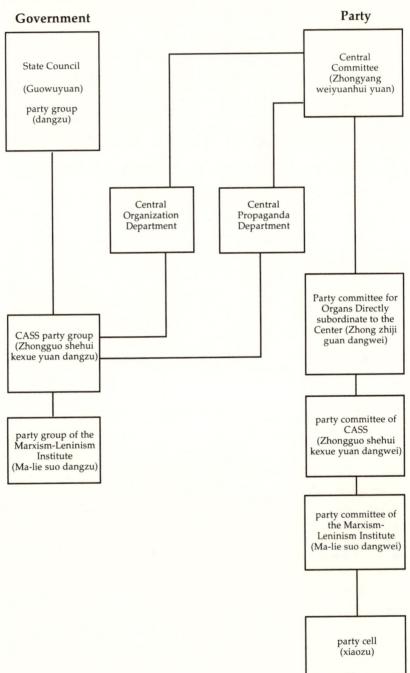

In most cases, the secretary of the party group is also head of the government organization and head of the party committee, though this is not necessarily the case. In the instance of the Marxism-Leninism-Mao Zedong Thought Institute, I was secretary of the party group and director of the institute, but not head of the party committee. The secretary of the party committee was responsible for routine party affairs such as organizing study sessions and determining the acceptance and discipline of party members.

The position of party group secretary is more important than either of the other two positions, because as party group secretary one represents both CASS's party group and the State Council party group. His power includes both the administrative and party affairs. This line of authority ensures that the respective institutes are implementing the party line.

The secretary of the party group in an institute is appointed by the party group of CASS and reports to the Central Organization Department for its approval. Changes of party leaders in an institute must be reported by the party committee of CASS to the Party Committee for Organs Directly Subordinate to the center.

In the case of secretaries and deputy secretaries of the institutes' party committees, the Party Committee for Organs Directly Subordinate to the center has the authority to reject the decisions of lower-level units. In addition, that committee passes the decisions on secretaries and deputy secretaries horizontally to the Central Organization Department, which also has the authority to approve or reject the selections.

Because CASS is an ideological organ, it is also supervised in terms of content of work by the Central Propaganda Department, even though they are nominally of the same rank. Thus, each issue of CASS journals is sent to the Propaganda Department, and if the Propaganda Department finds something wrong with an article, it will pass the criticism along to the leadership of CASS, which will then inform the offending institute and author. When the general political atmosphere is fairly open, such criticisms can usually be refuted and ignored. At other times, when the situation is tight, the author may have to conduct a self-criticism and may be subject to inner-party discipline sanctions.

This censorship process is not one of prepublication review but rather postpublication criticism. It is the head of the institute and the secretary of the party group (usually the same person) who is responsible for the content of the institutes' journals. Hence, the process is one of self-censorship by the institute itself.

In addition, the Propaganda Department has the authority to approve or disapprove the research projects that are undertaken by an institute. At the beginning of the year, each institute submits a list of topics to be researched to CASS, which then forwards the list to the Propaganda Department. If the Propaganda Department objects to a particular research project, it must be dropped.

Structure of Communication

CASS has a variety of ways of communicating its views to the party and state. First, each institute has two journals, one that is circulated to the outside and one that is internal (*neibu*). Second, the institutes write various types of internal reference material (*neibu cankao ziliao*, usually referred to as *neican*). Such internal reference materials are taken each day to a large building known as the "exchange station" (*jiaohuan zhan*) where the internal reference materials produced by CASS are exchanged with those produced by other government organs. Those of other organs are brought back to CASS, where they are sorted according to their level of classification in the "secrets room" (*jiyao chu*). Depending on researchers' level of clearance, they can then read the appropriate level of documents.

For extremely sensitive materials, the director of each institute has the authority to send material directly to the leadership. This might go in the form of a "special newsletter," or *neican qingyang*, a type of document that is produced only in very small numbers and circulated among only the top leadership. For instance, when the United States and China were discussing the establishment of monitoring stations in China to monitor Soviet missile tests, Hua Di of the American Studies Institute wrote a report favoring this idea. Li Shenzhi, the head of the institute, then forwarded the report directly to the top leadership and to Deng Xiaoping.

The Informal Power Structure

CASS was established as an independent organ in 1977. The Chinese Academy of Sciences (CAS) was not necessarily sorry to see social sciences removed from its purview because their removal reduced the politicization of CAS, which had been exacerbated by internal disputes during the Cultural Revolution.

CASS was established as a think tank for the reform leaders who were coming back to power at that time. In the early period, power at CASS was held by three people: the president, Hu Qiaomu, and two vice presidents, Deng Liqun and Yu Guangyuan. All three were members of the State Council Political Research Office, which was then–Vice Premier Deng Xiaoping's think tank.

The relationship between the Marxism-Leninism Institute and the CASS leadership was directly affected by the personal relationships between these top three leaders. When CASS was first established, Hu Qiaomu, Deng Liqun, and Yu Guangyuan were of one mind in their opposition to the Gang of Four and Hua Guofeng's Maoist dogmatism. Later, however, when there was no common enemy, they began to diverge, for personal and ideological reasons. Yu Guangyuan was close to Hu Yaobang, whereas Hu Qiaomu and Deng Liqun were loyal to Chen Yun. Ideologically, Yu Guangyuan believed that the party must sum up not only the lessons of the Cultural Revolution but also the mistakes made in the seventeen years before the Cultural Revolution. Hu Qiaomu and Deng Liqun, however, wanted to restrict criticism to the Cultural Revolution period. Thus, Hu and Deng were often referred to as "restorationists" (*huigui pai*).

Personal relations were also important in the relationship between the Marxism-Leninism Institute and the Department of Propaganda. Such ties were separate from any formal structure of relations, and they varied over time, depending on who was in charge of the Propaganda Department. When Wang Renzhong was director, relations were not bad. Although Wang was conservative, he respected scholars and maintained good relations with them. When Deng Liqun became director, however, the relationship was antagonistic. Later, on the first day after the more liberal Zhu Houze took over as director, by contrast, he invited members of the Marxism-Leninism Institute to go to the Propaganda Department to discuss openly how they should study the party line.

Two Efforts to Abolish the Marxism-Leninism Institute

Twice in the decade after reform was inaugurated, conservatives tried to abolish the Marxism-Leninism Institute. Both episodes illustrate the weakness of formal procedures in China.

The first time was in October 1983, during the campaign against "spiritual pollution." At that time, I was criticized and a small work group was sent to the Institute by the Discipline Inspection Commission of CASS. My friends in the Translation Bureau told me that the Department of Propaganda had ordered the abolition of the institute and had suggested that the bureau accept some of the institute's staff. Yet we ourselves had heard nothing from the CASS leadership about this, and legally the party committee of CASS would have had to approve such a decision. I asked a member of my staff, Feng Lanrui, to go to party elder Bo Yibo to ask about the situation. Feng and Bo had a good personal relationship that dated back to the Yan'an period. Feng reminded Bo of a regulation that was in effect during the ongoing party rectification (launched in October 1983; Bo was one of the leading officials of the campaign). No organs were to be abolished; only after rectification had been completed were organs to be abolished if deemed necessary. Armed with this regulation, Bo was able to intervene and preserve the Marxism-Leninism Institute.

Around the same time, the campaign against "spiritual pollution" was stopped suddenly, so I went to see Mei Yi, head of the CASS party group, about the status of the institute. He said that he did not know anything about a decision to abolish it. Later, I was told that a meeting of the leadership of CASS had been held to discuss the issue, and at that meeting, Mei Yi had said that Hu Qiaomu and Deng Liqun were recommending the abolition of the institute and asked for a vote by ballot. At that time, CASS Vice President Yu Guangyuan was absent, on a visit to Japan. The suggestion therefore was passed with only one dissent, by Vice President Huan Xiang. He asked that the report express his dissent, but it did not. After Yu's return, Huan and Yu visited Hu Yaobang and told him the whole story. Hu Yaobang criticized CASS for its recommendation. Even now, I still do not understand why Mei Yi lied about this. One might say that neither the order to abolish the institute nor Bo Yibo's intervention to save it followed formal legal procedures. Both expressed the personal whims of top leaders.

The second time that the Marxism-Leninism Institute was threatened with dissolution was during the 1987 campaign against "bourgeois liberalism." At that time, Deng Liqun criticized the institute as a typical example of bourgeois liberalism. Yu Guangyuan was severely criticized, and I was removed from all my posts. This came about because there was a secondary list of people to be criticized for "bourgeois liberalism" (besides those key targets who lost their party membership—Fang Lizhi, Liu Binyan, and Wang Ruowang). Party elder Wang Zhen asked Zhao Ziyang why the people on the list had not been punished. Zhao said that the evidence was not sufficient to warrant punishment. Wang then asked Deng Xiaoping why they had not been punished. Deng forced Zhao to hold a Secretariat meeting on July 22 in Beidaihe to discuss the matter. The result was that four persons, including me, were to be punished (twelve persons were originally on the list). The decision was then forwarded to the CASS leadership. Only ten to fifteen days after the decision did Zhao Fusan, executive vice president of CASS, show me the decision. I asked why I was being punished; Zhao said he did not know.

All this was quite irregular. According to the regulations of the Chinese Communist Party (CCP), a person who is to be criticized must first be criticized in his party cell. In this case, that never happened. The evidence against the people on the black list was prepared in the Secretariat's Research Office, then headed by Deng Liqun. And the decision came from the

Secretariat to the CASS leadership. My party cell never discussed the matter.

At the same time, in the summer of 1987, Hu Qiaomu wanted to "abolish" the Marxism-Leninism Institute by combining it with the Marxism-Leninism Institute of the Central Party School. He asked Zhao to merge them. Zhao put this off by saying that he would consider it later. Finally in May 1988—when the political atmosphere was again more open and Hu Qiaomu and Deng Liqun had lost formal power—at an enlarged meeting of the Politburo, Zhao asked Hu Sheng (by then president of CASS) whether to abolish the institute. Hu replied that CASS should have a Marxism-Leninism Institute. This ended the matter. Zhao had used tactics of delay and an opportune meeting to effect a favorable decision.

Conclusion

The history of the Marxism-Leninism Institute at CASS reflects the non-procedural, unpredictable, and highly personal and political nature of Chinese decision-making. In conclusion, we may say the following:

1. China has rule of man, not law. Neither of the two efforts to abolish the Marxism-Leninism Institute, nor my personal punishment, followed legal procedures.
2. The party is above the government. Although CASS and the Marxism-Leninism Institute are subordinate to the State Council, in fact they must follow party dictates. This is why high-level party elders or leaders with no government positions can intervene in CASS affairs.
3. Personal decisions and personal relations are very important in China. For instance, the roles of Hu Qiaomu and Deng Liqun in arguing for the abolition of the Marxism-Leninism Institute and the roles of Zhao Ziyang and Bo Yibo in preserving it were very important.
4. The history of the Marxism-Leninism Institute illustrates the saying in China that "above there are policies; below, there are counterpolicies." Only by using "counterpolicies" can individuals and institutions survive in the atmosphere of Chinese politics.

Note

The author acknowledges Professor Joseph Fewsmith's assistance in preparing this chapter.

11

Political Work in the Military from the Viewpoint of the Beijing Garrison Command

Fang Zhu

China's civil-military relations since 1949 are characterized by both high military intervention in politics and remarkable loyalty to the party regime. Both of these two aspects of the People's Liberation Army's (PLA's) role in politics can be explained by a historical fusion between the civil and military organizations. Many party leaders have military backgrounds and strong personal ties with military leaders. Military leaders take part in party and government policy-making on local, provincial and national levels. The PLA has a higher percentage of party membership than any other group in society, and the officer corps is made up entirely of party members. Without a clear-cut institutional distinction between civil and military elites, the formal rule that the party commands the gun is ambiguous in actual practice. Military involvement in politics is not only normal but intrinsic in such a system.

By the same token, as the military elites are an integral part of the party regime, it would be self-defeating for them to try to topple it. Thus when we talk about party control we should not think of the party and the army as two separate entities with the former controlling the latter. The party-army blending blurs the institutional boundary between the two. Party control is achieved primarily not by coercion but by co-opting the military elites into the party leadership. By encouraging military participation in policy-making the party accepts incomplete civilian control in exchange for a guarantee of the ultimate survival of civilian control. This is the fundamental nature of civil-military relations in China.

The Central Military Commission (CMC) and the Party Structure in the PLA

Officially entitled the Military Commission of the Central Committee of the Chinese Communist Party (CCP), the CMC actually enjoys a great deal of autonomy from the jurisdiction of the Central Committee or the Politburo. Its membership usually consists of the defense minister, the chief of the general staff, the directors of the general political and logistic departments, the commanders of the air and naval forces, and commanders of some major military regions. As both an eminent organ of the party leadership and the pinnacle of the military high command, the function of the CMC could be interpreted in two very different ways. It could be considered the organ through which the party exercises political control of the PLA since it is officially under the CCP Central Committee. During Mao's time its chairmanship was always held by Mao himself, who was concurrently chairman of the party. This interpretation is also consistent with the 1975 and 1978 state constitutions, which stipulated that the chairman of the CCP Central Committee was the supreme commander of all the armed forces.[1]

On the other hand, the CMC's power could also be understood as a manifestation of military penetration into the party. The majority of CMC members are military rather than civilian leaders who concurrently sit in the Central Committee, some of them in the Politburo. They thereby participate in general policy-making. Both these interpretations contain some truth. In fact, the CMC could best be seen as the highest connecting point of party-army blending. All the policies or directives of the CMC bear equal authority of both the party and the military leadership. It is hard to distinguish any particular policies and directives of the CMC as representing purely party or military interests.

Party Committees

Directly under the authority of the CMC are party committees at each level of the PLA. As the highest authority in each unit, they decide on all promotions, political education, and military training.[2] At every level from top to middle, each military unit has three sections subordinate to the party committee, replicating the general department divisions under the CMC: the political department, the command department, and the supply department.

The *political department* is an executive body of the party committee in charge of the political work under the direction of the political commissar. However, it has its own director, who, without exception, also sits on the party standing committee along with the commissar, the commander, and the chief of staff of the unit. Sometimes the director of the supply department is also a standing committee member, but not always. Among the three departments, the political department is generally considered more important in many areas, other than military training and war operations, which are the command department's responsibility under the direction of the commander. At each level it gains its importance through control of all promotions and reporting, which gives it access and influence at higher levels. It has four subdivisions: (1) the cadre division for personnel matters; (2) the organization division to take care of meetings, reports, and so on; (3) the propaganda division; (4) the security (*baowei*) division. The political department is in charge of all background checks, since there is no security department within the military. This division is only in charge of internal security, concerning criminal cases in the unit and settlement of personal disputes among officers and soldiers. It is not targeted against hostile penetrations from outside in terms of anti-espionage or counterintelligence.

The command department also has four subdivisions: (1) military training; (2) guards; (3) military affairs (*junwu*, concerning daily routine affairs); (4) war operations (planning).

The *supply department* has four subdivisions: (1) equipment (not weapons); (2) finance; (3) production (farms and factories, including joint ventures with local authorities); (4) transportation (railroads, harbors, airfields, etc.).

Party structure in the PLA does not represent a separate system of civilian control over the military.[3] These committees are an integral part of the military hierarchy, composed of career military rather than civilian members. The only exception is the civilian party secretaries who concurrently hold the positions of political commissars in military regions and districts. A typical party committee usually includes the political commissar, the commander, their deputies, the director of the political department and the chief of staff of the unit. Composed of senior leaders of the unit, the party committees within the military are essentially the same as party core groups or committees in any unit of the government or party, respectively. Instead of serving as a separate system of civilian control over the military command, they are the military command itself.

Although the commissar usually also sits in the next higher level party committee and thus enjoys more access and influence than the commander, he should not be considered a representative of party control. This is because any given member of a party committee, whether a military or political officer, must obey military commanders at the higher levels as well as his political superiors. In other words, military commanders have just as much authority as political commissars of the same level over party committees and political officers of lower ranks. In order to create a separate system for supervisory purposes, the party and political organizations would have to be given some autonomy from their military superiors, which obviously has not been the case in the PLA. As power rests with the party committee in each unit, it is important to note whether the commissar or commander serves as the party secretary.

The norm is as follows: division level and below: commissar = party secretary, and commander = deputy secretary; army level: either commissar or commander = secretary, and the other is deputy; regional level: commander = party secretary, always.

Thus at the regional level, where there is power to move troops, the commander is given full, undivided military and political authority. This is to say that political commissars have less power vis-à-vis commanders at the army level and above. As a result it is very important to the political leadership to assure the loyalty of military region commanders.

Control over Troop Movement

Party control over the army as manifested in regulations for moving troops is ambiguous. The regulations are as follows: To move an army requires the signature of the CMC chairman; division, permission of the General Staff Department (GSD) and the CMC; regiment, regional party committee; battalion, army-level party committee; company, division party committee.

Examples of the regulations in practice show the precariousness of party control over the military. In late 1976, after Mao died, the director of the General Political Department (GPD), Zhang Chunqiao (a civilian and Politburo Standing Committee member) moved a division headed by Sun Yuguo (the hero of the 1969 Sino-Soviet border clash) to Beijing from Shenyang Military Region, where Mao Yuanxin (Mao's nephew) was political commissar. The CMC vice chairman and defense minister, Marshal Ye Jianying (a veteran career military leader), was angry, because only the CMC could give permission to move a division, yet he did not even know about the order. Consequently, the division was ordered back to its barracks.[4]

The significance of this event lies in the fact that Ye Jianying, who ranked lower than Zhang Chunqiao in the party hierarchy, was able to nullify Zhang's order in the name of the CMC. This was one of the events that alarmed the pragmatists in the party leadership, who soon collaborated in arresting the Gang of Four. This arrest, in turn, was a typical palace coup organized by Ye Jianying and carried out by the Central Guard Regiment known as the "8341 Unit" under the direction of its commissar and the director of the Central Committee General Office, Wang Dongxing.[5]

Another example of troop movement politics occurred during June 3–4,

1989. The Thirty-eighth Army commander received an order to move into Beijing through a telephone call from the CMC General Office. But he refused to do so, because he did not have the signature of the CMC chairman. As the party leadership was split on how to handle the crisis (the party general secretary, Zhao Ziyang, was opposed to military action) there was ambiguity as to whether the commander was to obey the party or the military high command. He was consequently arrested and put on military trial in the wake of the crackdown.

Armed Forces in the Capital

After Mao's death, important changes took place among the armed forces stationed in Beijing. More units are now answerable to different central leadership organs, responsible for the security of central leaders and central institutions located in the capital. One purpose for this pluralism was to provide some checks and balances. Although the CMC oversees all these units, they each have a different oversight unit for daily affairs.

The Beijing Garrison Divisions (in Beijing, *weishuqu*; in other cities, *jingbeiqu*) originally included four divisions—two for garrisoning the city proper, the other two mechanized divisions for guarding the outskirts of the city. Tasks include protection of the major regime (party, military, government) institutions and the key locations (such as the Jingxi Guesthouse, used for top party and military meetings), and military leaders' residences. Most of these fall under the first division, located inside the city, guarding west of Wangfujing Street. The second and third divisions, which have heavy weaponry, guard the perimeter of the city. The fourth division (five units) is responsible for guarding east of Wangfujing (including foreign embassies). In 1982, when the People's Armed Police Force (PAPF) was resurrected as an organization separate from the PLA, the fourth division joined the Beijing PAPF.

Besides the CMC, the garrison leadership is responsible to the Beijing municipal leaders. A Beijing party secretary is its first political commissar. This is one of the most important mechanisms of civilian party control over the PLA. Yet the penetration goes two ways. Both the garrison's commander and its commissar are members of the Beijing Party Committee's Standing Committee. The garrison headquarters is located next to the municipal party and government headquarters.

Communication within the garrison is given special attention. A typical political report from the office of a division's political department would be hand-delivered by a courier (twice each day, mainly by motorcycle) to the Garrison Command. Because of the sensitivity of the first division, it had its own battalion specializing in communication. One company was in charge of a separate military telephone system, including many "hot lines" (direct lines from the division up to the garrison and down to lower levels). A regular field army would have such a battalion; a division normally would have only a company for communication. The garrison itself had its own communication regiment, but only around 1,000 men, not the normal 1,500 in a regiment.

The Central Guard Regiment (Zhongyang jingwei tuan) is responsible for guarding top leaders in terms of both personal safety and residence; it is the same size and strength as a division.[6] After its long-time director, Wang Dongxing, fell from power in 1980, the famous "8341 unit" was reorganized and given a new five-digit number (beginning with 5), but everyone still calls it the "8341." It is not solely or directly under the Beijing Garrison Command, although the latter provides training. There is a triple command system, combining civil and military authorities—the Beijing Garrison, the CMC General Office, and the Central Committee General Office. The latter plays the key role; its approval is required for any action by the other two supervisory units, and it has normal operational control. The importance of this office in intraleadership conflicts was revealed on the eve of the Cultural Revolution when its director, Yang Shangkun, became one of the first victims of the unfolding political storm. Yang was dismissed at the end of 1965 and replaced by Wang Dongxing. The decision was announced internally on the same day as the publication of Yao Wenyuan's article that attacked "Hai Rui Is Dismissed from Office" by Wu Han, which marked the first shot of the Cultural Revolution.[7] The unit also played a crucial role in the coup against the Gang of Four in 1976.

The Central Committee General Office selects and promotes all doctors, secretaries, cooks, and drivers for leaders, and takes care of other aspects of their living conditions. But the CMC General Office appoints its 8341 unit guards and military secretaries, with Central Committee General Office approval. A leader's military secretary is in charge of all his guards; this secretary always accompanies the leader, although the guards do not necessarily travel with him. After 1985, a separate guard unit under the Garrison Command was established for military leaders and their residences, leaving the 8341 responsible only for party and government leaders.

The PLA Personnel System

The CMC has final authority over personnel decisions involving military region commanders and commissars, their deputies, and above, including the leaders of the Beijing Garrison Command (but not Shanghai or Tianjin

Garrisons). The "CMC" actually means the "top leader" (Deng or Mao Zedong) here. Thus, at the top levels, party control over the military personnel is realized mainly through the authority of the paramount leaders who control both the party and the military. The GPD is the CMC's "staff" for investigations, reports, and recommendations involving personnel. They send the lists for approval. The GPD has little influence over appointments at the very top level, but great power over personnel within the military regions. The norm for personnel authority is as follows: The head of an army is appointed by the Politburo; division by CMC; regiment by regional party committee; battalion by army-level party committee; company by divisional party committee; platoon by regimental party committee.

In the PLA, the political departments are involved, along with supply and command departments, in both recruiting and demobilizing regular soldiers. The main responsibility for recruiting lies with the political department, because of the importance of checking political reliability. The main responsibility for demobilization lies with the command department; the political department merely provides a political report for the person's file. For officers, however, the political department alone is responsible for demobilization and retirement since all officers are party members. The personnel section recommends the lists for approval by the party committee; the organization section does the actual detailed work.

Most important PLA schools are controlled by the GPD, although the General Staff Department (GSD) and General Logistics Department (GLD) each have a college of their own and the military regions have theirs. Graduates of the three general departments' advanced (*gaoji*) colleges became officers at unit-level and above. During the reform era, many younger officers were promoted directly out of the military schools, and therefore the personnel section had less influence. After June 1989, this trend was reversed, again making room for more promotion through patronage rather than according to professional criteria.

In the actual personnel process, the work of the party secretaries is extremely influential. The party committee assigns a secretary of the political department to do a background check on someone and then, if appropriate, to recommend a promotion to the standing committee (commissar and deputy, plus commander and deputy) to make a collective decision. Several formal meetings may be involved in the process; discussion and decision rarely take place at such meetings but rather occur informally during the process.

Fall was the time for annual PLA nationwide recruitment. "First pick" always went to the 8341 unit; Beijing Garrison got "second choice" and the Beijing Military Region came thereafter. The 8341 unit normally did its own recruiting, but sometimes would delegate this to the Garrison Command, since the latter had more personnel for recruiting and selected from more localities. Sometimes, the garrison would voluntarily recommend an outstanding recruit to 8341.

A Garrison Command recruiting team of ten would be in charge of one county. They would look at over twenty thousand files of persons recommended by the village party secretaries, conduct selected personal interviews in the villages, and choose only twenty recruits for the garrison from each county. Criteria for recruits were: age seventeen to twenty-two, North China origin (for a proper Beijing accent), usually middle school or high school education, and political reliability (by far the most important criterion). This meant having a poor peasant family origin, with rarely an exception, plus a good record of personal behavior.

Case Studies of Political Campaigns in the PLA

The PLA tends to be very self-protective. The party committee of the Beijing Garrison hardly ever witnesses an internal power struggle or mutual accusation; it demonstrates a unified front in dealing with higher levels, as the following case studies reveal. In both cases, no purge resulted from a change in political line, revealing a strong tendency within the PLA to feign compliance successfully, even with a major turn in political direction. The CCP is so concerned about PLA unity that it bends over backward to avoid the destabilizing purges that occur in civilian sectors.

In general, less factionalism arises within the PLA than in civilian organizations precisely because the CCP is so sensitive to division or dissent at all levels that it is promptly nipped in the bud. Discipline is very strict. As a result, problems are often covered up or resolved at each level out of self-protection, and the end result is to lessen power struggles in general.

Case One

In the early 1970s, the Gang of Four had created three model PLA units, one of them a company in the first division of the Beijing Garrison Command. Mao's wife, Jiang Qing, had visited the company of the Beijing Garrison Command for two months during the campaign against Lin Biao and Confucius. The party committee of the first division had written a letter pledging loyalty to Jiang Qing and promising that the committee would support anything she wanted to do with this unit. A group was sent for her to use as personal staff, headed by a deputy commissar; this group wrote articles for her during the campaign.

Obviously, this became a major political problem after the overthrow of the Gang. An investigation team was sent down by the CMC, composed mainly of GPD officers. The committee was asked to explain who had drafted the letter, who had decided and how it had been decided to send it. The process of the investigation was as follows: During the first week, "brainwashing" was conducted to reorient the committee; members studied documents criticizing the Gang. Next, in group meetings, each person was questioned with regard to involvement in the incident; precisely what they had done and when and with whom. Since most of the committee members were relatively new and had not been involved, they "weren't active." Most of those responsible were retired as advisers (still in uniform and on the books, but "on leave" and inactive on a daily basis), but they all attended these meetings. Each guilty person confessed and conducted a self-criticism. All passed the buck by saying, "I was tricked (*chi pian*) by Jiang Qing and wasn't firm enough in resisting." In the end, a final conclusion was reached and a formal report sent to the CMC.

A group process of writing the report produced many drafts, as the party committee labored word by word, seeking to avoid accepting responsibility. The final report was just half a page, saying, "Jiang Qing's black hand got into our unit. The majority tried to stand firm against the counterrevolutionary plot, but we failed, and thus gave her an opportunity with serious consequences for which the party committee is partially responsible. The lesson is that we must keep alert and stand firm on the side of the correct party line." (The implication was that the "black hand" was Jiang Qing herself; no other individuals were responsible.)

The actual story behind the scenes was that Jiang Qing had initiated a contact with the company directly, since it was a very important unit, responsible for guarding Jingxi Guesthouse, the site of many top party and military meetings, and she was anxious to develop influence within the PLA. First, she held an informal discussion meeting about the current political campaign with company officers; after hearing their talks, she encouraged them to publish them. The company reported on this contact to the first division's party committee, which saw it as a great opportunity to get special attention and favors. So the committee sent some of its personnel to the company to help write their articles.

The result of the investigation and cover-up was that no one in the committee was punished. One lower-level scapegoat was found, a division party committee propaganda section official, and demobilized—ostensibly for other reasons. The cover-up succeeded because the GPD team conspired with it; they didn't want to know what really happened, as evidenced by the fact that they showed up for the investigation meetings only occasionally, leaving it largely to the committee to decide on its own.

Case Two

In 1978–80, political study sessions were held within the first division party committee to "study reform." In reality, the majority of committee members, including the commissar, disagreed with the reform policies. The result was study sessions that were almost like a script for a play or movie. They would begin with general statements like "I support Deng Xiaoping," but quickly would move on to griping about "society getting worse, more corrupt, materialistic." Then the commissar would politely but not forcefully or genuinely "correct" these views. (A generation gap was very evident in the exchange of opinions.)

After the study sessions, a party secretary was asked to draft a resolution supporting reform. He was personally enthusiastic and so wrote a very positive first draft, which the commissar disagreed with and which he watered down considerably.

The report was sent two levels above (up through the Garrison Command to the military region level) as was usual whenever an action was ordered from above. (Routine meetings dealing with internal matters initiated by the committee itself would be recorded, but reported up only if something of significance emerged.)

Conclusion: Party Control vs. Civilian Control

Both cases reveal that the PLA was required to take sides in intraleadership disputes over power and policy. As the intraleadership power struggle and policy disputes heightened, both sides of the conflict went out of their way to enlist military support. This shows that military involvement in politics is a systemic feature of PRC politics. In the first case, the first division leaders responded to Jiang Qing's overtures both because they felt pressured and because they took it as an opportunity for potential career advancement. They were later criticized not for their involvement in political affairs but for taking the wrong side by supporting the Gang.

This reflects a fundamental difference between the Chinese principle of party control and the Western professional ethic of civilian control over the military. In China, the party has never been just "civilian." It includes both the civilian and the military. For a long time before 1949 it was more military than civilian. Throughout the history of the People's Republic of China (PRC), the military elites have enjoyed as much legitimacy in political decision-making as their civilian colleagues because of the structural party-army blending.

Moreover, the Chinese concept of party supremacy is never abstract. It always has particular political and policy implications. For instance, the central theme of the political indoctrination in the PLA after 1959 was obviously factional and policy-oriented, centered on the building of Mao's personal cult. PLA members were told to engage in class struggle between socialism and capitalism. They were to safeguard Mao's "Three Red Banners" Great Leap Forward policies against "political right deviation."[8] Party control, to the PLA, meant the control of those party leaders, military or civilian, who represented the "correct line" of the party in the class struggle between Marxism and revisionism. On the eve of the Cultural Revolution, Mao and Lin Biao were believed to represent the "correct line" of the party. It is thus not surprising that the PLA intervened on the Mao-Lin side without worrying about violating the principle of the party commanding the gun. Instead of restricting military intervention in politics, party loyalty requires active military participation in the political conflicts on the "correct" side. Party control can thus even be understood as the opposite of civilian control.

Almost two decades have passed since Mao died in 1976. Yet little discussion has taken place in the Chinese official press about the misuse of the PLA during the Cultural Revolution. Despite all the condemnation of the Cultural Revolution as a "disaster" and "internal chaos," only passing mention has been made of the fact that military intervention was a deeper cause of the national tragedy.[9] All the propaganda since the end of the Cultural Revolution has tried to show how the campaign should not have been launched in the first place, but has not tried to understand how a party minority headed by Mao and Lin was able to prevail despite the majority will of the Central Committee and Politburo. This failure reflects the fundamental acceptance among CCP members and in the general society of the military as an intrinsic part of the political process. The reluctance to condemn military intervention as wrong regardless of circumstances indicates that the party leadership today is still not ready to exclude the military from political affairs. In fact the leaders are careful to preserve their prerogative to use the army in future emergency situations such as occurred in the spring of 1989. The Chinese party-state has a long way to go before it can endorse the principle of civilian control and nonintervention for its armed forces.

Notes

This chapter represents some of the author's dissertation findings and is based largely on interviews with a former People's Liberation Army officer who served in the Beijing Garrison Command for ten years until 1985. As a secretary in the political department of a division of the command, the officer's duties included arranging and convening meetings, taking notes, drafting forms and reports, doing an annual analytical summary of the year's work, and recruiting.

1. In the 1954 and 1982 constitutions, however, the state chairman was designated as the commander in chief of the military. This is generally considered cosmetic; the real power of the state chairman was never comparable to that of the party chairman. The same is true with the state CMC created in 1982, which turned out to be identical to the Standing Committee of the party CMC.

2. Cf. "Political Work Regulations for the Chinese People's Liberation Army" issued on March 27, 1963, in Ying-Mao Kau, *The Political Work System of the Chinese Communist Party: Analysis and Documents* (Providence: East Asia Language and Area Center, Brown University, 1971), 231–38.

3. This view was, for instance, represented by John Gittings, *The Role of the Chinese Army* (London: Oxford University Press, 1967), 106.

4. For an account of these events, cf. Andres D. Onate, "Hua Kuo-feng and the Arrest of the Hua Kuo-feng Gang of Four," *The China Quarterly*, no. 75 (September 1978): 540–65.

5. Wang was also the director of the Security Bureau of the CMC and a vice minister of public security. See Huang Zhenxia, *Zhonggong junren zhi* (Annals of Chinese Military Men) (Beijing: Dangdai lishi yanjiusuo, 1968), 744.

6. The "8341" was estimated by Kang Mingshu as the size of an army corps with 35,000 to 40,000 men, including two guard divisions, one independent armored regiment, and some independent antiair, engineering, and communications regiments and battalions. See *Sirenbang shijian qianhou* (Before and After the Incident of the Gang of Four) (Taipei: Shibao wenhua chuban gongsi, 1978), 51, 52, 57, 58.

7. Ma Qibin, *Zhongguo gongchandang zhizheng sishinian* (Forty Years of CCP Rule) (Beijing: Zhonggong dangshi ziliao chubanshe, 1989), 264.

8. Cf. "The Resolution of the Enlarged CMC Conference Regarding the Strengthening of the Political Work in the Armed Forces," made by the CMC on October 20, 1960, in *Zhongguo remin jiefangjun zhengzhi gongzuoshi* (History of PLA Political Work) (Beijing: Defense University Press, 1988), 165–68.

9. Cf. "The Resolution on Some of the Party's Historical Issues Since the Founding of the PRC." This document was drafted under Deng Xiaoping's personal direction and was passed by the sixth plenum of the Eleventh Central Committee in June 1981. For the entire text see *Mingci jieshi* (Explanation of Terminology) (Beijing: Changzheng chubanshe, 1981), 20–30.

Part III
Experiments in System Reform

12

The Decision Process Behind the 1986–1989 Political Reforms

Chen Yizi

Patriarchal rule is typical in a totalitarian state like China. The pattern of policy-making usually takes the form of "head scratching,"[1] meaning that policy-making begins with an idea generated in the mind of one or more top leaders, whether it be idealistic or realistic. Because of the resulting irregularity and unconventionality of policy initiation, the ensuing policy, from initiation to formation and finally implementation, usually requires new temporary institutions and personnel alongside the formal bureaucratic system, with mass campaign methods operating alongside formal bureaucratic procedures. This is the origin of the numerous leading groups and temporary organizations in the Chinese political system at all levels. Statistics in 1986 showed more of these informal institutions than of formal institutions at most levels of governance.

From Mao Zedong to Deng Xiaoping to Zhao Ziyang, the nature of the "ideas" that initiate policies shifted from idealism to utilitarianism, then to rationalism. And the pattern of decision-making shifted from one leader's "snap of a finger" to a group of leaders' "joining heads," then to the experimental "crossing the river by groping for the stones."

The decision-making process on political reform between 1986 and 1989 may provide us with some insight into this evolution.

The Origin of Political Reform

To trace the origin of the political reform, we have to go back to the late 1970s. It is generally agreed that the economic reform program began at the turning point provided by the third plenum of the Eleventh Central Committee at the end of 1978. Two different types of political reform emerged after the Cultural Revolution: one in 1978, and the other in 1986; they were quite different in nature, goal, scope, and method.

After Mao's death and the downfall of the Gang of Four in 1976, many people, especially intellectuals, began discussing the weaknesses of the Chinese political system. Discussion revolved around the question of how to eliminate political elements that produced such forces as the Gang of Four and how to change the one-man rule of Mao's era. In 1978, when the Cultural Revolution officially ended, people began to contemplate seriously how to prevent another such disaster.

Still, implementing political reforms at that time was nearly impossible for two reasons. First, after the ten years of the Cultural Revolution, the country was economically weak, and the people were living in poverty. The majority demanded an improvement in living standards. Only intellectuals, who were a minority, asked for political change (as reflected in the 1979 Democracy Wall movement). Second, the leaders who had been attacked during the Cultural Revolution, once reinstated, were no longer motivated to change the system that gave them political and economic power along with special privileges. They believed that China's socialist system basically was adequate and it was only a few leaders who misdirected it temporarily.

However, after economic reform was launched in 1978, it soon became clear that economic reforms could achieve only limited success without political changes. For example, the deepening of agricultural reforms led to hiring of labor, which, in turn, aroused opposition on the grounds that "capitalism is being reborn." When intellectuals brought up the issues of freedom of the press, freedom of creativity, and freedom of speech, orthodox Communists initiated campaigns against "bourgeois liberalism" and "spiritual pollution."

The First Wave of Political Reform

The first wave of political reform, launched at the end of 1978, was widely known in China as "restoring order from chaos and returning to normal" (*boluan fanzheng*). This political reform was aimed at negating the Cultural Revolution and resurrecting the political system as it existed before the Cultural Revolution. All the orthodox Leninist party and government institutions were gradually reconstructed, discipline restored, and former bureaucrats returned to office. Among the 201 members of the Central Committee at the end of the 1970s, more than 80 were reelected former officials. All the old senior leaders were rehabilitated one by one, among them Chen Yun, Peng Zhen, Bo Yibo, and Wang Zhen. Unlimited political power was returned to them. This political reform is most properly called conservative in nature because except for the critique of the Cultural Revolution, it was confined within the formal ideology and tradition of the old Chinese Communist Party (CCP); it did little to touch the core of the Communist political system. The culmination of this stage of reform came with the twelfth party congress and the third session of the Fifth National People's Congress (NPC) in 1982. To do it justice, this stage of political reform undoubtedly had a positive effect in the aftermath of the disastrous Cultural Revolution, and it also made some marginal system changes at the local level such as the abolition of the commune system. Maybe it was the best possible choice, but it left two hidden problems. First, it left serious systemic difficulties that would surface more and more as obstacles in the later reform period. Second, it formed two conflicting groups in the reform camp (which had defeated the Maoist faction), one being the conservatives headed by Chen Yun, the other more liberal and open-minded leaders headed by Deng Xiaoping. Both labeled themselves reformers, and both carried the banner of reform, but they really meant completely different things.

That is the background for Deng Xiaoping's failed political reform from the top before 1986. The emergence in the 1980s of the idea of separating the party from the government—the heart of the later political reform—was a good example. That idea was originally put forward by none other than Deng Xiaoping himself. As early as 1941, he realized that problems existed in the newly established democratic government in the liberated areas during the anti-Japanese war. Before that time, the issue was not salient because the party's central task was to win the war. There was only the integrated party and army, but no government. Faced then with a strong tendency among party members to reserve for the party powers rightly belonging to the government, Deng strongly criticized this as an evil passed on by the Kuomintang (KMT). He pointed out that "the malady of ruling the country through the party institutions was the best way to paralyze our party, corrupt our party, sabotage our party, and separate our party from the broad masses."[2]

After the founding of the People's Republic of China (PRC) in 1949, such problems were no longer mentioned among the new leaders. Only at the end of the 1970s was this issue again brought up by Deng Xiaoping. At first, the separation of the party from the government was not directly raised, but debate revolved around the need to strengthen and improve party leadership. This obviously was Deng's major political concern during the late 1970s and the early 1980s. He began talking about this quite frequently both in private and on public occasions. Nevertheless, with the mountains of problems to be solved at that time, the true meaning of this issue attracted little attention at first. Deng became impatient and frustrated about this. In 1978 at a preparatory work conference before the third plenum, he condemned the practice of putting the party in place of the government at all administrative levels and bluntly pointed out that strengthening party leadership did not mean the party taking over everything or intervening in everything. By the same token, overall party leadership did not mean the integration of the party and the government or the replacement of the government by the party.[3]

By this time, the idea had begun to sink in among other leaders, and it caught the public eye in March 1978, when Deng spoke before the National Science Conference. In his speech he explored the issue further. His important message was better developed and more comprehensive than before. In addition to expanding his earlier ideas, he defined the connotation of the "leadership of the party," which had not yet been done by other leaders, including Mao. Deng said:

> The leadership of the party committee should be primarily political leadership, the guarantee of the correct political orientation in the unit concerned, seeing to it that the party's line, principles and policies are implemented. . . . It is impossible for all work to be done by the party, solved by the party; there should be a separation of responsibility. . . . The party committee should be acquainted with government work and check up on it, but should not attempt to take it over.[4]

This speech was drafted by Bao Tong, later to become the director of the political reform office, who was then the director of the state Science and Technology Commission's general office and already a strong advocate for economic and political reform. The Science and Technology Commission was then a stronghold for Deng's reform ideas. The phrasing no doubt reflected Bao's understanding of the meaning of political reform, but Deng made clear to him the points he wanted to address and to emphasize both before and while the speech was drafted.

After the conference, Deng took this issue to the Politburo. It was picked up quickly by other leaders, like Bo Yibo and Peng Zhen. Later, Deng asked Li Xiannian to emphasize this topic again at the April 1979 Central Committee work conference, which Li did.[5] Other top leaders, including Hu Yaobang and Zhao Ziyang, were even more enthusiastic about this. They talked about party-state reform in many of their speeches during the period. Although they may have had much more in mind concerning this, they were careful not to go beyond the meaning of Deng's words. The pace for action was also set in accordance with Deng's guidance.

Among several important speeches Deng made on the separation of the party and the government from the last half of 1978 through 1980, the most influential, which later played a crucial role in the 1986 political reform, was Deng's speech at the enlarged Politburo meeting of August 18, 1980. The speech was called "On Reform of the Party and Government Leadership System," in which he pinpointed the problems involved in the Cultural Revolution and indicated the deficiencies stemming from the party's acting as the government's surrogate. He implicitly called for a change in the system. Deng progressed from the previous call for "improvement of party leadership" to "reform of the system of party leadership." The message was very clear that this time he wanted a drastic and systemic institutional reform rather than an improvement in style and discipline.

Deng Xiaoping later disclosed that two things had mainly led him to this new approach. One was the serious situation in the economy, especially in the industrial sector during 1974-75, when he first returned to lead the central party and government, and again in the late 1970s and 1980s. As vice premier, he could very well have experienced the tug-of-war caused by the interference of the party bureaucracy in the government, which hindered the implementation of his policies; and as party vice chairman, he saw that he had to take on a lot of government responsibilities. Finding no efficiencies there, he realized that the key problem lay in the overconcentration of power, first in the central government, then in the party. It was more a political than an economic problem. His endeavor to pump up economic growth and present himself as the new savior of the country would surely fail unless the problem were solved. The other motivation was the suffering and humiliation he had experienced during the Cultural Revolution. His being purged three times was unique and troubled him a lot. He wanted to prevent such things from happening again and realized that to do so he must make systemic structural changes.

But after 1980, this surge for party-government reform gradually died down; it was not a main theme at the twelfth party congress and Deng addressed this topic less and less during his meetings with party and government officials and foreign guests, for four reasons.

First, after the elimination of the leftists led by Hua Guofeng, the recurrence of movements like the Cultural Revolution no longer seemed a pending threat.

Second, there were differences inside the ruling circle concerning the extension of political reform. The powerful Chen Yun camp took a more moderate stand than did Deng's. They believed that the problems of the Chinese political system could be addressed most effectively through internal party reforms. During the entire period when Deng advocated a system reform of the party and state, never once did Chen Yun even mention these words in his many public speeches. Instead he stressed the problems of cadre behavior, slack party discipline, and lack of ideological commitment, which he regarded as the result of the post-1958 negligence of traditional party work methods and the Maoist assault on party authority during the ten-year catastrophe. What he was most concerned about was defects in "work style" and the decline in the credibility and legitimacy of the party. Chen's ally, People's Liberation Army (PLA) veteran Huang Kecheng, said, "In the 1950s we would send cars to take our children home from the primary boarding schools on weekends without hearing any complaints from the masses; now things are different. Even sending an aide to take the children home from school is criticized."[6] At a time when Deng needed Chen's cooperation both in the economic field and political field, certain compromises had to be made.

Third, the priority of the party shifted to a more urgent agenda: reconstruction of the collapsed economy. Fighting over Hua's draft ten-year plan was not yet over, and forming a new adjustment program was difficult. By the time of the fourth session of the Fifth National People's Congress in December 1981, Chen's view had gained more acceptance among the leadership. The original "three years of readjustment" was extended to 1985, and Zhao Ziyang announced "ten important principles" that incorporated Chen's balanced growth philosophy. But the session failed to ratify the annual plan or the 1982 budget or discuss the long-awaited draft five-year plan for 1980–85. While all agreed on the principle of "readjustment," evidently debate on the actual allocation of resources remained tense. Deng did not want to risk any further big political ventures without some economic cushion.

Fourth, the excited discussion of political reform and democracy in 1980 went beyond Deng's limit. In the discussion and debate, intellectuals advocated (1) a change in the nature and form of the state from a proletarian dictatorship to a socialist federation; (2) abolition of life tenure for the paramount leader; (3) the study of Western democracy's separation of powers; and (4) defining the goal of political reform as the establishment of democracy. All this was more than Deng could tolerate. Deng smelled something dangerous from the "right." One day in 1981 he called together the heads of the propaganda departments and pointed out very seriously:

> Some people recently made a great clamor; the content of a lot of their speeches was much worse than the rightists in 1957. . . . In essence, what they want is to discard socialism, to get rid of the leadership of the party, and spread bourgeois liberalism. . . . From now on, we will not launch an anti-

rightist movement, but we will fight mercilessly the various wrong trends whenever necessary.[7]

So the early 1980s political reform ended up with an anti-liberal movement and a compromise with the conservatives. Deng refrained from any drastic party-government reform. Instead, a bureaucratic streamlining and some small-scale experiments with various institutional reforms at the grass-roots level were carried out. Given these circumstances, when I raised the necessity of political reform with Zhao Ziyang in early 1984, Zhao avoided the subject.

The Second Wave of Political Reform

It was not until the end of 1984, when the comprehensive economic reform program had been endorsed by the Central Committee, that the request for a political reform began to arise again among intellectuals, students, and local government leaders. The intellectuals and students called for freedom of the press and speech, while the local leaders believed that the existing political system hindered further economic reform. When the triumvirate reformist leadership of Deng, Hu, and Zhao had been consolidated, the issue of political reform resurfaced. In late 1984 and early 1985, when I briefed Hu Yaobang and Zhao Ziyang on the subject of political reform, they agreed that without political reform, the further advancement of China's economic reforms would face great obstacles. Hu had already repeatedly addressed the issues of freedom of speech, press, and creativity. Zhao also said, "If we don't proceed with political reform, it will be very difficult to proceed with economic reforms. If the party/government and government/industry relationships are not separated, then enterprises can never truly reach the stage of having control over their own profits and losses." Beginning in 1985, Deng showed up in public more frequently and began picking up the old themes again, although the content did not go beyond that of his 1980 speeches.

The motivation behind this was the pressing need for economic reform. Never in his wildest dreams did Deng want democratic reform in its true sense. Politically he did want some relaxation, but that was all he intended in 1985–86. Economic reform was the central cause of his interest, as was explicit in Deng's talks in early 1986. At a July 28 meeting of high officials Deng pointed out that "political reform and economic reform are reciprocal, and dependent on each other. They should be well coordinated. There surely will be a dead-end for the economic reform unless the political reform keeps up, since the first obstacle you meet with will be people's interests." Later Deng took up the issue with every foreign guest he met, telling some Japanese visitors, "Without a big stride in economic reform, the necessity for political reform became more apparent."[8]

In 1986, urban economic reform met with serious problems. All kinds of conflicts of interest appeared, the conservatives stepped up their opposition, and there was a lot of dissent in society regarding the injustice and inequality produced as a by-product of the reform. Even the reformist circle encountered difficulties in reaching consensus on various policies. Besides the difficult economic and social situation then, more and more economic decisions eventually affected political issues, especially the power and role of the party and the way it operated. As the economic reform deepened, it apparently could no longer be confined to economics.

The Economic Reform Institute, of which I was the director, in early 1985 organized ten working groups to investigate the progress of economic reform in ten counties. The final report of the investigation, which was sent to Hu Yaobang and Deng Xiaoping, concluded that only when the foundation for a democratic political system was laid at the end of this century could China achieve full modernization. If the problems of the political system remained unsolved, the future of China would be unpredictable and, recalling the death of 43 million people from starvation in the early 1960s, the CCP's reputation in history would be open to question.

By 1986, the problems encountered in the deepening of economic reforms caused people to become increasingly vocal in demanding political reforms. All kinds of forums were held in Beijing. In July, I presented a speech called "Economic Reform and Political Reform" at the Central Party School. I stated that political reform was the guarantor of economic reform, and that if political reform was not carried out, economic reform could not make progress. Although Hu Qiaomu criticized the speech, Zhao Ziyang and Deng Xiaoping gave their approval. As premier, Zhao Ziyang was eager to push for political reform to clear the way for economic reform. He wanted to enlarge the power of the government when it needed it most, while restricting the power of the party. Deng worked closely with Zhao Ziyang in economic reform all through the 1980s, so it was impossible for Deng to put aside the critical issue any longer. In 1986, Deng stepped up his effort to begin political reform. He planned to put the political reform formally on the agenda at the sixth plenum of the Twelfth Central Committee late in the year. Because of the complexity of the issues and the lack of preparation, Deng wanted to be sure that political reform was carefully planned and the risks at a minimum. In any case, this agenda was very clear now.

On September 13, Deng attended the work reporting session of the Central Finance and Economics Leading Group. At this session he assigned

Zhao Ziyang the new task of organizing the research and design of political reform for approval at the Thirteenth National Party Congress scheduled for late 1987. Deng told Zhao that it was time to begin the discussion on the range and content of political reform. He then spoke of several guidelines that he had been considering for some time. Deng said at the meeting that the "goal of this political reform should be to motivate people's initiative, raise efficiency, and get rid of bureaucratism. The key should be the separation of party and government. How should the party exercise its leadership? How can they be good at this? This is very important. The second goal of political reform should be the decentralization of power. The third goal should be the streamlining of the bureaucracy. And don't forget the issue of efficiency."

Further direction from Deng followed, setting the boundaries for the political reform: (1) socialist principles should be upheld in the whole political reform process; (2) there should be no talk of the Western-style separation of power among the branches of government; (3) the design work of the political reform should be kept away from the public, lest an early leak cause social instability. These limits would later be repeatedly emphasized by Deng during the process of policy-making.

Given the political tradition and procedure in China, it was unconventional for the premier to take charge of the country's political reform. Although Zhao Ziyang also held a top party position as a member of the Politburo Standing Committee, it is the rule that each standing member take care only of the work in his own domain, which is decided when a new Politburo is formed. Political affairs are usually the responsibility of the party general secretary, and Hu Yaobang was still general secretary at the time. One possible explanation for the choice of Zhao to lead political reform was that Hu was losing Deng's favor and his power was rapidly diminishing after the June Politburo meeting during which Deng criticized him concerning their disagreement on criticism of bourgeois liberalism. Giving Zhao this assignment may have been a further harbinger of Hu's later fall from grace.

Another possible explanation is that by that time, a reshuffling of top party and government leaders was in process before the thirteenth party congress, during which it was planned that Hu would take charge of the Central Military Commission and also become president of the country, leaving the position of party general secretary to Zhao Ziyang. Deng and other old leaders gave Hu so many hints and applied so much pressure that, at a Politburo meeting in September, Hu himself recommended that Zhao Ziyang be in charge of political reform, and the Politburo approved. This meeting gave the procedure more legitimacy in the eyes of the many puzzled officials involved.

Institutional Reform Arrangements

After the Politburo decision, Zhao immediately sent a written report to Deng and the Politburo, saying, "To establish socialism for the long term, and maintain stable administration of the country, we must accelerate the pace of political reforms." He proposed the establishment of a five-member Political Reform Research Group (Zhengzhi tizhi gaige yanjiu xiaozu), the equivalent of a central leading group. The intent and major function of this group was to provide suggestions and advice to the Politburo on political reform. The group consisted of Zhao himself, Hu Qili (secretary of the Central Secretariat), Tian Jiyun (vice premier), Bo Yibo (vice chairman of the Central Advisory Commission), and Peng Chong (vice chairman of the Standing Committee of the National People's Congress). Bao Tong, who was then Zhao's personal secretary and political secretary of the Politburo, drafted Zhao's report, which was quickly approved by Deng. A Political Reform Office was soon set up under the Political Reform Research Group as its operational organ. The office was organized as a temporary institution at first, with leadership brought in from Zhao's government economic reform team. The office director was Bao Tong, chief of staff for the premier's office and vice minister of the state Economic Reform Commission. The deputy director was He Guanghui, also a vice minister of the commission. To provide some political balance, Zhou Jie, a deputy director of the Central Committee General Office, later came as deputy director of the office. He was a protégé of Hu Yaobang and Hu Qili, as well as Hu Yaobang's main speechwriter and policy aide.

Zhao gave Bao Tong carte blanche in organizing the office and choosing the research staff. Zhao only emphasized that he wanted most of the staff to be comparatively young and to include some people from local government. It should be mentioned here that Zhao was the first Chinese leader in his generation to sincerely embrace the younger generation and open up to fresh ideas: He would often summon young economic specialists to his office and listen to their ideas for hours. This is very rare in a system that emphasizes seniority and rank so much. His economic think tanks were filled with talented young people, so he wanted to do the same with the political reform. Zhao acted as a bridge in connecting two generations.

On September 18, Bao Tong invited me to be in charge of daily operations in the Political Reform Office. Several leading intellectuals, including Zhou Jie, Wang Fei, Chen Fujing, Chao Zhi, and Yan Jiaqi, were recruited to this office, which was ultimately expanded to twenty people. The overcentralization of power in China creates a lot of evil, but it has also an advantage. When a person with high authority seriously wants something done, it happens simply and quickly. Such was the case with the formation of our office and our work. There was no red tape in the establishment of the institution, and no dragging of feet in the appointment of personnel.

The first meeting of the office staff was held on September 23. After the meeting, the office immediately began gathering materials on comparative political systems on a broad scale and held seminars discussing subjects ranging from the modernization of socialism and the goal of peaceful, stable administration, to crucial issues in political change. In addition to domestic resources, the office wrote to PRC embassies in more than twenty countries for information about foreign political systems.

The Political Reform Research Group held meetings periodically, about ten times between September 1986 and June 1987. The meetings were usually initiated by the Political Reform Office according to the schedule set by the Research Group, and prepared by the Central Committee General Office. Before each meeting convened, the office would get everything ready; Bao Tong would then report to the Research Group at the meeting, explaining all the important points and answering the leaders' questions. The decisions made at these meetings were usually prepared by the office and already discussed with Deng Xiaoping beforehand. At these meetings, the leaders would listen to the office reports; then a tense deliberation would follow.

Zhao Ziyang usually talked a lot, all through the meeting. The staff had the impression that he was very intelligent, thoughtful, and open-minded. He was also warm, humorous, and deeply concerned about the existing problems. Sometimes the staff wondered how, with the economic schedule so full at that time, he had time to think about all these issues and even of what lay ahead. Zhao's style was relaxed and steady, and he was always vivid in expressing his ideas. Once, when talking about grass-roots democracy, Zhao told the people at the meeting about the old "red bean democracy" in the liberated areas before 1949. He said that even at that time, there existed secret ballots and competitive elections. The candidates for the village head would stand in line, each holding a rice bowl behind his back, and the peasants would drop a red bean into the bowl of the one they chose (while talking Zhao stood up, holding his hands behind his back, showing people how this was done). The person who got the most red beans would be elected village head. Then he asked, why, so many years after the founding of the PRC, are we still afraid to carry out competitive elections? Why can't citizens' political rights be guaranteed? And it was at that meeting that the idea of competitive elections in the party and in the people's congresses was put forward. Later this new election method would first be tested at the thirteenth party congress, and Deng Liqun would be the famous first victim.

Other leaders usually inserted only a few words, except for Bo Yibo, who did not hesitate to speak his mind. When these meetings convened, sometimes all the staff would attend the meeting when it concerned a general topic, such as the discussion of the framework of the political reform. At other times only part of staff concerned would attend, because the topic was very specific. At each meeting, some tentative policy would be approved for further discussion in the Politburo.

These Research Group meetings witnessed the only formal working relations among the five leaders. After each meeting ended, they would go their own way to attend to their routine business. Other communication between them on the political reform occurred in the Politburo meetings convened during that period, as well as through the huge amount of paperwork the office sent to them regularly. They would sometimes write their opinion and sign their approval on the documents and have them sent back to the office. Bao Tong was in contact with Zhao Ziyang almost daily, and Zhao was well informed about whatever happened in the political reform policy design. Deng Xiaoping never appeared at any formal meetings, but he would be informed about all the important decisions.

Issue Identification and Policy Elaboration

In late September, the Research Group held its first meeting, which declared that the first stage of work should be clarifying the meaning of political reform. Several forums were held thereafter; the participants included well-known scholars such as Xue Muqiao, Yu Guangyuan, Su Shaozhi, Zhao Baoxu, Gao Fang, and Liao Gailong; PRC ambassadors from around the world; and former officials such as Li Ximing, Zhou Hui, Liu Jie, and Gao Yang. After months of discussion outside and within the Research Group and its office, a report was sent to Deng Xiaoping, stating that the current leadership system—while appropriate during times of war, class struggle, and mass movement—was unsuited to times of peace and construction. Political reforms in seven dimensions would resolve the problems of the party and government leadership system. These seven dimensions included: 1) separation of the party and the government; 2) development of inner-party democracy; 3) delegation of power (decentralization) and administrative reform; 4) party organizational reform; 5) personnel reform; 6) expansion of socialist democracy; and 7) perfection of a socialist legal system.

After reading the report in November 1986, Deng gave his approval and support, saying "The ideas in this report are very good." Deng usually says only one word about the important documents sent to him by the office, either "good" or "feasible." This time it was a "very good," so everyone sighed with relief. Other leaders in the Research Group also read the reports sent to them; they would usually make some suggestions and offer improvements, but they always left the decisions to Deng Xiaoping and Zhao Ziyang.

In late November, seven small groups under the Political Reform Office were formed, with the following assignments: (1) Wen Jiabao, director of the party Central Committee's General Office, in charge of the separation of party and government group; (2) Zhou Jie, deputy director of the General Office, in charge of the inner-party democracy group; (3) He Guanghui, deputy director of the state Economic Reform Commission, in charge of the delegation of power and administrative reform group; (4) Chao Zhi, deputy director of the Central Organization Department, in charge of the organization and personnel reform group; (5) Hu Sheng, the president of the Chinese Academy of Social Sciences, in charge of the socialist democracy group; (6) She Mongyu, deputy secretary general of the Central Political and Legal Commission, in charge of socialist legal reform group; and (7) Liao Gailong, a noted theoretician who drafted Deng's 1980 speech, in charge of the group on general principles of political reform. Each group recruited scholars and experts from across the country to help design an overall plan for political reform. The office also established liaison channels with the ministries concerned and with most of the provinces so the situation and problems there would be quickly known.

To reinforce the reform study, seven similar groups were organized in the Central Party School under the direction of Chen Weiren, vice president and party secretary. These additional groups compared findings and enabled the investigation to proceed from different perspectives.

The Political Reform Office published two periodicals and distributed them to the elders and researchers. To maintain confidentiality, the staff members of the office obeyed strict regulations prohibiting contact with outsiders, especially foreigners.

During the internal discussions, many sensitive issues were touched upon and different opinions heard. For example, different possible relationships between the party, the NPC, and the government were discussed. Questions were also raised, such as what political system was most suitable for China and how to make the transition to a democratic system. In discussing the delegation of power, some proposed a federal system while others suggested reducing the size of provinces and districts, along the lines of those in the United States, which were smaller and easier to administer. Still others proposed increasing the autonomy of cities while decreasing that of the provinces and substantially diminishing the domination of the central government.

Between January 1987 and August 1988, the Political Reform Office published 40 million words of text on political reform, which were collected or written by four hundred experts. These publications, based on scientific and historical fact, compiled much political knowledge—past and present, domestic and foreign—to provide reference for China's political reforms. Studies ranged from Plato to Napoleon, Washington to Lincoln, and Sun Yat-sen to Chiang Kai-shek, and schools of thought of significant leaders from the Soviet Union, China, the United States, and other countries.

Because of the high risk and sensitivity of this political reform project, and because of the possible controversy and reversals in policy, the office skillfully protected the process in three ways. First, it invited other important party and government institutions to join the effort to win their cooperation. Second, it closely followed the political reform progress in the Soviet Union. The office demanded regular reports from the International Liaison Department and the Ministry of State Security to keep up with the political reform progress there. These departments had excellent Soviet and East European specialists. The underlying message was that if these things could be done by the Soviet Communist Party, we could do them, too. Third, it linked all the policies to Deng Xiaoping's ideas and words. The office usually sought approval from Deng well before any major new concepts went to the Research Group or Politburo. If Deng said something was "good," no one would say otherwise. The chief editor of the *Selected Works of Deng Xiaoping* worked in the office; since he was so familiar with the works of Deng Xiaoping, he could always find justification and legitimacy for the new policies in Deng's words.

Overcoming the Opposition

The political reform attempt encountered strong opposition, expressed intensively during the "anti–bourgeois liberalism" campaign of early 1987, which started after the suppression of student demonstrations at the end of 1986. Through 1986, discussion of political reform took place only internally and was not allowed to develop into a broad public discussion. People who heard that the effort was under way became discontented that these reforms did not proceed more quickly and democratization did not progress further. Students, in particular, became increasingly vocal in expressing their discontent with the many problems accompanying the reform program, such as inflation, unfair disparity in the distribution of wealth, loss of status for teachers, and continuing lack of freedom of speech and of the press. At the end of the year, the students took to the streets. Conservative leaders such as Li Peng (then vice premier in charge of education) and his ally He Dongchang (vice chairman of the State Education Commission) labeled the demonstration "bourgeois liberalism," and the movement was soon suppressed.

During this period, reformist leaders such as Hu Yaobang and Zhao Ziyang were attacked by the conservatives for their tolerant attitude toward the student demonstration. Hu was removed from his post as party general secretary. Not long after the "anti–bourgeois liberalism" campaign launched in January 1987, conservative leaders turned on Zhao and claimed that the "Hu/Zhao" leadership as a whole needed to be censured. They believed that "political liberalization stems from economic liberalization and the latter has planted the seeds for the former. This economic liberalization began with the household responsibility system in the villages." The shift in attitude toward reform was exemplified by Beijing Party Secretary Li Ximing's support of such reforms in a 1986 forum, but his criticism of them in February 1987, when he said, "Political reform is absurd and will weaken our party's leadership."

At that time, some leftist ideologues held a meeting, protesting, "We fought the Japanese for eight years and succeeded, yet failed when we attempted to clean up spiritual pollution for twenty-eight days." They asserted that "this time, in our battling against 'bourgeois liberalism,' we must persist to the end." Wang Renzhi, the new director of the Central Propaganda Department (who attained his position via the "anti–bourgeois liberalism" campaign), said that during the eight years of reform the party, under Hu Yaobang's leadership, made serious mistakes, resembling those of the Gang of Four. He claimed that these had to be corrected in order to improve long-term ideological consciousness. Hu Qiaomu, the leading ideological conservative, stated that "now Marxists within the party are in the minority. In recent years, the power of the leadership has no longer been in the hands of Marxists. There has been a complete retreat, reversal, and repudiation of revolutionary ideals."

To meet the challenge, Zhao took several actions. First, he limited the "anti–bourgeois liberalism" campaign to within the party, not allowing it to spread to the public. Later, he confined the campaign strictly to politics. His shrinking of the scope of the campaign was enforced through the well-known central document number four of 1987, based on Zhao's now-famous speech of May 13 on the issues of economic reform, which halted the "anti–bourgeois liberalism" campaign and allowed reforms to resume at a faster pace.

In spite of Zhao's effort, his position on political reform was not assured, as his view sometimes differed from Deng Xiaoping's. For example, Deng Xiaoping looked at the issue of separating the party from the government from a utilitarian standpoint, while Zhao looked it from a rational stand-point. Deng's main concern was how to change the party's method of control in order to consolidate it. But Zhao's concern was how to diminish the party's role and establish the government's authority. No words can better reveal his view of socialism than his well-known quote: "What is socialism? No one can clearly define it." Once he said that if all state institutions were established by the party, there is absolutely no reason to regard the state as an antagonist and put it into a state of limbo. The historical task of the party is to take political power; when this is done, the party should step back to second place.

During most of the political reform policy process, Zhao Ziyang was both the premier and interim general secretary, that is, from the fall of Hu Yaobang in January 1987 until the thirteenth party congress in October. During the entire time, he still worked at his state office and considered policies more from the government angle. Until June 1987, Zhao Ziyang was still maneuvering not to succeed Hu at the thirteenth party congress; at the same time the Political Reform Office was considering plans to strengthen the government and premier's power by establishing the institution of the Premier's Staff as one measure of the policy to separate the party from the government. Even the location of the Political Reform Research Group's meetings was a State Council meeting hall; the only meeting held at the party headquarters was the last one.

But by June it had become clear that Zhao could not avoid his new appointment, and new candidates for premier (including Yao Yilin, Li Peng, and Tian Jiyun) were already being put forward. Deng Xiaoping said, "If the party general secretary is changed twice in one year, the impression left on the world will not be good. In my opinion, the party general secretary should not be changed. As for the premier, there is least dispute over Li Peng, so Li Peng can be the premier." Later, at one of the meetings, Zhao told Bao Tong and the office to omit the plan for establishing the Premier's Staff and not to bring up this plan again.

Although Zhao adjusted his position in policy-making, his advocacy for limiting the power of the party never wavered. As reluctant as Zhao was to assume the post as general secretary, he was even more reluctant to expand the power of the party over the state. Zhao's policy later resulted in the serious accusation of neglecting party work and weakening the construction of the party.

It was interesting to note that Hu Yaobang, also a main figure in the reform camp, was not so enthusiastic about the separation of the party and the government. When the issue was first brought up for discussion in the Secretariat and Politburo, he insisted that it would be better to use the expression "division of work between the party and the government." His opinion was seriously considered by the office together with many other proposals concerning the issue, but finally the concept of "separating the party and the government" prevailed, because it is more accurate, more to the point, and best serves the purpose.

The Final Decision

The final decision came after all seven groups had finished their research in mid-1987. The last session of the Political Reform Research Group was held on July 7, at which a general plan for political reform was passed and sent back for further adjustment and revision in the office according to the suggestions put forward. The next stage was waiting for final confirmation by the Politburo, and, most importantly, by Deng Xiaoping.

The general plan designated political reform in the following issue areas:

1. To separate the party and the government. The party, the NPC, and the government should have different and separate functions. The party's control of economic organizations should be abolished, and the party's function should be changed from leadership to supervision. The manager responsibility system should be implemented in the more than four hundred thousand state-owned enterprises.
2. To widen socialist democracy. Majority rule in elections and regulations for the operation of the Central Secretariat and Politburo should be established. The NPC should be given independent legislative rights, and its rubber-stamp function should be changed. The NPC should have the capability to supervise government. The functions of the Women's Federation, Communist Youth League, and Trade Union Federation should be redefined to increase autonomy.
3. To reform the personnel system. The core issue here was to change the party's control of all cadres. The party's organization department should control only politically appointed cadre. A civil service system should be established and the promotions and dismissals of civil servants must be regulated according to the civil service system.
4. To increase the efficiency of the bureaucracy and simplify the administrative structure.
5. To establish an independent judicial system.

In July 1987, a central work conference was convened; discussion of the general plan for political reform was high on the agenda. All Central Committee members in Beijing, all government ministers, and all provincial leaders attended the conference, and for the first time, the result of the eleven months of work was exposed for review and criticism. Everyone at the conference appeared extremely interested, especially the provincial leaders. They were very curious and made every effort to grasp the meaning of the program and to keep up with the new policy. During the conference several hundred suggestions and proposals on the plan were sent back to the office. There was no strong objection to the policy. The office considered each proposal carefully, and the drafting team made all the necessary changes, big or small, incorporating all the proper new ideas into the draft.

Deng finally gave his approval after assessing the plan, although he later recalled his dislike of the West's "separation of powers" and warned that he sensed those features in the plan. The plan, later known as the "General Program for Political Reform," was approved by the seventh plenary session of the Twelfth Central Committee on October 20, 1987, and then incorporated in Zhao Ziyang's political report delivered at the Thirteenth CCP National Congress on October 25, 1987. Zhao's report made the political reform decision official, even though its implementation encountered many difficulties in 1988 and was halted after the Tiananmen Incident in 1989.

The Failure in Implementation

After the thirteenth party congress, the specification and implementation of the political reform plan was to be carried out by the formal institutions in the relevant party and government institutions. Although the Political Reform Research Group faded out from existence, the Political Reform Office was retained and transformed into a permanent, formal party institution subordinated directly to the Central Committee. It was given very high status for the convenience of coordinating and overseeing implementation of political reform. Beginning in late 1988, when political reform was in jeopardy and political conflict was apparent, the office gradually became a kind of special office to defend General Secretary Zhao Ziyang. It was running around like a fire-fighting team. That in itself was a clear indication that the party system was no longer obedient to its boss, and Zhao's power was eroding.

The political reform decision approved at the thirteenth party congress seems limited from today's perspective. However, given the conditions of China at that time, this decision had already pushed or even gone beyond tolerable political limits. Many leaders opposed it and complained from the very start; by mid-1988 political reform had already been aborted.

Why did political reform meet with strong resistance during implementation? The fundamental reason was that political reforms intimately affected the power and interests of a large group of leaders. While economic reforms brought about some adjustments in the interests of some cadre, they did not affect the high-level leaders. Political reforms, in contrast, limited the high-level leaders' powers. Years of ingrained habit made these leaders bitterly complain that the reforms weakened the party leadership while helping to promote "bourgeois liberalism."

Under these circumstances, although the thirteenth party congress reached a decision on political reform, the implementation of political reform quickly ran into great obstacles. For example, the effort to separate the party and the government immediately ran into opposition from many party leaders. The implementation of the civil service system also confronted barriers. In 1988, important members of the conservative faction, such as Song Ping, the director of the Central Organization Department, wrote memoranda stating that conditions were not ripe for implanting the civil service system. Under the old system, the department held great power, overseeing cadre at all levels. If the political reforms were carried out, the Central Organization Department would still control the ministers, provincial party secretaries, and provincial governors, but they would not be able to control these officials' deputies. Thus the personnel reforms would significantly retrench the capabilities and affect the interests of cadre in the Central Organization Department.

Administrative reforms offer another example. Although considered to be the shallowest and least-important aspect of political reform, even this effort faced great obstacles. When the ministries heard of the plans to merge ministries and commissions, they all claimed that their institutions were indispensable. Thus administrative reform not only failed to progress from moderate to major changes, but turned into an insignificant "Band-Aid" type remedy.

Political reform, which took about two years from the beginning of conceptualization to the completion of decision at the thirteenth party congress, thus failed to be implemented.

Notes

This chapter is based on the author's personal experience as told to Suisheng Zhao and on chapter 5 (translated by George Lee) of his book *Zhongguo: Shinian gainning yu bajiu mindong* (China: Ten Years of Reforms and the 1989 Democratic Movement) (Taibei: Lianjing chuban shiye gongsi, 1990). The author wishes to thank Suisheng Zhao for redrafting various versions of this chapter.

1. This term was used by Vice Premier Wan Li in his speech "An Important Issue in Political Reform: The Democratization and Scientific-ication of Policy-making in

China," at the National Soft Science Conference in Beijing, July 31, 1986.

2. *Party Life* magazine, published by the Party Northern Regional Bureau, no. 15, 1941.

3. Speech by Deng Xiaoping at the central party work conference, December 13, 1978.

4. Speech by Deng Xiaoping at the opening ceremony of the National Science Conference, March 18, 1978.

5. See Li Xiannian's speech at the central party work conference, April 5, 1979.

6. Speech by Huang Kecheng at the meeting of the Central Discipline Inspection Commission, November 1980.

7. Deng Xiaoping's talks with heads of the party Propaganda Department, July 7, 1981.

8. Deng's talks with the head of the Japanese political party Komeito, September 3, 1986.

13

Separating the Party from the Government

Hsiao Pen

Separating party and government functions was a main theme and key policy in the 1986–89 political reform. Of all the policies involved, it was the only one that was not just on paper but was partially implemented. Two major concrete steps were put forth on the separation of the party and the government in the General Program for Political Reform. The first step involved the separation of decision-making, including abolition of the practice of party secretaries without government positions being in charge of government work; abolition of the concurrent holding of the top government positions by the top party leaders at different levels; and elimination of the cross-system intervention in government affairs by party supervisory departments. The second step involved the separation of the organization and personnel system, including abolition of the party core groups in the government and nonparty organizations; abolition of the party counterpart departments corresponding to the government departments and bureaus; abolition of the enterprise party committee leadership system; and reform of the party's cadre personnel management system.

It should be emphasized here that during the political reform, the policy-making and implementation were not so clearly differentiated but rather proceeded side by side. Small-scale experiments and feedback were indispensable to policy-making.

Separation of Decision-Making

Beginning with the founding of the People's Republic of China (PRC), the party's "overall leadership" and "absolute leadership" were constitutionally guaranteed. Decision-making power at various levels, from lawmaking in the National People's Congress to the decisions in the local governments and enterprises, was in the hands of the Communist Party organizations and party officials.

A 1951 Central Committee document stipulated: "All the laws, regulations, decrees, and legal codes concerning state and government affairs should be initiated and drafted by the Central Committee. Then they will be passed on for discussion by the national Committee or Standing Committee of the Chinese People's Political Consultative Conference. They will be ratified and implemented by the people's government or State Council."[1]

In 1953, the Central Committee reinforced the regulation, stating, "From now on, the decisions on all major and important strategies, policies, plans and key affairs of the government departments should first be referred to the Central Committee, and they should be put into effect only after discussion by and approval of the Central Committee . . . the various government departments should report on a regular basis to the Central Committee concerning the implementation of these party policies and decisions."[2] These decisions were followed afterward as strict rules binding all decision-making.

This later developed to such a degree that the party committees at different levels took over all policy-making, big or small, from government organs at the same level. It was common for all important policy documents concerning government affairs at the national level to be issued to the country under the name of both the Central Committee and the State Council, or sometimes under the name of just the center. The same practice was used at provincial, municipal, and county levels. During the Cultural Revolution, the documents were issued jointly in the names of the Central Committee, the State Council, and the Central Military Commission. It would not be surprising to find a document on economic statistical work issued by the center.[3]

Former Vice Premier Dong Biwu, a famous nonparty government leader, said in 1951, "The laws and decrees issued by the central people's government are all initiated by the party; many of the declarations and documents were drafted by the party; there exist no resolutions that have been prepared without the party."[4] Through the years, this practice produced low efficiency, policy failures, intense conflict between the party and government system and leaders, and great waste and damage to the economy.

In the 1987 General Program for Political Reform, "party leadership" was formally defined for the first time as "political leadership," which means leadership in ideology and political guidelines to provide correct political principles, political direction, political line, and major general policies. It also means the recommendation of important officials by the party to the government. It was now considered wrong to interfere in or take the place of government in decision-making power, to participate in every decision and attend to every detail, in the work of government. Greater initiatives should be encouraged in all walks of life.

In the General Program, it was decided that a powerful government system would be established and strengthened from the State Council down to the local level. From then on, work concerning government responsibilities should all be considered and decided at government organs. The documents would also be issued solely by them. The party's Central Committee and local committees would no longer make such decisions and issue such documents.

When this issue was discussed at the Political Reform Office, confusion arose as to how to define a "small, trivial decision." If the party should decide only the most important and general policies, then what are such policies? It was very difficult to draw the line. So even though the main points were adopted, there still would be possibilities for abuse of power by the party. This defect in the policy reflected the contradiction between orthodoxy and pragmatism; it reflected the fundamental dilemma of the political reform.

Abolition of the Practice of Party Secretaries and Committee Standing Members with No Government Positions Being in Charge of Government Affairs

This practice began in early 1952, with the slogan "the party secretary in the lead." Informally, this is called *guikou,* (proper channels), which means that a party secretary is in charge of directing and supervising every counterpart. Therefore there usually were many party secretaries in each party committee, a first secretary, second secretary, third, . . . These party secretaries at the local and provincial levels were often nicknamed the "agriculture secretary," "industrial secretary," "education secretary," and so on. For example, if the cultural bureau of one provincial government planned to organize a cultural activity and needed a certain amount of funds, the official from whom he would seek permission and help would first be the party secretary in charge. Only after obtaining his approval could he then go to the deputy governor in charge of financial affairs. It did not work the other way around.

After the thirteen party congress, the Politburo passed on political reform plans and the Central Committee issued separate documents to the provincial and local party committees concerning the implementation of the policies. The procedure was carried out without much trouble. All the *guikou* secretaries and party committee standing members gave up their government duties. Those who originally had specific responsibilities in the party system minded their own business. Those who had no specific duties in the party were given other positions.

Abolition of the Concurrent Holding of Top Government Positions by Top Party Leaders at Different Levels

In China, the usual practice is for high-level party leaders to hold concurrent positions in both the party and the government. The top central party leaders were usually the heads of the central government and State Council. Mao Zedong was once both chairman of the party and of the republic. Other important government and judicial positions were also divided among members of the Politburo.

At the provincial and local levels, most of the standing members of the party committee would hold government positions as governor, mayor, deputy governor, or deputy mayor. The administrative heads who did not hold positions in the party would be inferior in status to those holding concurrent party positions.

After the thirteenth party congress, the Central Committee issued a document on the implementation of the new policy. From the provincial government down, important party officials such as party secretaries or deputy party secretaries were not to hold concurrent positions in government. After giving up their government positions, party officials were to concentrate their energy on improving party work. Those party officials who were better suited to the government job were to give up their positions in the party and be transferred to government work. The party committee and organizational departments at provincial and local levels quickly adjusted to the new rule. After the end of 1987, the old practice no longer prevailed.

Cessation of Party Cross-System Intervention and the Return of Decision-Making Power and Function to Government Institutions

Before the reform, the very powerful party supervisory departments—the Propaganda Department, Central Organization Department, United Front Work Department—used to directly take over government functions. For example, the Propaganda Department was in charge of newspapers, magazine publications, the political science curriculum in the schools, the arbitration of copyright disputes, and previously was even in charge of cultural education, sports, and health care. The United Front Work Department managed some joint ventures, private enterprises, and the industrial and trade coalition, and even established its own "economic bureau."

The implementation plan included guidelines for distinguishing between separate functions. After the thirteenth party congress, these functions were gradually returned to the respective government institutions.

Separation of the Organization and Personnel System

After the PRC was founded, the party could tightly control government and other nonparty organizations from both outside and inside. Layers of party organs overlapped the nonparty organizations, especially government institutions. Those were the places where the integration and interplay took place, where separation of the party and the government began.

Abolition of the Party Committee Leadership System in the Government Economic Institutions and State Enterprises

The separation of the party and the government first began at the enterprise level. The party committee leadership system in the enterprises was set up at the eighth party congress in 1956. Later, during the Great Leap Forward, the system was a model for guaranteeing that "politics come first." The party engaged not only in policy-making but also in day-to-day management. This was called "concentrating big power and distributing little rights." The party committee leadership system in state enterprises was known in China as "managerial responsibility under the leadership of the party committee." Under this system, the party committee and its secretary had not only policy-making power in every field but also the authority to run the economy, ranging from the production plan to the employment of workers and managerial personnel. The state enterprise party committees were, in turn, subordinate to the relevant party committees in the government economic institutions according to their trade or subordination of ministries.

During streamlining in 1982 and again in 1987, some of the government economic departments were changed to administrative corporations, but the party system remained and the party committees in the state enterprises were only subordinated to the "new" old boss.

Beginning in July 1981, the Central Committee and the State Council tried to adjust the leadership structure in state enterprises. They issued several temporary regulations in this regard, including "Temporary Ordinance for Work of State Enterprise Managers," "Temporary Ordinance for Organization Work of State Enterprise Party Grass-roots Party Organizations," and "Temporary Ordinance for Work of Grass-roots Party Organizations in Finance and Trade Enterprises." But while these documents emphasized the importance of managerial power and redefined the party leadership in the enterprises, they retained the old party committee system.

At the third plenum of the Twelfth Central Committee, a big step was taken in the historic Decision on Economic Structural Reform to change relations between the party and enterprises. It was decided that the party committee leadership system was no longer valid and would be replaced by the "managerial responsibility system." But afterward this policy was experimented with on only a small scale, in only a small percentage of all state enterprises. Thus the old style of party leadership in enterprises still persisted.

In March 1986, after listening to the report of an urban economic system reform conference, Zhao Ziyang reiterated, "The 'party in charge of the cadre' system doesn't mean that every cadre should be appointed by the party. I want to reemphasize here that in those enterprises that already have set up a 'managerial responsibility system,' the authority of appointing medium-level officials belongs to the manager. This will not be changed."[5]

When the Political Reform Research Group discussed the issue in late 1986, attention focused on large-scale implementation. The major policy pushing the new system to cover all the state enterprises was included in a document titled "Supplement to the Previous Three Ordinances." On October 25, 1986, when the issue of the "Supplemental Ordinance" was covered at the discussion conference of provincial and municipal leaders initiated by the Political Reform Office, local leaders suggested that the position of enterprise manager should more clearly be defined as the juridical representative of the enterprise and the center of power in the enterprise. Bao Tong suggested that the system be summarized as "[only] one enterprise manager" (*yi chang zhi zhang*). Hu Qili, who was present at the conference, basically agreed with the notions Bao put forward. After the conference, Zhou Jia, deputy director of the office, asked Wu Guogang to work on the proposals and suggestions from the conference and forge them into the final definition of the status of the enterprise managers.[6] It was also planned that, under the new system, the enterprise party committees would no longer be subordinate to party committees in the relevant government ministries and administrative corporations, but would be subordinate to the city district or residential community party committees according to their locations. This would greatly reduce their authority and cut off their vertical connection. All this was to be written into the draft "Supplemental Ordinance" and brought to a meeting of the Secretariat for approval.

During the policy-making, while taking into account the problems that

arose in experiments, several options were considered. For example, because of the long-time practice of the party committee leadership, many
party secretaries were familiar with production, capable, and held authority
in the eyes of the employees. So the new system was very difficult to accept
and the result was also unsatisfactory. Some staff in the office suggested a
step-by-step reform. Chen Yizi proposed that it might be feasible to first
change the composition of the leadership structure, switch the really capable party secretaries to the position of manager, and the manager could
become the party secretary, inferior in status to the manager. Then could
begin the next step of setting up the new system.[7] When the decision went
to Zhao Ziyang, he did not want to prolong the process or make it too
complex. He had already determined by this time to push the policy through
in a single step.

On November 11, the Supplemental Ordinance was approved by the
party Secretariat and was issued in the name of the Central Committee and
the State Council. The final program on the manager-centered enterprise
leadership system was formally ratified at the seventh plenum of the
Twelfth Central Committee in 1987. It was carried out by the Central Organization Department, all the industrial ministries concerned, and at the local
level by the provincial and municipal party committees and the government
departments concerned. By 1989, the new "manager responsibility system"
was set up in over 400,000 of the big and medium-size state enterprises, and
gradually took root.

Abolition of the Party Core Group System Inside the Nonparty Government and Lawmaking Bodies*

After the founding of the PRC, at a time when the united front policy
placed many nonparty celebrities in various government positions—even
as vice president, vice premier, and minister—the core group system was
strengthened as a counterweight, in order for the party to be in actual
control. This party core group system has been one of the party's most
effective weapons in controlling all nonparty political organs, especially
in the government.

The party core group system can be viewed as an inner-government
apparatus since it exists as an integral part of its host government bodies,
actually the real authority and functional centers. The party core group
members in each government department at the national level are appointed
exclusively by the Central Secretariat. Their counterparts down the line are

---

*See appendix on page 163.

appointed by the relevant provincial and local party committees. The party core group at each level answers to the party committees above, to which they owe their appointments.

A party core group usually is made up of four or five party members who hold senior posts in the government administrative organs. The secretary of the party core group would normally also be the director of the administrative organ. In the rare instance that the director or minister was not a party member, the first (executive) deputy director, who then had to be a party member, would hold the party core group's secretary post, which means that he would have more authority than the director or the minister, technically his senior. The party core group's secretary always had the final say in all the organ's affairs, and the documents were often issued in the name of the core group.

The party core group's main task was overseeing the general activities of the government organs in which it existed, especially in the areas of policy-making, policy implementation, and personnel appointment. The party core group ensured that the party's current political line was fully endorsed by government as well as other nonparty organizations. Through the party core groups, the party actually took over administrative power.

Because the power held by core groups and the important role they played in controlling and interfering in administration, abolition of party core groups was regarded as the most important part of separating party and government. When the policy was made, therefore, feasibility studies were conducted and every detail was considered very carefully, especially the settlement of the dismissed personnel, which was politically sensitive. Bao Tong thought this core group system was absolutely unnecessary, because even in the U.S.S.R., the party was not in control to this degree. This policy reached consensus at the top without much difficulty, at least at first, and was written very clearly in the General Program for Political Reform and the thirteenth party congress political report.

But this policy met with strong opposition and aroused a lot of controversy later, during implementation among the officials at the provincial and local levels. They thought this policy seriously weakened the party's leadership.

Debate continued, and the Politburo and the top leaders hesitated in putting this policy into effect, as shown by the related policy document issued in early 1988. The policy was not carried out until August 1988, when the Central Committee finally decided to approve and issue the plans made by the Central Organization Department and Discipline Inspection Commission to abolish the party core groups in the State Council administrative organs and also to abolish the discipline division within each core group. The document stated, "This is one of the most important measures in the political reform; it will benefit the institutionalization and efficiency of the government."

Implementation proceeded as follows: The core group system in the State Council was well organized and was dismantled gradually and partially, in tandem with streamlining the bureaucracy. In those organs that were to be abolished, the party core group was cut off. For those that were to be retained or merged, the core group would be kept during the process to guide the process through a smooth transition. Afterward, when the new government institutions began working, the core groups were then to be disbanded. The details of the abolition of the party discipline division of the core group would be decided by the core group, with some details required to be reported to the Central Discipline Inspection Commission for approval. After the change, most of the core group secretaries would retain only their position as director of the administrative organ, with officials reassigned to new jobs. All the work of the core group would be transferred to the administrative board.

At the same time, the central party reinforced the work of each unit's party affairs committee (*jiguan dangwei*), a purely grass-roots organization. By June 1989, most core groups no longer existed, yet the system was still far from extinguished and was easily revived in the wake of June Fourth as a primary means for the party leadership to regain its grip on government and society.

Abolition of the Administrative Counterpart Departments in the Party

This system was set up in the mid-1950s. In October 1955, a policy was proposed by the Central Organization Department and ratified by the Central Committee to establish in the central-, provincial-, and municipal-level party systems a set of departments with the same functions as the administrative sectors in the government, such as the Industrial and Transportation Department, Trade and Financial Department, Education and Cultural Department, Agricultural Work Department, and City Planning Department. Over time, more such counterpart departments were set up.

Distinguishing between party and government functions became very difficult. For example, besides decision-making in agricultural affairs, the party agricultural work department would even be in charge of administrative redistricting of rural areas and training accounting and bookkeeping personnel. Also, the work process became very confused. Administration organs would also have to be responsible to both higher-level government and party counterpart departments. To ensure party leadership, the party departments held higher status than the government organs. It thus appeared that policies adopted by the government organs would have to go simultaneously to the higher government official in charge, to the party counterpart department, and to the relevant party committee for approval. The person with the final say was usually the party secretary in charge of such affairs. Policy documents were often issued cosigned or triple-signed.

By 1987, statistics showed that the counterpart party organs at the provincial and independent municipality levels were 15 percent of the total party and government institutions; at the city and county level, 50 percent of the total. The policy to abolish the counterpart party departments was very clearly written in the General Program as well as in the thirteenth party congress political report. The main idea was that the smaller the party was, the better. The Central Organization Department and the Central Committee General Office later worked out detailed policies and a document was issued in mid-1988 in the name of the Central Committee. The process of implementation also proceeded in tandem with streamlining the bureaucracy, because this also was a big deflation of the large bureaucratic system. During the process, some party departments were simply abolished, with the personnel either transferred to the relevant government department or reassigned to other positions in or out of political institutions. Others were merged into the relevant government departments. All the functions belonging to the party departments were turned over to the government. This policy was carried out quite thoroughly. Although it met with no small protest, the whole thing was so natural and reasonable that there were few reversals later on.

Reform of the Party's Cadre Management System

This policy was set up mainly to change the situation wherein the user of the personnel had no say in its appointment or management, while the person who did appoint them did not have to bear the responsibility of using them. The reform plan was an ambitious one—to abandon existing tradition and establish a completely new government civil service system. This was a sizable, relatively independent endeavor, and it failed to be implemented after the thirteenth party congress.[8]

In the eyes of many people, the political reform in 1987 failed before it even began. But the facts show that this is not true. If we take a closer look, we will find its traces everywhere in China today, not only in relations between the party and the government but also in the enterprises, and in the behavior of the average citizen.

Notes

1. Central party document, 1951.
2. Central Committee document, 1953.
3. Central party document, 1962.
4. *People's Daily,* March 1, 1951.
5. Speech by Zhao Ziyang at the report session of the urban economic reform work conference, March 15, 1985.
6. Interview with Wu Guogang, August 1992.
7. Discussions at the Political Reform meeting, according to interviews with office staff members.
8. See chapter 14 by Yan Huai in this volume.

APPENDIX: EVOLUTION OF THE CHINESE COMMUNIST PARTY CORE GROUP SYSTEM

The party core group (PCG) method of political control is as important as it is unique to the Chinese political system. It has served in one form or another since the late 1920s as a powerful organizational tool of the Chinese Communist Party (CCP) in directly controlling nonparty political organizations and government institutions, especially administrative and legislative bodies.

The PCG system was exclusively created by the CCP, evolving over a long period of time as the CCP struggled to achieve power, beginning in the guerrilla war bases and in the liberated zones. This system even surpassed the control organization of the Soviet Communist Party and fully exhibits how odd relations between the CCP and the Chinese government can be. Other Communist countries have no core groups in either the military or in the government, only in the parliament or social organizations.

The CCP long ago established two sets of organizational apparatus at each level of governmental, which should not be confused: the PCG (*dangzu*) and the unit party affairs committees (UPAC) (*jiguan dangwei*).

The PCG system might be termed an "inner-structural" apparatus as it exists as an integral part of its host organization. PCGs may appear similar to political party caucuses within the U.S. Congress but they are quite different in nature. Unlike the caucuses, they are the real authority over the government bodies within which they exist and are these bodies' functional centers. PCG members from national to the local levels answer to the party committees to which they owe their appointments.

In contrast to the PCGs, the UPAC network is an "outer-structural" apparatus. The UPACs belong more to the party organizational system than to the government institution to which they are appended. UPAC members are elected by party members working in the relevant government body. Their main task is to take care of more fundamental party affairs, such as recruiting party members, directing political study and ideological work, and collecting membership fees. The committees usually do not interfere with government work.

The UPACs answer to the next higher-level party committee as the PCGs do, but at the same time they are under the direction of the PCG at their own level.

Background of the Party Core Group System

In surveying the CCP's various constitutions and other key documents produced between 1921 and 1927, covering the period from the party's first congress through its fourth congress, nowhere is found mention of an organizational structure resembling the PCGs. This not surprising since during the first United Front period in the 1920s, the CCP joined the Kuomintang (KMT) as a whole and was operating inside the KMT structures.

The PCG concept first appeared after the break with the KMT in June 1927, in the document "The Decision of the Third Revision of the CCP Constitution," and later in the constitution endorsed at the sixth party congress in 1928. At that time, the party units were called party leagues, not PCGs, but their function was similar. It was stated in both documents that "in every nonparty mass organization and in all administrative bodies (such as in the government and in workers' and peasants' unions), if there are more than three CCP members, a party league should be organized. Its main task is to increase the influence of the party and to implement party policies among the nonparty populace." In the constitution endorsed by the sixth party congress, one more task was added: "Supervising activity of party members working in nonparty organizations."

It was not surprising that after 1927 the party put so much emphasis on the party league apparatus. It was a time of turbulence and uncertainty. The CCP had just been ousted by the KMT (after the successful completion of the Northern Expedition) and in the process, the party had almost perished during the KMT-inspired "white terror" against the Communists. The party was struggling just to survive and could no longer operate openly.

Instead of trying to find a way to adapt to the realities of the Chinese situation (as Chairman Mao Zedong later did in organizing a peasant revolution and guerrilla war), the Central Committee clung to Leninist doctrine, still giving priority to activities among workers and the general populace in the large urban centers in the so-called white territories, hoping to organize major uprisings against the KMT. The party league was the key to this effort.

As to how party leagues should be formed, it was decided in the 1927 decision that "the executive committee, or secretariat of each party league, should be appointed, given its power to oversee the routine work of the whole league." The sixth party congress also ruled that "an election should be held to select the secretary of the party league executive committee, with the approval of the relevant higher-level party committee."

The 1927 decision set out six guidelines on relations between the party league and relevant party committee: (1) When the relevant party committee addresses an issue concerning a certain party league, the league can send delegates to participate (but not to vote); (2) party leagues must be subordinate to the relevant higher-level party committee and must strictly follow the party line; (3) when differences arise between a party league and party committee, the party committee should convene a league plenary meeting to discuss the disputed issue again; the league must accept the decision of this meeting; (4) whenever a party league discusses a political issue, the party committee can send delegates to attend; (5) when party league members vote in nonparty organizations, they must do so in accordance with the party line; if they do not, they will be punished according to party discipline; and (6) party leagues should have all nonparty issues discussed in league meetings or executive meetings.

The document also stated that "the local party committee can add or withdraw party league members but should explain the reasons for doing so." In reference to finding party members to fill nonparty positions, the document states: "In putting up party league candidates for nonparty positions, the league must consult the party committee so that the decision can be made together. The same applies in the case of any change of position."

The term "party core group" first appeared in the constitution endorsed by the seventh party congress in 1945. It emphasized that "in every leading government body, workers' and peasants' unions, as well as in other mass organizations, if there are three party members who hold leading positions in the body concerned, a party core group should be formed. The main task of these groups is to direct party members in the organization concerned to increase party influence and implement party policies." The term "party league" was dropped and the numbers of PCG members were dramatically reduced from what they had been when these organizations were called party leagues.

In the late 1940s, rapid progress in the Chinese Revolution was accompanied by some big changes concerning the PCGs. Most of the PCGs were then established in the Chinese government bodies and their own nonparty organizations, which had been set up in the vast liberated areas. Emphasis was now put on the leading organ of each nonparty organization. The designated three party members who were to form PCGs had to be the leading members of the relevant organization. The PCGs no longer had the task of supervising the routine activities of party members within the relevant organizations. This became the task of the UPACs.

After the PRC was founded in 1949, the constitution endorsed by the eighth party congress in 1956 offered a more carefully defined task for the PCGs, namely, that they be "responsible for the implementation of all party policies and resolutions. They should strengthen unity with nonparty cadres, keep close contact with the broad masses, consolidate the law of the party and state, and fight against bureaucracy."

At this time, after the first congress of the Chinese People's Political Consultative Conference in 1949, a new united front government was set up. There were nonparty heads of state, nonparty directors of more than half a dozen administrative departments, and nonparty heads of other important organizations. The party was very concerned about how to seize real power without damaging the illusion of coalition government. This was achieved by putting the PCGs in a dominant position in all government bodies. The PCGs played such an important role in this effort that nonparty heads became little more than democratic window dressing. After the Great Leap Forward, there were PCGs in every ministry down to the bureau level, in every army group down to the division level, and in the provinces down to the bureau level.

During the Cultural Revolution, with the consequent collapse of bureaucratic institutions, the PCGs were also paralyzed. The central Cultural Revolution Leading Group and subordinate "revolutionary committees" took over everything at every level of both party and government. In the constitution endorsed by the ninth party congress in 1969, PCGs were not mentioned. There was only an emphasis on "overall party leadership" and a recommendation to set up bodies with the task of connecting the party to the masses without re-creating a vast bureaucracy. At the tenth party congress of 1973, however, there was a foreshadowing of the return of the PCGs. "In government bodies and mass organizations, a party committee or party core group may be formed," the document said.

In the constitution endorsed by the eleventh party congress in 1977, the leading position of the party was again emphasized. The phrase "*overall* party leadership" was replaced by "*absolute* party leadership" and it was also stated in the document that "PCGs should [as opposed to 'may'] be formed." This reflected a still confused ideological framework and mixed way of exercising authority that was put forward by both the neo-Maoists and the post-Mao reformists.

Gradually, in the process of rebuilding institutions, the PCGs were fully restored. In the constitution put forward by the twelfth party congress in 1982, the PCGs were given great emphasis and their functions were again defined in detail. The constitution said: "The main task of the party core groups is realizing the party line and its policies, implementing the tasks assigned to them by the party and the state. The core groups are to be appointed by relevant higher-level party committees remaining under their leadership and following their decisions. The party committee conferences should require important core group leaders to attend." It was also stated in the constitution the "party core groups should direct the work of the unit party affairs committees." The congress constitution also allowed for changing some of the PCGs in vertically, highly centralized administrative organs into independent party committees.

Process and Problems within the System

With progress achieved in the economic reforms begun in the late 1970s and the launching of tentative political reforms in late 1986, the deficiencies of the PCG system became evident. The PCGs may have suited Maoist rule, but in the era of reform following the Cultural Revolution, they became obstacles to changing the CCP's monopoly role in society. They were hindering the institutionalization of government, causing ineffectiveness, overlapping of policy-making and functions, and blocking progress toward democracy.

By the 1980s, since lists of core group leaders overlapped almost completely with "professional" leaders of government organizations, foreign specialists surmised that party core groups had become redundant and could therefore be easily abolished. But the desire to abolish the core groups actually arose from the continuing chronic conflicts of interest and opinion between core group leaders and professional leaders. Under the dual lines of control, provincial core groups were answerable to the center, while provincial committees were answerable to the governor, for example.

The Secretariat determined which work units would have core groups whose secretaries would report to the Secretariat, mainly from a political (policy) perspective. The minister of a government unit reported to the State Council, mainly from a professional (administration) perspective. This is where problems would arise when leaders got conflicting orders. Under normal procedures, issues would be dealt with along *both* of the dual lines of authority, going up in the party to the secretary and in the government to the minister/governor, who would hold individual meetings to resolve them. "Regular, normal" (professional) matters would be decided in an administrative meeting held by the minister, who would then hold an expanded minister's work meeting to inform subordinates of the decisions. General guidelines, personnel arrangements, or "problems" (issues producing conflict) would be decided in Central Secretariat or core group meetings held to achieve consensus, but only after the party secretary had informally consulted his superiors and decided how to resolve the issues. These separate meetings might be followed by joint party-government consultation in an expanded core group meeting.

Under normal conditions, such as during a political campaign, once the secretary was in charge of the campaign, he would make all decisions. If he were in political trouble, the Secretariat might send in a work team to run things temporarily. By such means, political campaigns would increase the power of the party in the system.

Any unit without a core group likely had problems regarding personnel conflict, for instance, inability to decide on the right person or being in transition while a successor leader was groomed. The following are two examples, the first being the state Economic Reform Commission. Before 1988, the secretary of the core group was Vice Chairman An Zhiwen and its deputy was Bao Tong. In 1988, the commission did not abolish the core group. A reformer, An tried to avoid the political showdown of 1989 by going to Shandong, but Li Peng ordered his return to Beijing, where he entered a hospital. Today, An is still head of the core group. Second, the Chinese Academy of Social Sciences has no core group, although two-thirds of its institutes do. The reason for this is that CASS leaders are not party members and party members are not acceptable to the scientists as leaders.

In 1987, the Political Reform Office recommended the abolition of core groups (and political departments) in stages, beginning with economic units. By that time, there were few remaining political departments (responsible for personnel, political affairs, foreign affairs), mostly in the paramilitary sector of the economy—such as the Ministry of Petroleum or the Railway Administration—which operated along military lines and supervised enterprises nationwide. The remaining political departments most often were involved in negotiating conflicts between workers (such as coal miners) and management over poor wages and working conditions. These political departments answered to party core groups, not military organs.

It was decided in the political reform policy process that the PCG system should be abolished in executive and administrative bodies but remain in some elected bodies such as the National People's Congress, the Chinese People's Political Consultative Conference, and in some mass organizations. This decision was set out in the Political Reform General Program that was ratified at the thirteenth party congress. In 1988, this decision was implemented with considerable success.

14

Establishing a
Public Service System

Yan Huai

The report to the Thirteenth National Congress of the Chinese Communist Party (CCP) Central Committee in 1987 announced that reform of the cadre and personnel system should focus on the establishment of a public service system. This was the first time that the CCP had approved of and set out to build up such a system. This chapter describes the process of that decision, based on my experience as director of the Beijing Institute of Organizational and Personnel Studies, which initiated the process.

Setting Up the Institute of Personnel Studies

The Beijing Institute of Organizational and Personnel Studies published a study report in the first issue of *Lingdao kexue* (Leadership Science) in 1988, entitled "Tentative Ideas on Restructuring China's Cadre and Personnel System." The editor's note pointed out that this report had been used as an important reference for drafting the report to the thirteenth party congress.[1] This is an indication of the role played by the institute in the decision made on the issue.

After the national representative conference of the CCP in 1985, a group of middle-aged reformers ascended to the central leadership.[2] As a result, a new political situation characterized by leniency, tolerance, and benevolence began to emerge, especially in the field of propaganda. The trend toward reform was gaining momentum. However, in the Central Organization Department, conservatives still had a strong hold and the reform process was very difficult. At the end of 1985, I, as a cadre in the Young Cadre Bureau of the Central Organization Department, suggested to the department leadership that an institute be established to study the reform of the cadre and personnel system for the following reasons: first, political reform is a must; it is only a matter of starting sooner or later. The personnel issue forms an important part of the political system. It is necessary to have a research organization set up specifically to pioneer discussions on the theory and plans for reform of the personnel system. Second, almost all the nearly 100 organs directly under the center have attached to them some sort of research institute, except for the Central Organization Department, commonly known as "the first department under heaven." This cannot meet the needs of the present situation. But Cao Zhi, deputy head of the Department and former director of the COD's Political Research Office, insisted that no other research institute be established. Wei Jianxing, director of the Organization Department, instructed that the proposal be shelved on the grounds that there was neither a precedent nor an instruction from the central authorities.

At the beginning of 1986, however, Jin Jian, deputy secretary of the Beijing Municipal Party Committee, expressed his support for this proposal. The Municipal Party Committee wrote to the Central Organization Department, requesting my transfer to organize a "Beijing Municipal Institute of Organizational and Personnel Studies."

In June, Deng Xiaoping raised the issue of political system reform again, and the Central Organization Department suddenly shifted its position. It consulted with the Beijing Municipal Party Committee and suggested jointly organizing the Beijing Institute of Organizational and Personnel Studies (note that "Municipal" is omitted to reflect the joint central and city sponsorship). The institute was to study issues of restructuring the cadre system nationwide, under my supervision. In mid-1986, I set about the establishment of the institute and began the study of the public service system with a team of postgraduates in political science and sociology and other personnel of reformist spirit.[3]

The Study of the Public Service System

In September 1986, a Political Reform Research Group headed by Zhao Ziyang was set up. Bao Tong was assigned to take charge of its general administration. In November, seven study groups were established to cover the various subjects under political system reform. Cao Zhi took charge of the "Personnel Group," which had ten participants from the Political Research Office of the Central Organization Department. The Beijing Institute of Organizational and Personnel Studies had wanted to collaborate with them to pave the way for the successful approval of a "public service proposal." However, after several rounds of talks, we found too many differences between us. The Personnel Group members, all from the Central Organization Department, held that a "public service system" was too radical and made it clear that they intended to monopolize the drafting of the reform scheme. The Beijing Institute of Organization and Personnel Studies had no choice but to carry on its independent study of the "public service system."

In June 1987, Chen Yizi asked the Institute for tentative plans on reform. I spent an entire afternoon talking about the "public service system" at the Political Reform Office. Chen Yizi indicated his support but Cao Zhi was opposed. Bao Tong could join only in the last part of the discussion. He recalled that he had been unable to tell whether he was a political appointee or a professional public servant when he had been asked during his European trip as director of the Premier's Office the year before. He showed his agreement by saying that the "public service" concept was such an important topic it should be studied diligently, and it could be tried out when the time came. Because he had served in the Central Organization Department and knew how conservative it was, however, he did not commit himself explicitly on this sensitive issue.

At that time, a strong aversion to the concept prevailed in the party in reaction to the cry of some people for emulating the Western civil service system. An even greater furor was caused when the Institute put forward its proposal to implement the public service system within the party's organizations; this was regarded as undermining the sacred principle that the "party commands cadre."

In July, the first version of "A Draft Plan for an Overall Political System Reform" was completed. The portion on personnel reform was drafted by the Personnel Group from the Central Organization Department and referred to as a "plan for graded and classified administration" (*fenji fenlie guanli fang'an*). Graded administration means reaffirming the existing principle of each administrative grade controlling the grade below it, for example, the center controlling cadre in the provinces, the provinces controlling cadre in the prefectures, and so on. Classified administration refers to changing the existing practice of the organization departments of the party controlling all leading cadre into one in which leading cadre in enterprises (factories and companies), undertakings (educational, scientific, cultural, and health institutions), and secondary mass organizations (writers' unions, etc.) are handed over to the personnel departments of the governments.

Our institute was of the opinion that serious faults of the existing cadre and personnel system, such as a lack of clear-cut definition of the concept of "state cadre" and an overconcentration of control, were not directly addressed by the Draft Plan. Under the new arrangement, control would still be overconcentrated. The main problem was that the organization departments did not want to reduce their control and the party organizations refused to relinquish their vested interests.

The Beijing Institute of Organization and Personnel Studies, dissatisfied with the plan for graded and classified administration, after several days and nights of hard work, brought out a counterplan. Its sketch for a new public service system contained the following underlying principles: (1) build a state public service system composed of two categories of officers, political and professional; and (2) scientifically classify the existing body of state cadre into party, enterprise, undertaking, and social organization cadre to form a personnel system with relatively independent groups. Then the institute began lobbying actively for its plan.

Making the Decision

Sometime toward the end of July 1987, at our request, Song Ping, the newly appointed director of the Central Organization Department, listened to a briefing on our plan. We tried our best to sell him this plan. Having worked for long periods in government departments and localities, Song had personal experience in the problems of excessive control and overconcentration of power. He even offered some examples. However, he criticized our use of such sharp words as "serious abuse, feudalism, and patriarchal despotism." A student at Qinghua University in his youth and at one time vice minister of labor, he knew about the public service (civil service) system and agreed that it should be practiced in China at some time in the future. However, he still had many reservations about its feasibility in the near term and the steps to be taken, as well as the ideological and theoretical implications.

We explained the results of our studies, which were summarized as "three unities": the unity of party control and legal control of cadre; the unity of political democracy and administrative efficiency; and the unity of stability of the state and of social development. Song advised us to write these points into our plan to make it easy for the party leaders to understand. As the question of a public service (civil service) system affected the whole situation and could exert extensive influence, he wanted to give the matter careful thought before expressing a definite opinion.

In August, the institute divided into three groups: Key theoreticians stayed behind to polish the draft according to the suggestions of Song Ping to make it easier for the higher authorities to grant their approval; Chen Weilan (the daughter of Chen Yun, chief of the Young Cadre Section under the Beijing Organization Department and concurrently deputy director of our institute) and I went to Beidaihe to win the approval of the party elders; Wang Shen, the son of Wang Lin (who had once been Song Ping's superior), continued to talk to Song so as to gain his support.

By the beginning of September, these three tasks had been completed. "Tentative Ideas on Restructuring China's Cadre and Personnel System" was formally submitted to Song Ping by the institute through the correct administrative channel. Meanwhile, by going through the "back door," I also passed one copy to a friend at the Xinhua News Agency to be published in its *Internal Reference Material.*

On September 16, "Tentative Ideas" was distributed by Xinhua in *Restricted Current Domestic Information* (Guonei dongtai qingyang), a "top secret" document circulated among the central leadership and at the ministerial level. This may have pressured Song Ping to expedite his declaration of support, for the very next day, he wrote on the institute's report: "Comrade Ziyang, this report has offered some useful suggestions that could be used as reference for the political system reform. Please read and give your instruction."

On September 18, Zhao Ziyang wrote his comments: "Comrade Song Ping, this study report is very good. In my opinion, the public service system can be carried out. It would be better for public servants to be divided into two categories, political officials and professional public servants. Please ask Comrade Bao Tong to consider including it in the report to the thirteenth party congress."

On September 20, Bao Tong asked us to see him at his office to discuss the implementation of the instruction of the general secretary. The institute submitted a "Table of a Classified Management System for the Existing Body of Cadre" to Bao for his perusal. The table is divided into 120 cells formed by the intersection of fifteen rows across the page from left to right and eight columns from top to bottom.

The fifteen vertical cells from top to bottom at the left of the page divide state cadre into: political public servants (legislative, administrative, and judicial = 3 cells); professional public servants (legislative, administrative, and judicial = 3 cells); party functionaries (responsible persons, working personnel, and grass-roots leaders = 3 cells); enterprises (managers, staff = 2 cells); and others (head, administrative personnel = 2 cells). Altogether, they make up six categories and fifteen subgroups.

The eight horizontal cells across the page from left to right at the top classify the following particulars about the above groupings: (i) the laws applicable to them, (ii) method of appointment, (iii) tenure of office, (iv) method of assessment, (v) supervisory organs, (vi) nature of responsibility, (vii) value orientations, (viii) type of talent required. These cells arranged along the top row across the page from left to right and the first column on the left hand side of the page contain the headings. The other cells (below them and to the right of them) provide the space for the particulars of each subgroup of cadre to be filled.

After reviewing the chart, Bao Tong had his secretary print and distribute it immediately as a document of the Politburo. He then said: "China has a cumbersome administrative force that we have failed to streamline for years. In this table of 120 squares crossed by fifteen horizontal columns and eight vertical ones, you have classified cadres into six categories and subdivided them into fifteen groups. Just as when the Great Yu harnessed the flood waters, it appears to be orderly and clear at a glance. This will steer our personnel management onto the right track."

Then I talked with him for two hours about a comprehensive program for political and personnel system reforms; Bao Tong agreed with much of what I said. At the end of the meeting, I expressed my dissatisfaction with that part of the report to the thirteenth party congress which dealt with personnel reform. Bao shared the same opinion and told us to complete its redrafting in three days.

At the dinner afterward, Bao Tong confided to me: "At the last briefing session, it was inconvenient for me to say anything. And you understood the difficulties Ziyang was facing. You went to persuade Song Ping to give his consent first. This certainly pleased Zhao Ziyang. Thus he quickly expressed his approval and gave his instruction. Seeing that Song Ping had taken a clear-cut stand, other senior comrades have no reason to oppose the proposal any further."

On September 22, we handed over the institute's draft of the portion on personnel system reform for the report to the thirteenth party congress. Bao Tong found it satisfactory after reading it and directed it to be put into the report. This was how the fourth section of the fifth part on political system reform in Zhao Ziyang's report to the thirteenth party congress came into being.

Implementation Failure

On May 31, 1989, after the downfall of Zhao Ziyang, Deng Xiaoping said to Li Peng and Yao Yilin, "The political report of the thirteenth party congress has been approved by the Congress. Not a word can be changed." Thus China now is supposed to be promoting a public service (civil service) system, but practice is at variance with the spirit of the thirteenth party congress report. On September 4, 1992, the minister of personnel said at a conference of directors of departments of personnel, "In our public service system, there is no distinction between those handling political affairs and those doing professional work, in the Western sense. All cadre above the rank of vice minister are senior public servants, those below the rank of director of a ministerial department and above that of deputy director of an ordinary department are middle-ranking public servants, and those below that of a section chief are junior public servants." This is a retreat to the grading system of the 1950s. It appears China will have to go through a long and tortuous process before it can put in place a proper system of public service (civil service).

Notes

1. The note says, "The article 'Tentative Ideas on Restructuring China's Cadre and Personnel System' is a study report by the Beijing Institute of Organizational and Personnel Studies. It was used as one of important references when drafting the report to the thirteenth party congress on relevant issues."

2. This meeting was held in Beijing, September 18–23, 1985, and presided over by Chen Yun. At the meeting, Zhao Ziyang made a speech, explaining the draft proposal of the seventh five-year plan for national economic and social development. And representatives deliberated the partial reshuffle of members of the central organs. See Jiang Nianxuan and Zhang Weiping et al., *Brief Record of Meetings of the Chinese Communist Party* (Zhongguo gongchandong huiyi gaiyao) (Shenyang: Shenyang Press, May 1991), 726–72.

3. On January 6, 1987, both *People's Daily* (Renmin ribao) and *Beijing Daily* (Beijing ribao) reported that the Beijing Research Institute of Organization and Personnel Affairs was founded in 1986 as the first of its kind to study the reform of the cadre and personnel system.

15

Political Reform in Beijing City

Zhu Xiaoqun

This case study of the political reform effort in Beijing describes the interest conflicts in the decision-making process of local leaders and the process of power redistribution. It is also intended to illustrate how the participants tried to maximize their own interests in the political power struggle. My emphasis is on the primary problem inhibiting peaceful political change: the difficulty in setting up a new system that will not threaten the interests of those who still have the power to overturn the process of reform.

Background of the Reform

People from different groups had different motivations and purposes in the process of political reform, but all participants tended to maximize their own interests. The reason why Beijing municipal leaders became active in political reform and even took the lead in implementing local-level political reform plans was their calculation regarding the higher-level power struggle.

Looking back, the ups and downs of all Beijing leaders in Chinese history were always related to the power struggle at the center. Peng Zhen, the most famous Beijing mayor and a close aide to Liu Shaoqi, was ranked eighth in the hierarchy of the Chinese Communist Party (CCP). Thus he fell under suspicion by Mao Zedong and finally was labeled the head of an "antiparty group." Successive Beijing leaders, namely, Li Xuefeng, Wu De, Lin Hujia, Duan Junyi, and Li Ximing, have all been extremely cautious in trying to figure out the intentions of the top leaders. However, few of them have obtained any positive results.

In the early years of the Cultural Revolution, the Beijing first party secretary, Li Xuefeng, did not hold office very long before he was replaced by the second secretary, Wu De, because of his lack of support for the "rebels." Wu De stepped down with the Gang of Four after the Cultural

Revolution. The next Beijing first secretary, Lin Hujia, was unsuccessful because of his alliance with Hua Guofeng. When Hua lost his power, Lin had to resign.

The only exception in this dismal history was Duan Junyi. When he became the Beijing party secretary, Duan was following Hu Yaobang. He summed up Hu's personal opinions on work in Beijing and labeled them the "four instructions of the Central Secretariat on work in Beijing." These instructions became the guidelines for all policies adopted by Beijing. Then with Hu's support, Duan forcefully implemented a contracting system in the eastern suburb of Beijing, where the collective economy was fairly strong. Duan thus extended his stay, and retired at the right time to the Central Advisory Commission. Duan was fortunate in that this was the time of the "Deng-Hu-Zhao honeymoon," and the power struggle had not yet re-emerged at the top.

Li Ximing took the top Beijing position at the end of 1984 but did very little until 1987, when Hu Yaobang stepped down and Zhao Ziyang became general secretary. Li's personal advisers provided him with following analysis: During Zhao's premiership, the only time that he directly interfered with Beijing affairs was to give permission to the Capital Steel Company to increase its power of self-determination. This was often criticized by Beijing leaders and citizens because the expansion of the Capital Steel Company undoubtedly would cause extensive pollution, violating environmental regulations. Zhao, in turn, probably did not have a good impression of Beijing's leaders. Now Li's future depended on his ability to change Zhao's impression.

The Launching of Reform in Beijing

Political reform was put on the CCP agenda when Zhao became head of the Political Reform Research Group, established in September 1986. The group was to present its plan to the thirteenth party congress. Accordingly, Beijing's policy research office argued that political reform was probably Zhao's top priority. If Beijing could perform well in attempting political reform, then it would definitely be favored by Zhao and thus increase its status in the power struggle. The policy research office suggested that the city set up a working group to design a plan for political reform so that Beijing could hold its own party congress to endorse and begin immediate implementation of the reform. Li accepted this proposal, and both the Preparatory Working Group for Beijing's eighth party congress and the Political Report Drafting Group were created.

The first problem the Drafting Group confronted was the top secret nature of the national plan. In order to stay one step ahead of the competition, Beijing needed to gain access to this vital inside information. The secret information was finally obtained from a scholar who was also a member of the Drafting Group for the thirteenth party congress report. Then, after half a year, the Beijing plan was finalized. It included the following aspects.

The first aspect was a change in the status of the city party committee and an adjustment in its relationship with the Beijing people's congress and the city government. The general plan of the center had specific instructions on the functions of party committees at different levels. The Central Committee was the leading group for the country. The function of the grass-roots unit committees was "support and supervision." The local committees' function was not clearly defined, but by implication was somewhere in between.

Because of this stipulation, Beijing changed the decision-making process at the local level. Originally, the major decisions of the local people's congress and the local government had been drafted by the congress or the government and submitted to the party committee for approval. This was changed so that Beijing's congress and government could make decisions independently. The party committee was supposed to support the implementation of the decisions and supervise the government and congress in abiding by the central guidelines.

Beijing also changed the personnel arrangement process. The party committee lost its monopoly over appointments. Officials of the government and the congress were to be nominated only by the party and then elected or appointed by the congress or the government.

A second measure was a change in the work style and organization of the city party committee. The city party committee was no longer allowed to interfere in government affairs. Therefore, the positions in the committee that paralleled government positions were eliminated, including the deputy secretary or members of the standing committee who were in charge of industry, agriculture, finance, and city construction, as well as the subordinate industry department, agriculture department, and finance department of the committee. The party groups in some government agencies, like the Planning Commission, the Tourist Bureau, and the Financial and Fiscal Bureau, were also eliminated.

Third, the leadership structure of the grass-roots enterprises changed. Jurisdiction over the grass-roots party organization shifted from the vertical functional sector to the horizontal locality. The "managerial responsibility system" was enforced in factories and the "presidential responsibility system" was enforced in the schools and institutes. The function of the party committees in each became merely "support and supervision."

Finally there was a change in the party's relationship with mass (social) organizations, like the Trade Union, Women's Federation, the Communist Youth League, and the Students' Union. These organizations were now supposed to keep their distance from the party, represent the interests of their constituent groups, and conduct independent activities. The party committees were not to interfere directly and a system of discussion and dialogue was to be established so that the party could understand the interests of different social groups.

Conflicts and Compromises

The political reform plan for Beijing was highly controversial from the outset. The whole process of internal debate, verification, and actual implementation was one of continual conflict and grudging compromise. As a result, Beijing was plunged into a power struggle.

One of the main problems stemmed from very different understandings of the purpose for political reform. Some believed it should merely increase efficiency, while others thought it was to create a system of "checks and balances." Behind the argument over definition was the local party system's attempt to retain power. Deng Xiaoping's speech stating that he was not in favor of setting up a Western-style democracy with checks and balances greatly influenced the debate. He stressed the importance of maintaining the leadership of the party, which he believed to be more efficient than a system of checks and balances. He claimed the Western model was not efficient enough for China's economic construction and reform.

In the end, the different factions came up with a compromise. The long-term goal of political reform was determined as the establishment of a highly democratic, fully regulated, very vigorous, efficient, socialist political system. The short-term goals were to increase efficiency, overcome the problem of bureaucraticism and feudalism, and promote economic reform and opening through reform of the leadership structure.

Another area of conflict was the controversy over the function and power of the local party committee. The general plan of the center defined the function of local party committees vaguely as somewhere between political leadership and "support and supervision." In actuality, this would take away a lot of the power from the local party committees. Local party leaders were especially offended by Zhao Ziyang's comment that the reform could be conducted with reference to the Kuomintang's "provincial party branch" system. When the plan was discussed at the seventh plenum of the twelfth party congress in 1987, representatives from different localities all requested a change in that definition. Finally, draft sections stating the function of the local party committee were eliminated in the political report to the thirteenth party congress and held for later discussion and decision. Considering this development, Beijing modified its plan and stuck to the full political leadership of the local party committee. Thereafter, conflict between the Beijing Party Committee and Zhao's Political Reform Office intensified.

In this decision-making process, tension also existed between the Beijing Party Committee and the local people's congress. When the reform plan was implemented, the elections for the people's congress in the city and districts had just begun. Because of changes in the mechanism for personnel arrangements, some officials who had been nominated by the party committee were not elected, and some government officials appointed by the party committee were nullified by the congress. Even some candidates who were nominated by top leaders failed to get elected. There was therefore unanimous agreement that political reform weakened the party's ability to appoint "reliable people" to important positions.

Similarly, conflict arose between the Beijing Party Committee and the local government. According to the modified plan, the party committee was still the leadership; all major decisions had to be made within the committee. However, the relevant departments and positions in the committee had already been eliminated. Therefore, when meeting to discuss major issues, the party committee had to invite many people from the government to attend. This was a system in which the people who did the work could not decide and those who had the power to decide could not do the work. The relationship between the party committee and the government worsened.

Serious conflict also arose between the party organization and the grass-roots administrative system in the process of power redistribution within the leadership structure of the enterprises. In order to pacify the grass-roots party cadre, Beijing allotted certain degrees of power to the grass-roots party organizations. This compromise, however, contradicted the "managerial responsibility system" and as a result caused many problems in practice.

Fierce reaction from the party organizations put great pressure upon the Beijing party leaders. The political reform weakened the power of the party; the practical opportunities as well as the political and economic privileges for the political cadre were proportionately reduced. These people were very dissatisfied. Since they were the power base for the local party leaders, Beijing guaranteed all the privileges that they already enjoyed and also set out to organize some business companies for these people.

Facing these conflicts and pressures, the Beijing committee was forced to review its plans and concluded that they had underestimated the difficulty of reform. They decided to slow down the pace of reform and chose the Dongcheng district as the only experimental area for the reform plan. After the Tiananmen Incident in 1989, political reforms ceased altogether, the Dongcheng experiment was stopped, and the Beijing political reform plan was finally given up.

Political Impact and the Way Out

The impact of Beijing's failed reform was particularly significant because it helped tip the balance of power in the central political arena. The Beijing Party Committee, because of the failure of its political reform, began to suspect the legitimacy of Zhao's leadership. At the 1988 Beidaihe Conference, Beijing prepared two reports, one in favor of price reform, and one against. Li Ximing used the latter at the meeting and was criticized by Zhao. After that, Beijing politicians conflicted with Zhao and finally formed an alliance with Li Peng in 1989, helping to force Zhao's resignation.

These developments shook the foundations of the national political power structure. Although the party system retained most of its power, the reform attempt nevertheless conveyed a strong message to the party cadre. More and more people working in the party started to shift to government agencies or to business companies. The conservatives tried to reverse this trend after June Fourth, but could not stop this "brain drain" from the party.

The behavior of leaders changed. The political reform weakened the model of party appointment. The leaders realized that support from the party was no longer sufficient for their careers. They began to pay much more attention to the attitudes of the people. They would resist an order from the higher levels if the order was in conflict with the interests of the locality, branch, or unit. These leaders became representatives of special interests.

Why did the political reform fail to be implemented despite the approval of the thirteenth party congress and the completed planning in Beijing? The reason was that the reform threatened the interests and power of many professional party cadre. As one political scientist said, "If peaceful evolution to democracy were possible, then the first problem to be solved would be how to regulate the uncertainty without threatening the interests of those who are able to overturn the process of democratization." If the reform could not protect the interests of the cadre, they would fight desperately and peaceful evolution would not be possible. The success of the agricultural reform might point a way out, a new direction for political reform. The rural party leaders lost their power under the rural responsibility system and tried to oppose it, but the development of countryside enterprises provided many more opportunities for them so they all became supporters of reform.

Such a compromise arrangement may be unavoidable in political reform as well. The state may need to ensure that cadres gain access to economic resources in exchange for accepting some loss of political power. While this might lead to corruption, considering the fact that state property has always been under the control of the party, things could hardly be worse if the property was formally transferred to the party. In fact, reallocation of state-owned property is already taking place in practice. If this process could be regulated, it would increase the possibility for compromise among different groups and avoid the turmoil and economic depression that has taken place in the former Soviet Union and in Eastern Europe.

16

A Long Way toward a Free Press: The Case of the *World Economic Herald*

Meirong Yang

The Chinese Communist Party (CCP) has consistently asserted that the news media play a key role in consolidating the proletarian dictatorship. The party uses three means to control the media: the party organization, the personnel department, and the financial department.

All newspapers in China must establish a party organization. If a unit has more than fifty party members, it has to form a "party committee"; if the membership does not exceed fifty, then the unit has an option of creating a "general party branch" (*dang zongzhi*) or a "party branch" (*dang zhibu*) to oversee the "party cells" (*dang xiaozu*), depending on numbers. The Central Propaganda Department and each local propaganda department control the news media through these party organizations.

The editor-in-chief and the deputy editor-in-chief as well as the desk chief at all the major newspapers must be party members. In my observation, working for more than thirty years at the *Liberation Daily,* the official organ of the Shanghai Municipal Party Committee, 90 percent of the editors and reporters have been members of either the CCP or the Communist Youth League. Those who are not, like me, are few indeed. The great number of party and Youth League members makes journalists easy to control; propaganda authorities tell us what we can publish and what perspective we should take in editorials or commentaries.

The personnel department is totally controlled by the party, including the size of the staff, who was recruited, and the payroll. The editor-in-chief, usually head of the party organization, is appointed by the higher-level propaganda department; the head of each desk is appointed by the party committee after reporting to the higher propaganda department for approval.

The financial department is also controlled by higher-level financial authorities, to whom the budget, the revenues, and the expenditures of the newspaper all must be reported. The payment of salaries must also follow regulations set by the central financial authorities. Profits earned by the newspaper must be submitted to the higher-level financial department; even how the unit spends its own small reserve fund also must be approved by them. Since the early 1980s, the financial system has become somewhat more flexible, but it still is hard to say that a newspaper has financial autonomy.

These control mechanisms make it difficult to have press freedom or to launch an unofficial newspaper. Any movements toward freedom of the press are usually seen as dissident, and those who are involved are labeled "bourgeois liberals," which could entail drastic political and social consequences for them. Despite the dangers involved, some experienced journalists in China have not given up hope in their quest for freedom of the press. Over the last several decades, they have made their stance well known, claiming that the media should be not only the party's mouthpiece but the people's as well.

Since 1949, two key attempts have been made to establish press freedom and unofficial newspapers. The first came on the eve of the "anti-rightist movement," in the spring of 1956–57. The second was during the peak of the 1980s "reform and opening" period.

Wenhui Daily was a pioneer in striving for press freedom and in its efforts to become an unofficial newspaper in 1957. *Wenhui Daily* was established before the Communists took over China, funded primarily through private investments. It fell under joint state-private ownership under Communist government ordinances in 1953, yet retained many of its traditional features. *Wenhui Daily* served an intellectual readership, promoting ideas of liberalization and political freedom. When the anti-rightist movement began in 1957, *Wenhui Daily* became the target of a harsh editorial written by Mao Zedong for the *People's Daily* called "*Wenhui Daily*'s Bourgeois Orientation Should Be Criticized." The editor-in-chief and many other editors and reporters were denounced as rightists and suffered for two decades.

Along with the reform and open door policy after 1978, the market economy reemerged and large numbers of daily, weekly, and evening newspapers were created to meet readers' demands in all strata of society. These had their own special features and became a vital new force to break the monopoly of the party newspapers. The statistics showed that the newly established publications reached a total of 1,008, plus 769 old and reestablished publications, totaling 1,777 within the five years between 1980 and 1985. The ratio of party newspapers to the total dropped from 84 percent in the Cultural Revolution to 17 percent in 1985.

The main reason for this drastic turnaround can be found in the policies of Deng Xiaoping, whose main focus was economic growth; pursuing this required loosening restrictions on the media. Businesses and enterprises were allowed to start newspapers to promote the exchange of business information, as well as to provide a means of advertising. The most outstanding such paper was the Shanghai-based *World Economic Herald,* which was created in June 1980.

Qin Benli, the founder of the *World Economic Herald,* was a former party secretary and executive deputy editor-in-chief of *Wenhui Daily* who had been denounced during the anti-rightist campaign. He knew well that an unofficial newspaper must obtain relative autonomy in the areas of organization, personnel, and finance to get out from under government control.

To pursue this goal, Qin invited prominent scholars and officials along with other renowned economists and sociologists to serve on a board to set the paper's guidelines. As editor-in-chief of the *Herald,* he was appointed by the directors of the board, with the tacit approval thereafter by the Shanghai propaganda department. When he started the *Herald,* Qin hired only seven retired veteran journalists. He was bold enough to appoint some noncommunist deputy editors who had been denounced as "rightists" or as having "committed serious political mistakes" in 1957. It is not a great surprise that their appointments were not approved by the municipal propaganda department. Nevertheless, Qin recognized their abilities and gave them responsibilities, as well as the same privileges that a deputy editor would have at other official newspapers, such as first-class tickets for business trips, or the use of high-ranking cadre hospitals. When he recruited new staff members, he ignored the guidelines set by the propaganda department, recruiting young reporters and editors by public advertisement. Zhu Xingqing, a very smart young man who was not a party member but had made no "political mistakes," was appointed by Qin to be deputy editor-in-chief. overall, the staff included only a few party members, leaving many of the positions as desk chiefs open to noncommunists.

Qin started the paper from scratch, with no government funding. He obtained twenty thousand yuan of prepaid advertising money, and borrowed an office, desks, and some chairs from the Shanghai Academy of Social Sciences. The paper did not own any printing workshops or have typesetters, so Qin had to ask the *Liberation Daily* to print the paper for a fee. Material rewards for the staff was another aspect Qin introduced into the system. For instance, whenever an article was written or edited, or when advertising space was sold, a percentage of the reward would go to the staff member. This was a tremendous incentive, and as a result, the editorial staff devoted their time to writing more articles and increasing the output of publication. The financial situation continued to improve because of the increase in advertising sales. All these measures broke away from the higher-level financial department's strict regulations, giving the *Herald* a little more autonomy and freedom.

The *Herald* independently set its own guidelines at first. A main priority was to stay within the limit of the law. The *Herald* would be seen as a mouthpiece for the people, calling for reform and opening. The paper was designed to reflect the different views held by society in an unbiased and completely truthful manner. It also encouraged those previously excluded from self-expression to get involved under the motto "to help China understand the world, and the world understand China." Thus, the *Herald* was conceived of as a strong and unofficial voice, very different from other newspapers.

The newspaper became a good yardstick for measuring the extent of political liberalization in the country. The process was not as easy and straightforward as it may seem. In China, the stronghold of the central government is very difficult to break, and the *Herald*'s distinctive nature caused it to encounter numerous risks and barriers.

Attempts were made at shutting down the newspaper, especially during the 1983 campaigns to "eradicate spiritual pollution" and "ferret out financial criminals." This came about because of fear that enterprises like the *Herald* were gaining too much political and financial autonomy. Because the *Herald* had assumed responsibility for its own profits and losses, the Shanghai Foreign Economic Trade Committee assigned a task force to investigate the accounts, making sure that everything was in accordance with government regulations. Not surprisingly, the committee found the accounts out of order and unacceptable. This was all done in an attempt to oust Qin Benli in order to take over the paper in view of growing fear of its mounting prestige within the community. Efforts made by Qian Junrui (vice president of the Chinese Academy of Social Sciences and former vice minister of culture) saved the newspaper from the takeover.

After 1985, the *Herald* established a public relations firm and a publishing house and raised funds to build a new office building and printing workshop. Along with this came plans to launch an English edition in 1986, extending circulation outside China. At that time, the government encouraged foreign investors to build joint ventures in China. The *Herald* took advantage of this policy by entering into a joint venture with a Canadian enterprise, headed by a Chinese Canadian and a former Canadian official. The *Herald* would provide the news articles, and the Canadians would be responsible for printing and subscriptions. This initiative was approved by the director of the Shanghai municipal propaganda department. After this approval, the plan was then submitted to the Central Propaganda Department, which gave no definite reply. Even with this minor setback, Qin and the board intended to build an autonomous press called "Trust."

But this movement toward media liberalization was thwarted at the end of 1986 after a major government crackdown resulting from the student demonstrations late that year, and with the removal of Hu Yaobang from the leadership in 1987. A wave of repression against "bourgeois liberalism" arose. The plan for the English edition was rejected by the Central Propaganda Department. As a result, only one edition was published in Vancouver, and the Canadian investors lost one hundred thousand dollars in the failed venture. The scale and speed of establishing the public relations firm and the publishing house were forced to be reduced. Moreover, a resident task force was assigned by the Shanghai municipal propaganda department to force the *Herald*'s staff to undergo an overall examination on "bourgeois liberal" reportage in recent years and to submit self-criticism reports. Qin Benli denied that the *Herald* had participated in any such activities. However, at the time, it was well-known that Qin was considered an "intransigent offender," and some people wanted him to resign so that the *Herald* could continue publication without intense government scrutiny. The situation remained in stalemate for half a year until then–General Secretary Zhao Ziyang spoke out in support of the *Herald* for being on the frontier of reform, and asked his secretary Bao Tong to direct the Shanghai Municipal Committee to keep the paper afloat.

During that period, when it was difficult to get out from under manipulation of high-level authorities in the field of organization, the *Herald* focused on the freedom of speech. The reportage boldly expressed different voices and expressed what the people wanted to, but dared not say. In 1988, the *Herald* published Su Shaozhi's criticism of the Theoretical Conference commemorating the tenth anniversary of the eleventh Central Committee's third plenum. Su sharply criticized this conference, which sought to produce uniform public opinion and unified theory and thus deny the current crisis of socialism. This article had wide repercussions, enraging those at the Central Propaganda Department who had ordered that no newspapers could print it. At that point, even Zhao Ziyang felt compelled to say that Qin Benli had made a serious mistake and must be dealt with sternly. Only intervention by Deng Xiaoping eased the rising tensions over this issue.

Then, on April 24, 1989, the 439th issue, expressing public sympathy over Hu Yaobang's unfair treatment as well as with the student demonstration, was banned. This incident also showed clearly that the *Herald* at its peak was tending toward a truly free press.

Two days later, the Shanghai Municipal Committee dismissed Qin Benli and assigned a task force to take over the paper. Qin demurred, stating that the *Herald* had its own board and was an unofficial paper, with sole responsibility for its profits or losses. But the chief of the task force countered that the establishment of the *Herald,* as well as Qin's appointment, had been approved by the Shanghai municipal propaganda department. They declared that the *Herald* from its beginning had never been an unofficial newspaper, nor a "colleague-established paper"; there had never yet been an unofficial newspaper in China. In fact, Qin had never received formal certification or documentation regarding his appointment. This experience proved that China still has a long way to go toward an autonomous paper.

After nearly a decade of work, Qin and his desire for an autonomous paper and media liberalization abruptly came to a bad end. The *Herald* was not fearful of taking extraordinary risks toward a free press because its leader, Qin Benli, believed in the value of political freedom, with the hope of one day being able to forge a new path toward a free press in China.

17

Decision and Miscarriage: Radical Price Reform in the Summer of 1988

Cheng Xiaonong

During the summer of 1988, China's economic reform policy suddenly changed from a gradual strategy to a radical one, and then soon moved on toward stagnation. Deng Xiaoping tried to push an extensive price reform; however, his policy met with resistance from both conservative politicians and the masses, leading to socioeconomic instability and finally stagnation for the whole reform program. This succession of abrupt turns in policy, from gradual reform to radical reform, then again suddenly to retrenchment, provides a valuable case study of the economic reform policy-making process in China. This was a very important development in the history of economic reform in China and had decisive impact on the situation of 1989 and later. Most of the major actors in Chinese economic policy-making, from Deng Xiaoping and Chen Yun, to Zhao Ziyang, Yao Yilin, and technocrats of the State Planning Commission, participated in the decision-making process, and public opinion played an important role in the process as well. The decision was the only radical experiment for a thorough economic reform in the urban system and was the only case where an important decision by Deng failed so quickly and completely.

Based on facts that the author obtained while acting as a consultant on economic reform policies and also on official documents, this chapter analyzes the personalistic function of major Chinese leaders as well as the institutional and societal factors in the policy-making process from May to September 1988.

Among various types of policies, the economic reform policy discussed here falls into a special category of highly important or crucial policies that have the potential to change or greatly affect the whole economic system nationwide. Such a policy must be determined at the top level first and then be designed by technocrats. The personalistic factors in policy-making are obviously more significant than in more regular economic management policy-making, which is often handled solely by technocrats. However, this does not mean the institutional factors in policy-making are less important. The study tries to reveal the links between personal and the institutional authority, rather than simply emphasize one or the other.

Background

After the Chinese Communist Party's (CCP's) Thirteenth Congress in October 1987, all the elders were required to retire from the Politburo and a younger generation was promoted to the Politburo and its Standing Committee, but the latter still were not able to make policies independently. Deng Xiaoping still supervised policy-making within the Standing Committee, offering guidance or direct orders. Chen Yun also irregularly and informally did the same. Deng expressed his personal ideas regarding important policies in two ways: speaking with individual leaders or foreign visitors. Although his ideas were often not discussed with the members of the Standing Committee in advance, they had to follow them politically.

After Zhao Ziyang took the post of CCP general secretary in the autumn of 1987, his influence on economic policy-making significantly weakened. As party leader, he could use only the Central Finance and Economics Leading Group to discuss economic policies.[1] The group, however, did not have final authority in policy-making; his personal ideas expressed in meetings of the group did not bind the State Council, which was controlled by conservatives under Premier Li Peng and Vice Premier Yao Yilin.

The state Economic Reform Commission (ERC), the only ministry responsible for economic reform, did not possess enough authority to implement reform policies independently. And those ministries for economic management, particularly the State Planning Commission (SPC), were much less interested in thorough economic reform. The situation for the Reform Commission became worse when Li Peng became its director. In May 1988, Li curtailed its powers, ordering it to function only as a consultant, not as a policy-making institution.[2]

Policy consulting in China was then little developed, though there were many policy research departments under different ministries and under the State Council itself. Most of them still operated in the traditional fashion used before the reforms. Many research fellows in these departments lacked the knowledge and capability necessary for systematic economic research and analysis. As their nickname, "a group of document writers" (*xiucai banzi*), implied, they were responsible simply for drafting documents and taking surveys required by ministers.

Some form of institutionalized policy consulting from economists in the academic circle did exist before important policies were decided. However, many scholars, especially the older ones, were used to either simply praising current policy or expressing their opposing opinions on certain policies very carefully, closely following the lead of top officials. Among the top leaders, only Zhao showed an interest in policy consulting with scholars, and he understood modern economic analysis. He thus established and supported several institutes for policy research that were exceptions among China's policy research institutions. Young scholars with great enthusiasm for reform were able to do systematic and relatively independent policy research using modern theories and methods, and then provide policy proposals. Unlike Zhao, Li and Yao listened to the technocrats in ministries and seemingly did not trust those younger scholars, as will be shown later.

"Breaking a Path for Price Reform"

In the spring of 1988, China's economic growth rate was quite high, but the limited nature of the urban reforms to date had resulted in inflation and corruption. People's dissatisfaction with the reforms was obviously increasing, and signs of social instability emerged.[3] At the top level, opposing evaluations of the economic situation, and of the previous reform policies, first appeared between Zhao and Yao. At a meeting of the Central Finance and Economics Leading Group in February 1988, Yao suggested that the economic situation was so serious that China had reached the verge of economic collapse. This implied a negation of the reform policies of the previous ten years. To defend reform, Zhao indicated that the overall economic situation was good, and one should not "only look at the trees without seeing the forest," since economic growth, investment, and imports were all near normal levels in 1987, and the people's real living standard was growing then. He said that a certain degree of inflation was inevitable and that reform policies should not be changed although people showed their dissatisfaction toward inflation. Problems such as inflation and corruption should be solved only through more reform.[4]

Since Zhao was general secretary at that time, and Yao and Li dominated economic policy-making in the State Council, few ministers stood firmly by Zhao. One of the few who encouraged even more radical reforms than Zhao was Li Tieying, then still the director of the ERC, who believed that the only policy option was to speed up price reforms. At the end of March, he stated that the Chinese economy had approached a takeoff stage, and that this was a good opportunity to carry out a major price reform to eliminate the two-track system,[5] and to achieve economic success in the last decade of the twentieth century. Otherwise, the present limited reform could hardly produce a marked effect and might result in social unrest.[6] In the middle of April, he presented the idea at a meeting of the ERC: inflation was acceptable as the cost of implementing price reform. The longer the two-track system existed, the greater were the political risks.

However, the SPC's opinion was nearly the opposite. In April, its official view was that a timetable to establish an economic system dominated by new institutions in the next eight years seemed to be too hurried.[7] At the beginning of May, a meeting presided over by Deputy Director Fang Weizhong discussed the issue of price stabilization. The main theme at the meeting was the need to restore administrative control over prices.[8]

In early May Deng suddenly called for "breaking a path for price reform," a notion similar to Li Tieying's, perhaps due to Li's direct influence. Deng insisted that China was in a critical period of reform and should meet the stormy waves head-on while trying to complete price reforms in three to five years.[9] The Politburo Standing Committee convened in the middle of May to discuss Deng's pronouncement. A consensus on eight points was reached at the meeting: (1) the rice price index should be carefully monitored; (2) price and wage reforms should be carefully studied, and a five-year plan for reforms should be prepared; (3) inequality of income distribution must be resolved; (4) corruption should be fought against in the party and government; (5) industrial efficiency should be increased; (6) ideological propaganda should be reinforced and improved; (7) party discipline should be strengthened; and (8) a stable environment for reform should be created.[10] It was apparent that the Politburo Standing Committee did not actively respond to Deng's speech. The meeting did not decide to begin a radical price reform.

Shortly after that meeting, Deng pushed his price reform idea again. Three times in two weeks, he repeated his idea to foreign visitors, showing strong determination. He said:

> Price problems are a very heavy burden on our government, we cannot take a detour . . . though there are some risks. We have now already decided to take the risks, and to begin breaking a path and pass through the jungle. . . . Short-term pains are better than those that last over the long-term. . . . After the economic development of the past ten years, people now can bear more difficulties; there will be no unrest. Our state apparatus is still effective, and we also have enough experience to overcome difficulties; we should be bolder and not be afraid to take risks.[11]

Deng's open comments in fact implied that the decision to cut a path for a radical price reform had already been made and was going to be implemented right away. Undoubtedly, this created strong pressure on policymakers in the Politburo.

In quick response, the ninth meeting of the Politburo for 1988 was held from May 30 to June 1. Without any hesitation this time, it was decided to begin price reform. As a first step, Yao Yilin was appointed to be in charge of making a "price and wage reform program."[12] Although the policy had been made under pressure from Deng, divergent ideas about objectives and methods of the reform still existed among the members of the Politburo. Yao wanted to raise the sale price of grain for urban residents in order to reduce fiscal subsidies and was not interested in subjecting the prices of industrial raw materials to market conditions. Zhao pointed out that the rise of urban grain prices would stimulate inflation and suggested opening up the prices of raw materials first.[13] Li Peng did not even believe the economy could be adjusted by the market.[14] And Li Tieying, who supported Deng actively, thought that the price reform would create a perfect market economy even without private ownership.[15]

Although this was a crucial economic reform decision, and would affect the economy and society, it was not discussed by economists and sociologists in advance. There were no feasibility studies. Probably intended as a forum for professional input into policy-making, the "Symposium for Middle and Long-Term Economic Reform Programs" was held by the ERC.[16] Economic specialists from different institutions, universities, and government offices proffered nine long-term reform programs at the symposium; none of them supported the policy to start radical reform immediately. As a result of political imperatives, however, these research results did not have any impact on the price reform policy and were edited and published later as a purely academic book.

This was a policy initiated by politicians, and later designed by technocrats. During the process, Deng was the main policymaker and promoter, while the Politburo Standing Committee was an executive body for his decisions. Whether the members of the Standing Committee agreed with Deng's ideas or not, they first had to obey him politically. Deng did not know much about complicated socioeconomic problems and believed that the economic interests offered to people during the previous ten-year reform could be used in exchange for their political support of further reforms. But this quickly proved to be an erroneous political judgment.

"Price and Wage Reform Project"

Contradictory currents were evident throughout the policy design phase. Zhao Ziyang hoped to promote thorough reforms by taking advantage of the favorable situation created by Deng. His opinions, however, met with tacit refusal in the Politburo and in the State Council. Directed by Yao Yilin, meanwhile, the technocrats of the SPC used sophisticated means to change Deng's radical overall price reform policy into a modest regular price adjustment only for several goods. Later Chen Yun interposed his views, and a serious austerity program was also silently prepared in the SPC, simultaneously but contradictory with the price reform project. Official mass media routinely promoted Deng's radical reform policy, but this time the policy did not gain social support; on the contrary, it caused serious social dissatisfaction.

From June 2 to the beginning of July, a special group in the SPC drafted a "Price and Wage Reform Project."[17] The group was composed of directors of several bureaus, selected by Yao Yilin, whereas the ERC was completely excluded from the group. Even Tian Jiyun, the vice premier and Politburo member in charge of economic affairs, was not able to learn who participated in the drafting of the project until August.[18]

The Price and Wage Reform Project included such items as raising urban grain prices, increasing urban employees' wages, and raising the planned prices of coal and railway services gradually in the next two or three years.[19] Its main purpose was to reduce the state subsidies in urban grain supply, coal production, and railway services, rather than to be an overall price reform. Such a program resembled more a regular price adjustment project, common in almost every year even before the reform. Undoubtedly, the project was far from Deng's goal of completing price reform in several years.

Zhao was obviously dissatisfied with the result and repeated his own proposals. On July 1, he said, "The price reform and market formation is a very complicated process, and the key problem is not whether the increase of planned prices should be greater or less in the next step of the reform, but whether the whole economic system can be reformed simultaneously. The price reform is not simply a price problem, and it can hardly be successful without other reforms."[20] On July 11, when he held a meeting of the Central Financial and Economics Leading Group to discuss the Price and Wage Reform Project,[21] Zhao warned that the price reform would fail if enterprise reform did not take place simultaneously.[22] On July 20, he pointed out again at a meeting in Beidaihe that we should make clear what the key problems were in establishing a market system, and we should not simply suppose that a market system would appear after a price reform without reform of the public sector.[23] On July 22, during an inspection of Heilongjiang Province he said further that besides enterprise reform, political reform was also crucial for the success of the price reform.[24] He also told foreign visitors of his views.[25]

Zhao had an in-depth understanding of economic reform, but he did not possess effective means to influence the policy-making process in the State Council. Having replaced the price reform by a price adjustment project, Li Peng and Yao Yilin kept silent about the enterprise reform suggested by Zhao. Deng Xiaoping did not get involved with (and probably knew very little about) the details of the project. He only repeatedly expressed his determination to cut a path for a price reform.[26]

The Price and Wage Reform Project was discussed and revised several times during July. The original objective of the price reform finally became an abstract and remote desire.[27] Before the Price and Wage Reform Project was formally submitted for approval, Chen Yun gave a personal instruction to Yao and the SPC at the end of July. He said that the economy had become over-heated and that reform had caused economic chaos; it was time to straighten out (*zhengdun*) the economic system and readjust (*zhili*) the economy. Chen's instruction immediately launched an austerity project prepared secretly by a few senior officials in the SPC under Yao. Thus the SPC controlled by Yao was at the same time drafting two contradictory policy programs suggested by two supreme leaders with opposite positions. It made a show of political obedience to Deng, but implemented an antireform program.

Chen Yun, however, did not oppose the Price and Wage Reform Project openly then, and it was formally admitted at the meetings of the State Council on August 5 and 9 and of the Politburo on August 5–17.[28] During the process of drafting the price reform project, the official mass media received orders to promote the reforms to gain them extensive social support.[29] But unlike previous promotion efforts this one was not well received.

Since reforms first began, one strategy that the reformers adopted was to exchange economic benefits produced by the reforms for political support by society. This was effective in rural reform, as well as in the previous stage of urban reform, but proved unsuccessful in price reform, for price reform and enterprise reform would unavoidably damage the vested interests of urban residents, who are favored by the planned system. It is very difficult for the government to explain to urban residents why they must give up various benefits offered by a socialist system, and yet still be required to support socialism.

The official mass media therefore had to convince people of the necessity of price reform based on economic rationality, and for the sake of the state. This had quite weak appeal to the masses. The propaganda in fact increased urban residents' dissatisfaction and created panic over the possible losses due to this price reform. In a situation without freedom of speech, they were not able to criticize the price reform policy directly and openly and had to transfer their dissatisfaction to critiques of inflation and corruption. Official journalists at the time were hard put to find any supporters of the price reform policy among urban residents, except some managers and economists. During the summer of 1988, when the radical price reform was promoted, popular critiques of corruption and the injustice of income distribution became stronger and stronger, so Li Peng had to recognize them openly and promised to improve the situation.[30]

Abrupt Turn from Radical Reform to Stagnation

During the summer of 1988, a wave of mass panic buying burst out in Chinese cities. At the end of August, the Politburo decided to give up the Price and Wage Reform Project, which had been prepared and promoted for almost two months and had just been approved by the Politburo two weeks earlier. The austerity program was promoted instead.

The State Council proclaimed on August 30—only two weeks after formal announcement of price reform—that the government would promise to control the inflation rate of 1989 at a level lower than that of 1988, and that there would be no further price adjustments. Stabilizing the economy was also proclaimed a prime goal of the government.[31]

On September 2, the Politburo held its eleventh meeting of 1988 and decided that the economic policies of 1989 needed to be focused on stabilizing price levels through various administrative controls. The Price and Wage Reform Project was "temporarily" set aside. Zhao expressed his dissatisfaction with the methods of the austerity program, pointing out in the meeting that the old administrative methods would turn the reformed system backward. But no one paid attention to him.[32]

Ironically, while the retreat decision already had been made, the State Council continued to hold a meeting of experts and a meeting of the leaders of the "democratic parties" previously planned to seek opinions regarding the Price and Wage Reform Project.[33] At the meetings, Yao introduced the project, then the experts and leaders of the "democratic parties" seriously discussed it.[34] They did not know that the provincial party secretaries and governors were already on their way to Beijing to receive new instructions about the austerity program.

From September 15 to 22, the Politburo convened a Central Work Conference. Its main topic was how to implement the austerity program.[35] Afterward, the third plenum of the CCP Thirteenth Central Committee was held. In his report to the Central Committee, Zhao admitted that "the unexpected and serious inflation was discovered and treated too late," and as the general secretary of the party, he asked the entire Party to follow the policy of "rectifying the economy" (*zhili zhengdun*).[36]

The austerity program precluded further reforms. In the name of stabilizing the economy, the State Council began rapidly to exert various forms of administrative control over the economy in October. Economic reform then fell into stagnation. Deng Xiaoping experienced a complete failure and was forced to support the new policy. He said, "The austerity policy must be firmly carried out . . . even if it is overdone."[37]

Conclusion: Institutional and Personalistic Aspects of Economic Policy-Making

Both personalistic authority and institutional constraints on policy-making can be found in this case study. Both an institutional approach and a personalistic approach are frames of reference China scholars have often used to analyze policy-making in the post-Mao era. Among the various types of diplomatic, political, personnel, and economic policies in the reform period, economic policy is more often determined institutionally. The case study in this essay, however, suggests that sometimes personal authority in economic policy-making cannot be ignored.

For the purpose of analysis, Chinese economic policies in the reform period can be classified into four types according to their function, importance, and origins: (1) important policies that may change or affect the whole economic system nationwide, such as a large-scale price reform or enterprise reform; (2) the recentralization of macroeconomic policy to stabilize the economy; (3) those policies in particular fields such as industry, enterprise management, taxation, finance, foreign trade, and domestic commerce, aiming both at limited reforms in those fields and at improvement in macroeconomic management; (4) local policy such as the enterprise responsibility system, which is created at the lower level and promoted by some local leaders in the reform, and is then encouraged directly by some top leaders, thus finally being recognized by the central ministries, becoming a nationwide policy by an irregular route.

Among the four types, the third can best be explained by the institutional approach. Such policy-making usually follows an institutional routine; the octogenarians usually do not intervene and the members of the Politburo are often constrained by the regular policy-making institutions.[38] The policy is usually designed by technocrats in ministries and discussed repeatedly for coordination among them; sometimes economists are invited to join the discussion if the content goes beyond planning experiences of technocrats. Among members of the Politburo, only those who are in charge of economic affairs become involved and make the final determination, usually collectively. In this process, regular communication and discussion occur among these top leaders and between them and technocrats, by means of document circulation or meetings; the ideas of technocrats are respected; and the personal intervention of top leaders is significantly reduced.

The fourth type of policy often emerges first as a challenge from lower levels to the existing policies controlled by the central ministries. Support from some top leaders, therefore, is crucial for local leaders to resist pressure from the central ministries. Once top leaders become interested in the policy for their own purposes and thus encourage it, the central ministries may have to recognize it, and more local leaders may then follow the policy. A local policy thus is able to become a nationwide one without following the regular policy-making process at the central level. The personal influence of the top leaders is obviously very important in the process and is often elicited by clever local leaders. Top leaders, in turn, sometimes may use this approach to promote a reform policy from the bottom.

What is emphasized in this case study are the first and second types of policy, which usually have to be determined at the top level and then designed by technocrats in the central ministries. The institutional and personal aspects coexist in this policy-making.

Of the three levels in the central policy-making system of the late 1980s, two octogenarians, Deng Xiaoping and Chen Yun, are at the first level, the members of the Standing Committee of the Politburo are at the second level, and the central ministries are at the third.

Elders' Function in Policy-Making

Deng Xiaoping and Chen Yun have no formal positions in the economic policy-making structure; nevertheless, their personal decisions are still formally recognized and respected by the decision center of the party. As a result, the nominal system for economic policy-making differs from the real one, in which important policy decisions made by the top leaders at the second level must be reported to the elders and be approved by them either formally or informally. It could be said that their personal authority has been implicitly institutionalized in real policy-making.

The reason the two elders are able to exercise authority in economic policy is to be found in the power structure wherein the elders, especially Deng and Chen, still effectively control the second level by appointing those leaders in the Politburo. The members of the Politburo are responsible individually, and collectively as well, to the elders, when they are making important policy.

The two elders usually do not follow the regular official policy-making routine. They seldom attend decision meetings or write policy documents, so the communication about policy issues between them and others is abnormal. Both of them usually express their policy ideas to individual top leaders, even to foreigners, in "private talks." Chen Yun sometimes expresses his opinion by personal letters. The roles of the two elders are a little different. Deng is often more active than Chen, not only because he is in better health but also because he usually lives in Beijing, where he can obtain the latest information.

It is interesting that disagreement between Deng and Chen seemingly does not produce direct conflict in policy-making, since the two elders usually do not intervene in policy-making at the same time with openly opposing ideas. A rule of thumb between them seems to be that A would keep silent when B is talking, and wait for another opportunity to speak out when B's policy has met with some trouble. This may explain why Chen remained silent in May and June 1988, seemingly agreeing with Deng's radical reform decision, and then at the end of July when Chen expressed his opposite idea, Deng gave his tacit consent.

Although Deng Xiaoping has played a positive and active role in China's opening and economic reform, his personalistic style has resulted in some problems for the reform program as well. Being far removed from regular policy-making and largely isolated from society, he knows only a little of the economic and social information necessary for reform policy-making. He can only consider policy in a much simpler way than Zhao Ziyang or others can, yet acts as an exclusive initiator and promoter for some radical reform policies.

Such a system leads to three problems. First, policy is inappropriate. Deng tends to simplify a complicated economic reform policy as a political issue; its content, basis, and timing might be all or partly inappropriate. Second, policy can be inconsistent. When and whether Deng will intervene is unpredictable, and once he has made a decision, the reform program has to be readjusted to fit his idea, thus inhibiting the development of a systematic and coherent program. Third, policy is unreliable. Since a policy requested by Deng is usually highly abstract and different leaders at the second level are able to define or explain it according to their own preferences, Deng's policy can be distorted in drafting and implementation.

Policy-Making at the Second and Third Levels

In important policy-making, the second-level leaders need both support from elders and aid from technocrats at the third level, and thus may be constrained by either of them.

Before the members of the Standing Committee of the Politburo make important policies, they usually seek elders' personal support; if it is not yet available, they simply wait. Ideally, to make an important policy related to a nationwide reform or an overall change in the economic situation, the members of the Standing Committee seek either institutional authority, for example, the support of a majority in the Central Committee, or elders' personal authority, or both. The former authority, however, is usually not available for them, because it would be dangerous politically, or at least inappropriate for them to seek support from the Central Committee directly in order to make independent policy. The elders would view such action as a threat to their supreme power. Thus limited by an informal principle of party rule, the members of the Standing Committee have no right to hold a meeting of the Central Committee without the permission of the elders. The remaining authority for the subleaders, therefore, is that of the elders. Making policy under the elders' authority is obviously risk-averse, and thus is the usual option of subleaders. The younger and more experienced the subleaders are, the more careful they will be as long as the elders are still alive.

Once the elders have determined, or have given their support to, an important policy, all the subleaders first have to express their agreement, and those who really favor the policy may then use this opportunity to promote it actively and introduce their own policy intentions that are basically consistent with the elders'. In the summer of 1988, Zhao Ziyang's actions regarding the radical reform policy was just such a response. Yao Yilin then had to follow Deng's order nominally and routinely, though he was dissatisfied with the radical reform plan from the beginning; he waited to prepare an antireform austerity project until he had support from Chen Yun.

The members of the Standing Committee have much less personal authority, and their relations with the ministries are more institutional. Their influence in ministries is often determined by their division of labor. When Zhao Ziyang held the post of the premier, he was able to use the ERC as an active agency to directly promote many reform measures and to require the SPC and some other ministries to give up part of their macroeconomic control. When Zhao moved to his party post, his economic ideas immediately became less important. Li Peng was then able to weaken the function of the ERC through institutional means, and Zhao could say and do nothing about it.

At the same time, however, the institutional authority in a given ministry may be different for different top leaders, because of personal influence. Having worked in the central ministries for many years, Yao Yilin, for example, has an effective personal network in the ministries, which helps him to implement his own policy intentions. For the same reason, when returning to the State Council as vice premier, Zhu Rongji rapidly reestablished a new ministry on the basis of the former State Economic Commission, which was his previous "camp" but which had been abolished in 1987.

Without such personal resources, Zhao Ziyang had to find other institutional means to push his ideas. One of them was the Central Finance and Economics Leading Group. When he was premier Zhao held frequent meetings of the group to discuss and coordinate policies. Zhao also often invited both young scholars and ministers, sometimes even Yao Yilin, for a collective discussion, to analyze the economic situation and discuss policies in order to influence the ministries.

Theoretically, a more institutional system can reduce personal arbitrariness in policy-making. However, while both reformers and conservatives possess equal positions in the Standing Committee or the Politburo to maintain a political balance at the second level, a change of their party posts significantly influences mainstream policy-making. Without such a shift in the balance of power, majority support for an important reform policy could hardly emerge in the Standing Committee without Deng's outside promotion.

The political institutions in China during the late 1980s thus seemed to be an impediment to a thorough, or radical, urban economic reform. Under the control of octogenarians, a political balance among leaders with different intentions was maintained, making it difficult for the Standing Committee to decide and carry through a radical reform policy. This, therefore, unavoidably resulted in a reliance on Deng's intervention in the decision for radical reform in China.

Since the ERC, as the only ministry responsible for the economic reform program, did not possess enough power and authority, and those ministries for economic management, such as the SPC, controlled by Yao Yilin and guided by Chen Yun, were not interested in a thorough economic reform, Zhao Ziyang's intention and suggestions and even the push from Deng Xiaoping, could not be effectively transformed into concrete economic policy.

As a pragmatist, Deng supports only those economic reforms that he thinks would help consolidate the rule of the party. If reformers promote reform simply according to ideal reform goals, and thereby shake political institutions or arouse people's serious dissatisfaction, Deng may thus withdraw his support and isolate them. Conservatives then might easily find opportunities to suppress reformers through a power struggle. Moreover, after Deng's decision has caused a harmful outcome, such as in summer of 1988, Deng may then keep out of the difficult situation and let reformers take political responsibility alone.

Societal Impact on Economic Reform Policy-Making

In the post-Mao era, a significant difference from before is the increasing societal impact on economic policy-making. Since the beginning of the 1980s, the Chinese ruling party has gradually changed its old social control method from strictly political and ideological mobilization to material incentive. People have been encouraged to turn their concern to the progressive improvement of their living standard. People have become quite sensitive in measuring the changes regarding their newly vested interests, and public opinion is usually determined by that alone. Once they find themselves with greater losses due to an economic reform policy, extensive and strong social dissatisfaction may appear, which immediately makes the ruling party very nervous about possible socioeconomic instability and potential political dissident activities. The social impact of economic policy thus becomes an objective constraint on policy-making.

In urban economic reform, many reform policies may vary or reduce urban residents' benefits guaranteed by the residual socialist planned system, and thus may produce social dissatisfaction. Institutionalized communication between the public and the decision center might reduce the socioeconomic and political risks in policy-making. The political institutions in China, however, have not been reformed yet, and public opinion is still not able to influence policy-making directly or in advance.

In fact, the transmission of public opinion from bottom to top is almost the same as before the reform. The main and regular channel is restricted reports sent by official news agencies and local governments to the top leaders, such as the *Restricted Current Domestic Information* (Guonei dongtai qingyang) published by the Xinhua News Agency. These publications usually report only unexpected political, social, and economic events, and cannot regularly provide general information on public opinion. The first public opinion survey organizations did not appear in China until 1987, and remained highly restricted in their survey activities.[39]

The nominal representative system in China at the national level is the National People's Congress (NPC). It helps very little in transmitting public opinion to the central government. All its members are first appointed by the Central Organization Department, and then are nominally elected. They are politically dependent on the party and can hardly represent the people. They have never been given enough authority and opportunity to seek out public opinion. Their speeches, cautiously issued at NPC meetings, basically are their individual ideas, not necessarily public opinion.

Since people are not able to influence policy-making in advance, they have to express dissatisfaction with policies after the policy decisions are announced or implemented, and in noninstitutional ways. Such expressions usually takes the form of nonpolitical actions, such as slowdowns on the job, panic buying, withdrawal of bank deposits, or demonstrations for economic purposes. Once such actions have become widespread and have threatened socioeconomic stability or inspired political dissent, the top leaders have to respond and correct policy to prevent further unrest. The abrupt turnaround of the radical price reform policy in the summer of 1988 is a typical case of this. Such a means of policy improvement or correction may avoid policy disaster to some degree and at some times, but it also requires the nation, and the policymaker as well, to pay much higher economic, social, and political costs.

Notes

The author would like to thank Suisheng Zhao for his valuable assistance in various stages of preparation of this chapter and for his contribution to the theoretical conclusion.

1. In 1988, the group was headed by Zhao Ziyang. Its members included Li Peng, Yao Yilin, Tian Jiyun, Zhang Jingfu, Du Runsheng, and An Zhiwen. About fifteen staff members in the office were divided into three groups, respectively headed by Bai Meiqing (Zhao's personal secretary), Yuan Mu, and Wang Weicheng.

2. Quoted from the author's notes on Li Peng's first speech as the director of the Economic Reform Commission in May 1988.

3. Economic Reform Institute, "Social Stability Can Be Realized Only Through Thorough Reform," *World Economic Herald* (Shanghai), August 29, 1988.

4. Chen Yizi, *China: Ten Years Reform and the Democratic Movement in 1989* (Taipei: Lianjing Publishing House, 1990), 126–27.

5. The two-track system was adopted in the early 1980s. This system gives two different prices for many important commodities. One price was determined by the market and the other by the government. It was a transitional system in the early period of reform.

6. Quoted from the author's notes on Li Tieying's talk with the author and two other young research fellows in Li's office in Zhongnanhai on March 31, 1988.

7. Quoted from the author's notes on the speech of Wei Liqun, the director of the Reform and Law Bureau of the State Planning Commission, at a meeting to discuss long-term economic reform program in the office of ERC on April 23, 1988.

8. The author attended the meeting, which was held on May 1 and 4 at the State Planning Commission.

9. Quoted from the author's notes on May 7, 1988, when Li Tieying transmitted Deng's request to officials of the ERC.

10. The author took notes on the account given by Gao Shangquan, vice chairman of the ERC, who brought up the point at the Symposium for Middle and Long-Term Economic Reform Programs, May 30–June 3, 1988.

11. The author's notes on Li Peng's talk to the Symposium for Middle and Long-Term Economic Reform Programs, June 1, 1988, in which Li passed on Deng's recent remarks.

12. *People's Daily,* May 20, 25, June 4, 1988.

13. *People's Daily,* June 2 and August 19, 1988.

14. Quoted from the author's notes on a speech by An Zhiwen, vice chairman of the

ERC, who introduced Zhao's idea to the Symposium for Middle and Long-Term Economic Reform Programs, June 2, 1988.

15. Quoted from the author's notes on Li Tieying's speech at a meeting of the ERC on May 8, 1988.

16. The symposium was held from May 30 to June 3 in Beijing.

17. *People's Daily,* August 19, 1988.

18. Chen Yizi, *China: Ten Years Reform and the Democratic Movement in 1989,* 129.

19. The author's notes on Li Tieying's speech at the ERC meeting on May 8.

20. Quoted from the author's notes at a meeting held by the State Council on September 13, 1988.

21. Quoted from the author's notes on Zhao Ziyang's draft speech at a meeting in Zhao's office with six other young economists on July 1, 1988.

22. Quoted from the author's notes on Zhao's draft speech as transmitted by a senior official at the ERC.

23. Ibid.

24. *World Economic Herald,* August 8, 1988.

25. Zhao Ziyang's speech at a meeting with the delegation of the *Yomiuri Shimbun* of Japan at Beidaihe on August 16, 1988 (*People's Daily,* August 18, 1988).

26. Deng Xiaoping's comments to the president of Ethiopia on June 22, 1988 (*People's Daily,* June 23, 1988).

27. It was similar to the one the ERC already had at the beginning of 1988, and the crucial enterprise reform was excluded. The only thing left in the project was a limited adjustment of individual prices in the next two to three years.

28. *People's Daily,* August 19, 1988.

29. *People's Daily,* June 9 and August 24, 1988.

30. *People's Daily,* July 4, 1988.

31. *People's Daily,* August 31, 1988.

32. Quoted from the author's notes at a meeting of the ERC, September 1988.

33. The meeting was held on September 13 to 15, 1988, in Beijing.

34. *People's Daily,* September 18, 1988.

35. *People's Daily,* September 23, 1988.

36. *People's Daily,* October 28, 1988.

37. Ibid.

38. Some exceptions still exist. For example, elders or members of the Politburo are able to give financial orders to the SPC or the People's Bank of China for some special investment projects.

39. The State Council's Economic Reform Institute established the first public opinion survey organization, the Chinese Social Survey System, in 1987.

Part IV
Comparisons and Conclusions

18

Politics inside the Ring Road: On Sources and Comparisons

H. Lyman Miller

How does the Beijing regime work? How do we know what we think we know about how Beijing works? How have politics in Beijing changed over time? From these three most fundamental questions in the study of China's leadership politics sprout legions of related, subsidiary questions. But, basically, about the politics of China's national political elite there are only these three questions.

Certainly, these questions have been asked repeatedly in the past. There is, nevertheless, particular value in raising these questions anew. For one thing, many who follow China's contemporary politics agree that 1989 was a major turning point in the fortunes of the Communist regime after ten years of reform under Deng Xiaoping. During the decade before 1989, Deng introduced reforms to China's political system that changed it in substantial ways.

Characterizations of this evolution under Deng's reforms before 1989 also generally agree on the direction of change, even if not on precisely how. Andrew Nathan, for example, has suggested that the Deng reforms sought to change China "from a terror-based, totalitarian dictatorship to a 'mature' administered dictatorship of the post-Stalinist or East European type." Doak Barnett saw China's evolution under Deng as moving "from extreme totalitarianism toward liberalized authoritarianism." Harry Harding concluded that the Deng reforms "greatly relaxed the degree of political control over Chinese society without fundamentally altering the Leninist character" of the system. Zbigniew Brzezinski, not a China specialist but one of the most insightful observers of Communist systems in general, saw the reforms as sacrificing hard-line Communist tenets in favor of traditional Chinese cultural strengths—a "real cultural revolution"—and setting China down a promising (though not smooth) road to "commercial communism."[1]

Despite the overall consensus on the fact and general direction of change, however, the events of 1989 and afterward have produced no general unanimity of impressions on how far and fast political change in China will go. Many see the events in Tiananmen Square as truly a watershed—the beginning of the end of a regime that will go the way of the Communist regimes of Eastern Europe and the U.S.S.R., joining a "third wave" of democratizing revolutions. Others are not so sure. While they agree that 1989 was a significant landmark in the regime's fortunes, they suspect that the wounds of 1989 may not be fatal to the Communist government, and even if they are, the outcome is more likely to be another form of authoritarianism than democracy.

Because the outcome is portentous for everyone, inside and outside China, accurate judgments about where China is headed have a particular urgency. Addressing fundamental questions about leadership politics in contemporary China as precisely as possible may go a long way toward sorting out judgments about the future.

Second, the fundamental questions are worth asking again because the range and variety of sources at the base of our understanding have changed radically over the decade of Deng's reforms. As Michel Oksenberg has helpfully outlined, analysis of Chinese politics from 1949 to the Deng era was built mainly on a tripod of sources: China's official press and broadcast media; the travelogues and accounts of visitors to China; and interviews with and writings by émigrés from China.[2] Thanks to the "open" policies of the Deng regime and to the attendant expansion of Western access to Chinese officialdom at many levels and to Chinese society in general, information about many aspects of China's political system and process has expanded enormously. Important new studies about the operation and interaction of bureaucratic hierarchies, about village politics in the countryside, and about the interface between state and society among distinct social groups in Chinese cities all owe their success to this improved access and expansion of sources.

Émigré Cadre Literature

One important new source of information, providing new insight into China's leadership politics in particular, derives directly from the events of 1989. This source is the diverse body of memoirs, retrospective analyses, and interpretive judgments of cadre, all party members, who in the 1980s worked in the staffs and bureaucracies at relatively high levels of the central political system and who have now emigrated to the West as a result of events in 1989. This body of work is called here émigré cadre literature.

The émigré cadre literature, exemplified by the studies in this volume, is important in several ways. It draws directly on the experience of men and women who participated in the day-to-day operation of the political system at relatively high levels—frequently at levels just under the top leadership itself. Further, the cadre, such as the contributors to this volume, collectively had experience across a broad spectrum of institutions and hierarchies at the heart of the central political system. As a review of the careers of this volume's contributors shows, this experience spans *Renmin ribao*'s editorial section, the party Secretariat, reform research and drafting groups under the Secretariat and State Council, the State Planning Commission, and the Beijing Garrison Command, among others. These people share a natural and profound sense of alienation from and disappointment with the Beijing regime they once served. To some degree, these feelings echo those of the émigré interviewees who contributed to our knowledge before the Deng era. The latter, however, were usually not in positions that could give us insight into the leadership processes at the center of the political system.

This chapter explores how the accounts and analyses of our new émigré colleagues help us in addressing fundamental questions about central leadership politics. The approach taken in this assessment is comparative. Comparison proceeds here not in the nomothetic spirit of political science, which seeks to establish universal laws and frameworks for sorting and evaluating disparate political systems, but merely in the empirical spirit of history, as a perceptual mirror that aids understanding of the workings of a single government. In seeking to grasp precisely what one sees, it is sometimes helpful to observe what one does not see. Comparing what we know of China's politics to what is understood about other political systems—whether similar or vastly different—helps to illuminate gaps in what we know about China. This comparative approach is therefore not ambitious and far-reaching, as theory-building in comparative politics often is. It is, however, fundamental insofar as it aims at questions at the base of our understanding. It may contribute to better pictures of the present-day political system in China and its dynamics that will, in turn, provide better theories and better judgments about the future.

In applying this comparative approach, this chapter looks foremost at how Beijing works—first with regard to problems of institutional structure and formal procedure and then to problems of informal process, relationships, and implicit "rules of the game." A concluding section looks at broader questions of how the political system has changed and is changing and finally at issues of method, conceptualization, and interpretation.

Structure and Formal Procedure

The most immediately relevant field for comparison with what we know about China's institutional structure and the formal procedures and processes of leadership politics is the literature on the former Soviet system. What is striking about the body of secondary literature on Soviet leadership politics compared to that on China is the significantly greater degree to which Soviet institutions and formal procedures were known even before the snowballing revelations of glasnost during the Gorbachev era. A straightforward comparison of Central Intelligence Agency directories of Soviet and Chinese national elites reflects the disparate knowledge of organizational structure and institutional relationships.

Similarly, students of Soviet politics were successful in acquiring a more detailed knowledge of the routine formal procedures of the Soviet political process, including those of the highest-level decision-making. For example, the following picture of the operation of the Communist Party of the Soviet Union (CPSU) Politburo is typical of such descriptions in basic textbooks on Soviet leadership politics:

> The Politburo meets regularly once a week and since 1982 has published short reports of its deliberations. Its detailed operation is not known but it appears that in contrast to Khrushchev's adversarial style the modern General Secretary hopes to achieve unanimity rather than to impose decisions through voting. This is made easier by the detailed preparatory work carried out by the CC [Central Committee] Secretariat, where a consensus is hammered out. On most items there is no discussion, and Politburo members simply append their signatures to a prepared file. . . . Leadership of the Secretariat buttresses the General Secretary's position in the Politburo. The Secretariat usually meets on Wednesdays to draft proposals for the next day's Politburo meeting.[3]

This picture is admittedly rudimentary and perhaps simplistic. It may have been, moreover, that the formal routines of the CPSU Politburo were far less important than the various formal processes and informal politicking that preceded meetings of the Politburo. But Soviet specialists generally agreed on the essentials of this picture and its accuracy for most of the period since 1964, as more thorough and detailed analyses bear out.[4] This picture was confirmed and elaborated—supplying further details about Politburo agenda-setting, record-keeping and file procedures, attendance routines, patterns of debate, and division of labor—in studies summarizing the results of systematic interviews with émigrés formerly having access to the process.[5]

As much as scholars and analysts of Soviet politics complained about how much the CPSU Politburo and Secretariat were "shrouded in secrecy," their familiarity with the normal routine of those bodies far exceeds what is known about the Politburo and Secretariat of the Chinese Communist Party (CCP). China scholars share no working description of how the CCP Politburo operates, including basic information—valid for any period—about how regularly (if at all) it meets, what kinds of issues it discusses (if any), what the role of the Politburo Standing Committee is with respect to the full Politburo, how decisions are made (if they are), and what role the Secretariat plays with regard to agenda, and so forth. Glimpses and shreds of information are frequently contradictory, and so those scholars who have bravely sought to weave an integrated summary, like A. Doak Barnett, have been able to reach only tentative and provisional conclusions.[6]

As a consequence, the import of clearly major instances of institutional and procedural change at the top level has remained uncertain. In 1987, for example, the relationship of the Secretariat and the Politburo and its Standing Committee clearly changed in the wake of Hu Yaobang's removal as party general secretary, in part for "abusing" the role of the Secretariat. The Thirteenth CCP Congress in October that year revised party constitution stipulations on the role of the Secretariat, making it "the working body" of the Politburo and its Standing Committee rather than responsible for the "day-to-day work of the Central Committee under the direction of the Politburo and its Standing Committee." In his report to the party congress, new General Secretary Zhao Ziyang further revealed that a new "collective leadership system" would establish a routine of "periodic work reports" to the Politburo by its Standing Committee and "work rules" for the Secretariat, Politburo, and Politburo Standing Committee.[7]

The appointment of the Secretariat's new membership at the first plenum after the congress confirmed the impression that the Secretariat's functions had indeed changed. Since its restoration in 1980, the Secretariat had had ten or eleven members who, judging by their previous work and their patterns of public appearance, appeared to assume responsibility over distinct policy arenas or portfolios. After the thirteenth congress, however, there were only four secretaries, whose responsibilities (as secretaries) were not easily discernible. What all these constitutional and personnel changes added up to has remained unclear, and what we know about how the Politburo and Secretariat operate has not been substantially improved.

The reasons for the better picture of the formal processes in the Soviet Union are clear enough. Western access and contacts developed over a far longer period and continued even during episodes of tension and confrontation. Soviet official press and media sources have been far more extensive and revealing since at least the Khrushchev period. The Soviet émigré community included several people who once worked at relatively high levels of the Soviet system and who have since written and talked about their experiences. We have the memoirs of Nikita Khrushchev himself;

there is no memoir of comparable detail available for any Chinese leader at that level, and the few that have appeared—such as Marshal Nie Rongzhen's—have been highly selective and overwhelmingly anecdotal.

The Gorbachev years brought an explosion in all these categories of sources. Glasnost gradually produced a system of explicitly rival press voices within the Soviet political community. This, together with the Gorbachev leadership's investment in attacking the "deformations" of the past, resulted in massive but still selective revelations about major episodes in Soviet political history. Documentary series, memoirs and reminiscences, and hundreds of articles by Soviet historians filled huge holes in understanding how the system worked in the past. Frequently, CPSU Central Committee plenums in the last years of the Soviet regime were followed by publication of the speeches of the plenum's participants. Conflicts between various media organs, published interviews with editors and even propaganda officials, and deliberations over the new Soviet press law yielded deep insights into the operations of the Soviet press and its role in the political process. Meanwhile, Soviet officials were often accessible everywhere, in their offices and on American television news and discussion programs.

After the collapse of the U.S.S.R., it became possible for foreigners to gain access to those archives of the Soviet Foreign Ministry, the CPSU, and, for a time, even the KGB that survived the shredders. The problem for analysts of the Soviet political process since the mid-1980s rapidly became one of control and efficient sorting of a growing flood of information. As Werner Hahn has suggested, and as evidenced by his recent assessment of various accounts of the coup overthrowing Khrushchev in 1964, the work of Soviet analysis was increasingly like the work of "real history," involving the problem of critically sorting and evaluating various divergent accounts of the same event.[8]

For analysis of China, a parallel but limited revolution of sources has been under way since the beginning of the Deng period. Obviously, the revolution in Chinese sources has not proceeded as far as in the Soviet case, even before the events of 1991. But neither should the range and depth of information be underestimated. Access of foreigners to Chinese officials at various levels and opportunities for field research over the past decade have already significantly altered perceptions of the Chinese political system, not only in the details of its operation but also in the way it relates to Chinese society at large. Meanwhile, a far greater explosion of Overseas Chinese social contacts in China has brought forth a flood of reports, stories, rumors, and sometimes speculations and fantasies about political events in China, recorded by a diverse China-watching press in Hong Kong.

Media

There has also been the spectacular explosion of official press and broadcast media sources. Though still controlled at some level and shaped by regime purposes in its content, the scale of information now available from media sources has defied bibliographic control. On the eve of Mao's death in 1976, fewer than ten Chinese-language periodicals (mainly *Renmin ribao, Guangming ribao, Hongqi,* and two historical/archaeological journals) were available for foreign subscription. By the early 1980s the number available through the Beijing Post Office had passed 2,000 titles, and the numbers have continued to grow, though more slowly. Nearly every major policy sector has at least one and sometimes several journals that address it. Book publishing has undergone a similar revolution since 1978. In that year, according to the *1990 Chinese Statistical Abstracts,* slightly under 15,000 titles were published. By 1989, Chinese book publishers had surpassed 75,000 titles a year.[9]

The information contained in this mountain of source material has permitted a far better picture of some periods of China's political history. The categories of publications that contain useful information about the political system and its operation in the past include:

- documentary collections, including serial collections on party history like the *Zhonggong dangshi ziliao* (Materials on Chinese Communist Party History) series;
- speech collections by present and past leaders, including previously unpublicized speeches;
- reminiscences by major leaders, such as the recent recollections of Nie Rongzhen, and also by secretaries, assistants, and bodyguards of high-level leaders like Mao Zedong and Peng Dehuai;
- serious biographies, such as the recent account published by the Central Committee's Document Research Office of Zhou Enlai's life until 1949, with hundreds of footnotes drawing from unpublished documents in the party and government archives;[10]
- histories that tell far more about previously (and certainly still) sensitive periods of the party's past;
- docudramas recreating in minute detail—including purported dialogue and the thoughts of protagonists—dramatic episodes of the past, like the 1990 account published by the Central Party School of Ye Jianying's role in bringing down the Gang of Four;[11]
- handbooks on party and government organization, including detailed diagrams of structure as well as detailed question-and-answer guidance on routine and procedure for lower-level organs;

- biographic compendia of leaders including basic information that formerly had been held secret—like dates of birth and previous posts; and
- press accounts depicting purportedly normal leadership routines and policy processes intended to make China's leadership politics more transparent after decades of Maoist secrecy, such as the regular series carried in *Liaowang* (Outlook) magazine beginning in 1980 on the work of the Politburo and Secretariat, eventually published as the book *Zhongnanhai de chuntian* (Springtime in Zhongnanhai).[12]

All these publications from China's publishing system have opened a window of still unsurveyed dimensions on China's political system. In addition, the steadily widening flow of publications from China's "internal" (*neibu*) publication system may take us considerably farther. The scale of the internal publishing in China is still not possible to estimate with any reliability—the figures cited above presumably refer only to the open publishing system, and the internal system is said to be even larger.

Internal Publications

The open and internal systems serve entirely different functions in the Chinese political process. Internal publications include all the same categories of writings relevant to understanding the political process enumerated for the open system above, but they are not subject to the same political controls. Open publications are disseminated publicly without restriction; but because they are public, they are in some sense official, and so their content is regulated. Internal publications are restricted (sometimes perfunctorily) in circulation. Because they are not public, they are therefore not official, and their content is therefore not regulated. As the chapter by Ching-chang Hsiao and Timothy Cheek in this volume bears out, the former serve regime purposes of explanation and mobilization once decisions have been made; the latter serve the process of general information and policy deliberation.

Care must be therefore taken to recognize the different purposes of materials from each publication system. But, used alongside open materials, internal publications contain information that is frequently extremely valuable. Documentary collections such as the *San zhong quanhui yilai zhongyao wenxian xuanbian* (Selected Important Documents Since the Third Plenum), first disseminated through the internal system and later made openly available, included numerous speeches and party documents not published in the open media and publications system as well as more complete and unaltered versions of some that were.[13] The internally published selection of Chen Yun speeches includes several that are not in the three-volume *Selected Works of Chen Yun* published in the open system.[14] Internally published histories of the party routinely include details and whole episodes not included in even the most revealing histories published in the external system. The *Lushan huiyi shilu* (The True Account of the Lushan Meetings) written by Mao's confidant Li Rui and published internally in 1989, appears to be the most complete and intimate account of the fateful 1959 Lushan conferences and plenum.[15]

Émigré Cadre Literature and Formal Processes

Systematic examination of the most promising of the categories of published materials will prove all the more illuminating when pursued in conjunction with the analyses and accounts of events provided by the post-1989 émigré cadre writers.[16] Used together, these sources promise to illuminate poorly understood incidents and events in the China's political past. Michael Schoenhals's sensitive dissection of "using words" in Chinese politics, for example, provides a stimulating example of what can be done by combining the insights of émigré cadre with rigorous analysis of *neibu* and openly published materials.[17] But beyond clarifying mysterious episodes of past politics, and of more immediate value for current analysis, all these sources used together will provide a better-grounded picture of the institutional structures and formal procedures within which politics plays out in normal times.

Ruan Ming's study here, for example, sheds important new light on the operation of the Secretariat and its relationship to the Politburo during its "golden era" under Hu Yaobang, previously a dimly understood area as described above. In chapter 4, Yan Huai's dissection of the overall institutional system provides insight from a Chinese party organizational perspective that is often missed in Western accounts, while Yan Jiaqi's discussion of the organization of leadership systems confirms and fills in the picture worked out painstakingly but tentatively by Carol Lee Hamrin in an earlier study.[18]

The émigré cadre literature advances our understanding in other areas into which it has been extremely difficult to gain much insight. George Yang's picture of the Ministry of Foreign Affairs' organization and procedure bears out and takes considerably further the snapshot developed by Doak Barnett in his examination of China's foreign policy decision-making system. Fang Zhu's account of the organization, personnel arrangements, and work processes of the Beijing Garrison Command in the 1980s provides unique information about that unit's place in both the central military and political systems.

Another key aspect of the central leadership system that the analyses in this volume illuminate is the central documentary system. Understanding the significance of a particular document requires some knowledge of where it fits within the larger documentary system that produced it. The relative place of a specific document within the larger documentary hierarchy of a given institution, the range of its dissemination, who decides which level of document should be issued for which specific circumstances, and who drafts specific levels of document are all essential to gauging its importance. Michel Oksenberg and Kenneth Lieberthal made pioneering efforts to delineate these systems. But both their efforts preceded the explosion of contacts and published sources, and their joint volume on policy-making in the energy field, while important in many other ways, does not move significantly beyond their earlier individual works on this score.[19] Guoguang Wu's authoritative analysis of "documentary politics" in this volume takes us well beyond where we were.

Similarly, systematic use of émigré cadre literature in conjunction with other internal and open published sources may produce a better picture of the various patterns of leadership meetings that prepare the way for publicized meetings like Central Committee congresses, plenums, work conferences, and so forth. Again, Kenneth Lieberthal's *Research Guide to Central Party and Government Meetings in China* (and its updated version in collaboration with Bruce Dickson) have proven invaluable but also could be significantly expanded from the émigré accounts.[20] Chen Yizi's account here of the organizational procedures and steps taken beginning in 1986 to prepare the thirteenth congress's decision on political reform in 1987 is illuminating in this respect and useful well beyond the arena of political reform.

No policy cycle is more predictable and yet so perennially contentious in all political systems than the process of planning budget allocations, which inevitably brings normally separate policy sectors into direct competition. Aaron Wildavsky describes the U.S. federal budget as the focus of all "the victories and defeats, the compromises and the bargains, the realms of agreement and the spheres of conflict in regard to the role of national government in our society" and so as "the heart of the political process."[21] Though the bases and structure of power are profoundly different, it is hard to believe that the shape of the state budget and its relationship to the larger process of drafting annual and longer-term plans are not at or near the heart of the political process in China as well. Economists studying China have worked hard to examine trends in the Chinese state budget in economic terms. But the political implications of both the budget and planning processes and their outcomes are only beginning to be explored. Here the insights of Wang Lixin, in collaboration with Joseph Fewsmith, into the role and procedures of the State Planning Commission take us considerably farther, shedding light on not only the routines but also the institutional and cross-institutional agendas that the planning and budget processes engender.

Informal Processes

Hedrick Smith's *The Power Game—How Washington Works* is a sensitive and penetrating account of the complex ironies of American national politics conducted in the capital—"inside the beltway." [22] It illuminates how the system's explicit goals and established processes are distorted, displaced, paralyzed, and sometimes subverted outright by actors within the system who pursue a range of goals—some personal, some legitimately representational, others not so legitimate. In Smith's account, political players pursue a bewildering array of informal "power games" seemingly at odds with the ostensible missions of the system's organizational components, the rational allocations and divisions of authority within the system, and its expected norms of behavior.

The formal structure and procedures of the U.S. political system appear to incorporate several strengths. They provide for responsive and efficient representation of popular will through well-developed mechanisms of interest articulation and aggregation and pluralistic competition. They delineate a well-defined allocation of authority throughout the system through checks and balances. They foster a high degree of orderly leadership turnover through routinized succession processes. They maintain strong barriers against encroachment of the state on society through a mature legal system and a vigorous open press.

The system that Smith describes "inside the beltway" looks somewhat different, however. He describes a system having a polycentric and non-hierarchical structure in which political power is "fluid, fragmented and floating." These features emerged from a series of watershed changes in 1974, including:

- the proliferation of congressional powers vis-à-vis the president, concurrent with a loosening of Congress's internal discipline;
- dissolution of congressional baronies in favor of polycentrism and a "more piecemeal, jumbled, adversarial brand of politics";
- an explosion in the size of congressional and executive branch staffs, with a concurrent loss of the "coziness" that facilitated compromise in the past;
- a comparable growth in parapolitical agents—the lobbyists, lawyers, and journalists;

- the massive influx of big money into the political process, brought about by the resurgence of business lobbying and the rise of corporate political action committees, linking wealth and power to an unprecedented degree; and
- the rise of television as the primary mediator between candidate and voter ("Boss Tube Replaces Boss Tweed"), accelerating centrifugal trends and the diffusion of power.

Out of these changes has emerged a political process that looks less like the seesaw balance of power between Congress and the president that textbooks describe than a game of water polo in which players bob and struggle to stay above water, in which the flow of the action changes instantaneously, and in which scoring can occur from anywhere in the field of play. Powerful cross-cutting "iron triangles" vie to shape policy and appropriations with little reference to legislative-executive divisions of authority. Personal associations and networks among politicians assume an increasing importance in getting anything done in a polycentric structure of power.

Proliferating staffs assume enormous power over policy and agenda because of their substantive expertise, as elected politicians are forced increasingly to turn their attention to protracted campaigns and fund-raising for reelection. Despite provisions for a political process open to anyone, the advantages of campaigning in office and the financial demands of campaigning mean that there is only marginal turnover—to a degree that would seem to confirm C. Wright Mills's notion of a "power elite" in American politics. Politicians build staffs of media advisers because of the increasing need to manipulate and control their media personae and, above all, visibility (good or bad) on television.

These "background games" of access, visibility and credibility, staff-building, and networks lead to the larger power games over control of the national agenda, coalition-building to govern, control of public image, and containment of internal divisions, especially in foreign policy.

Rules of the Game

The great value of Smith's portrait of the American political process for students of China's political system is its description of the diverse informal practices and processes that make the system work within and frequently in spite of the formal aspects of the system. The American and Chinese political systems have profound differences, to be sure, but sometimes the parallels are surprising and, at times, downright unsettling. This reader was struck by how frequently Smith's description of American federal politics resonates with commonplace descriptions of how the Chinese political system operates. Just the terminology used to describe various political groups is suggestive—references to "factions" and "renegades" abound. (In the same vein, one finds Peggy Noonan in her fascinating account of her work as a Reagan speechwriter referring to White House cliques as Chinatown gangster "tongs.")[23]

But more than that, Smith's picture of the American politics suffused with power struggles built on complex networks and coalitions of interest and bureaucratic imperative, at first glance, seems not irretrievably distant from impressions of how Beijing works. In analyzing the politics of the White House staff, for example, Smith presents the struggle for power and influence within the White House between chief policy adviser Edwin Meese and then chief of the president's staff James Baker. Ultimately, Baker the "pragmatist" defeated Meese the "ideologue"—a man whose connections, views, and experience put him at a vast advantage in the struggle for Ronald Reagan's attention and influence—because he patiently and successfully employed what Smith calls the "five keys" to White House power:

- divide duties so as to control access to the president;
- develop credibility with and the trust of the president;
- get the best talent that is also unquestioningly loyal to work for you;
- build networks and focus on the process to control the action sequence; and
- focus on action and short-term results, not long-term planning and structure.

With some allowances, perhaps, these "keys to power" would seem to work credibly well in Beijing.[24] This is not as implausible as it seems: Lieberthal and Oksenberg have already pointed to the relevance of studies of the executive branch in understanding central bureaucratic politics in China.[25] One may wish to contemplate in this regard the great overlap of Baker's keys with the "rules of the game" postulated by Yan Jiaqi in chapter 1. Arguably, they are also visible in the tactics used by Chen Yun and Yao Yilin in overturning Deng Xiaoping's and Zhao Ziyang's radical price reform proposal in 1988, as analyzed by Cheng Xiaonong in chapter 17.

However such comparisons pan out in detail, the vividness of Smith's portrait of the American system's informal aspects invites us to contemplate how some of the informal aspects he finds relevant in understanding the American system might operate in the Chinese context. At least two broad areas—leadership routines and bureaucratic "power games"—suggest themselves.

First of all, Smith describes several informal aspects that derive from and in turn influence the power of top leaders. For example:

Physical Location and Layout of the Offices of Leaders and Their Staffs

Smith relates how the physical location of offices in the White House translates into access to the president. It may be instructive to know even the general configuration of Zhongnanhai, especially in terms of which leaders work near each other. In the same vein, Chen Yizi in chapter 12 recounts Zhao Ziyang's decision to retain the State Council offices as his primary workplace even after becoming party general secretary, a decision made in recognition of the implication of physical location for his own power and ambitions.

Information Flows to Leaders at Various Levels and Control of Information Dissemination in the Policy Process

Control of what the president reads and whom he sees, Smith shows, is the key component of a staff chief's power. Smith also underscores the importance of "Schattschneider's law" in the American policy process: those who seek policy closure because they are winning seek to keep the information loop small; those on the losing side of an ongoing policy battle seek to widen it. The émigré cadre analyses in this volume enhance our sense of both the range of documents, reports, and other materials top-level leaders read and of instances where significant information purposefully was not allowed to reach them.

Schattschneider's law, moreover, is clearly visible in the Chinese policy process. Cheng Xiaonong, for example, describes how the drafting of the price reform proposal was co-opted by Yao Yilin and the State Planning Commission in June 1988, how Zhao Ziyang and Tian Jiyun institutionally were cut out of the loop on the proposal, and so how the resulting proposal reflected few of its originally intended goals. In a reverse direction, Ruan Ming in chapter 2 shows how Hu Yaobang used Secretariat document dissemination prerogatives to circulate a Central Party School inspection report on Shenzhen to undermine opposition to the Special Economic Zones in the early 1980s. Wang and Fewsmith mention the use of leaks—the selective creation of *xiaodao* rumors, in tried and true "inside the beltway" fashion—by State Planning Commission bureaucrats to create the expectation that Hu Yaobang was about to fall.

Leadership Interaction

Top leaders in the American system rarely interact directly. Especially in periods of policy confrontation, the main arena of interaction is at the staff level. How do China's top leaders interact? Do they meet on any regular basis, collectively or one to one? Do they talk to each other on the telephone, communicate via memo or notes, or just scribble notations on mutually circulating documents? Some of the studies here—Cheng Xiaonong's comments on the interaction between Deng Xiaoping and Chen Yun, for example—confirm the general impression that Chinese leaders, especially the elders, frequently deal with each other not face to face but through their staffs. Chapters by Guoguang Wu and Chen Yizi suggest that leaders deliberate on policy decisions indirectly, via comments on draft policy documents.

Media Manipulation

Smith cites former Representative Tony Coelho (R-Calif.) as stating, "What is power? . . . drafting an op-ed article."[26] Stories of direct intervention and manipulation of the press by Chinese leaders are legion, and a glance at Mao's annotations and emendations to Xinhua dispatches in the 1940s and 1950s, as well as some telling references in Deng Xiaoping's *Selected Works,* shows such intervention to be routine. Cheng Xiaonong's study provides a clear example of how media reporting intended to prepare the public for pending price reforms was used instead to prepare the way to overturn them and introduce a more conservative package of economic policy adjustments. Ching-chang Hsiao and Timothy Cheek's chapter on the dual function of the media also provides instances of how internal and open media are manipulated for policy purposes.

Some informal aspects of the political process are not dealt with directly among the studies collected here, but the émigré cadre could tell us much about them, namely:

Public Visibility and Staff Dependence

Smith describes U.S. politicians in some measure as prisoners of their public appearance schedules, a circumstance that, together with the increasingly technical nature of the policy issues they confront, increases their reliance on staff to tell them where they should be and what they should be saying. Though the responsiveness of Chinese leaders to public opinion is driven by very different imperatives than in the American case, many—especially

Jiang Zemin, Li Peng, Qiao Shi, and Li Ruihuan among the present leadership—spend a great deal of time meeting foreign delegations, posing for photographs with provincial and local groups in Beijing for conferences or at award ceremonies, and generally pressing the flesh on tours of the provinces. Is there consequently a similar dependence on staff? It would seem likely, and though the studies collected here give little direct confirmation, a detailed account of a central leader's activities and their coordination by his staff would likely bear it out.

Folkways

Smith observes that the "conceit of Washington" is no less than that of Paris or Moscow. Leaders moving to Washington for the first time discover that they must learn the political culture distinctive and peculiar to Washington "inside the beltway" to be effective. Are there parallel "folkways" inside Beijing's ring roads? Certainly many chapters here, such as Su Shaozhi's, suggest a culture of comparable manipulation, requiring a finely tuned political sense for survival. Yan Huai's description of the hierarchical "grid" underscores the high sensitivity to status. Both Yan and Tong Zhan, moreover, point to a tightly disciplined, workaholic lifestyle among staff of the party Central Committee departments.

Ideological Cultures

Politicians bound together in groups out of common ideological and political predilection signal their membership through a various means—including dress, office decor, and idiom—that are instantly recognizable to participants in the political process but may escape the notice of outsiders. Peggy Noonan describes some of the cultural emblems of the Reagan revolutionary vanguard in the early 1980s:

> Everyone wore Adam Smith ties that were slightly stained from the mayonnaise that fell from the sandwich that was wolfed down at the working lunch on judicial reform. The ties of the Reagan era bore symbols—eagles, flags, busts of Jefferson—and the symbols had meaning. I had a dream: The ties talked; they turned to me as I walked into the symposium. "Hi, I'm a freemarket purist!" said the tie with the little gold curve. "Hello there, I believe in judicial restraint!" said the tie with the liberty bell. "Forget politics, come fly with me!" said the tie with the American eagle.
>
> You'd be in someone's house and on the way to the bathroom you'd pass the bedroom and see a big thick copy of Paul Johnson's *Modern Times* lying half-open on the table by the bed. Three months later you'd go back and it

was still there. Everyone had read Jean-François Revel's *How Democracies Perish* and could discuss with ease Jeane Kirkpatrick's analysis of authoritarian versus totalitarian regimes.[27]

Since people inevitably create markers of status and identity in even the most egalitarian and oppressively conformist of political cultures, it is worth inquiring what the emblems and badges of ideological and political identity are in Beijing. Some chapters in this book suggest strong generational and educational components to political identity that separate "reformers" and "conservatives," for example.

Out of all these various aspects, and in combination with an improved acquaintance with the formal rhythms and routines discussed in the preceding section, it may eventually be possible to build a realistic picture of a day in the life of a Chinese leader, whether Politburo member or ministerial executive or Central Committee apparatchik. In such a picture, the work style and interactions of individual leaders would fit into the larger framework of portfolio responsibilities and predictable meeting and policy cycles marked by Beidaihe retreats, Central Committee plenums, National People's Congress budget and planning sessions, and so forth. A better sense of leadership and policy routines for any given period would, in turn, help by supplying context for the ongoing political process. In providing the means to identify departures from normal routine, this picture would aid in identifying episodes of policy tension and crisis.

With regard to the respective bureaucratic politics played out in each capital, two areas of particular comparative interest are, first, the patterns of proliferation of bureaucracies and staffs, and second, the spectrum of diverse "power games" played among them. In the American system, Smith describes a two-wave pattern of proliferation of staffs, research offices, and functional bureaucracies: first, stemming from the expansion of congressional powers at the expense of the executive branch after Watergate; and then a wave of new executive branch bodies springing up as the presidency sought to reassert itself, especially under Reagan.

As staffs and bureaucracies proliferated on both sides, mediating groups—some informal and transitory, and others more firmly established and permanent—evolved to bridge bureaucratic hierarchies both across the congressional-executive divide and within branches. The reasons Smith cites for these developments conform with basic tenets of social science theories of organization process and behavior.[28] One reason is the increasingly technical nature of governing and an increasingly complex society and economy. Another arises from problems of interbureaucratic coordination. Some supraministerial bodies in China like the state Science and Technology Commission, for example, were created in part to harmonize the disparate bureaucratic agendas of State Council ministries that have a voice in significant policy areas. Another reason is the predictable pattern of organizational life cycles. Organizations rigidify and become defensive in terms of turf and mission, taking on new missions and tasks only cautiously; so new tasks frequently require new organizations. There are also the imperatives of political competition—the need for political buffers and for information and research that serves the political agenda of specific groups and leaders.

Certainly, the proliferation of bureaucracy is a commonly noted feature of political life in China. As Lampton, Lieberthal and Oksenberg, and others have shown, Western organizational theory has great salience for analyzing Chinese behavior in this respect. Despite the rhetoric and actions taken by the Deng leadership to streamline bureaucracy in the reform period, Chinese leaders themselves acknowledge the failure of these efforts, noting that bureaucracy has actually grown, not shrunk.

The specific causes for bureaucratic proliferation in China are similar to those in the United States, as the émigré cadre literature in this volume confirms. Chen Yizi's account of the 1986 initiative on political reform, for example, shows new organizations arising both from problems of rigidification in existing bureaucracies and from imperatives of political competition.

Smith's description of the various strategies that actors follow in the larger Washington "power games" also merits scrutiny because clear parallels are at work in the Chinese system. Smith points, for example, to the primary role played by leaders' staffs and the bureaucracies in the process of agenda-setting and policy initiation. Hough saw a similar phenomenon in the Soviet political process, as Lieberthal and Oksenberg do in China.[29] Smith also notes the "iron triangle" of shared agenda among Pentagon planners, defense contractors, and senators, representatives, and staff on defense appropriations committees that subverts the intended balance of authority between the executive and legislative branches and between public and private.

Comparable "iron triangles" of mutual interest certainly exist in China. Conflicts over power and policy among top leaders like Hu Yaobang, Zhao Ziyang, Yao Yilin, and ultimately Deng Xiaoping and Chen Yun, in the 1980s can be understood at least in part in terms of inter- and intrainstitutional warfare over the direction and implementation of economic reform. Figuring large in these conflicts were the bureaucratic battles between the State Planning Commission, on one hand, and the State Economic and Economic Reform Commissions, on the other, sketched in the chapters by Wang and Fewsmith and by Cheng Xiaonong. These battles are ultimately intelligible in terms of complex triangles of interest and agenda among party organization, ministry, enterprise management, and trade union and workers' congress constituencies.

Single bureaucracies are themselves not monolithic political actors. Smith describes how the Pentagon's "Early Bird"—a kind of *Cankao xiaoxi* (Reference News) for the American military establishment—is used by a "dissident triangle" composed of the Pentagon's internal whistle-blowers, Pentagon critics in Congress, and the press to alter and even defeat the political agenda of the Pentagon leadership.[30] Similarly, Yan Jiaqi describes the use of the internal reporting system under the supervision of the Propaganda Department to "frighten the elders" by exaggerating the tenor of protests in the student demonstrations in the fall and winter of 1986. And Su Shaozhi shows how internal party regulations and personal connections were used by reformist actors in the propaganda sector to defend their institutions and personal standing.

All these factors make inter- and intrabureaucratic dynamics complex and often highly fragmented processes. Scholars like Lampton, Lieberthal, and Oksenberg who have applied Western political science theories of bureaucracy and policy implementation have with considerable justification, therefore, concluded that the Chinese political system shows a similarly diffused and fragmented structure of authority. The resulting policy process, at least in some policy sectors, approximates the process of "bargaining" at work in Western bureaucratic systems and recalls in sometimes startling ways Smith's description of the American system as "fluid, fragmented and floating."

Appreciation of these centrifugal dynamics, however, needs at the same time to be tempered by renewed study of the single institution that seeks to integrate all individual bureaucracies and agencies at work in the Chinese political system: the Communist Party. The presence of the party and its methods of enforcing its system of "unified party leadership"—the party committee and core group system, the system of appointment and promotion, the concurrent party standing of state bureaucrats, and functional systems (*xitong*) of guidance—are the main feature of the Chinese system that overwhelmingly differentiates it from Western ones, and studies that attempt to apply Western organizational experience need to take it more strongly into account.

This is one area in which the émigré cadre literature differs in assumption from the thrust of recent Western analyses of contemporary Chinese politics. The overwhelming thrust of the émigré cadre analyses is the continuing presence and force of the party and its apparatus in all political arenas and the relative weakness of all nonparty institutions against it. From

Yan Huai's dissection of party domination throughout the institutional structure, to Wang Lixin's account of Hu Yaobang's efforts to use the party apparatus within the State Planning Commission to overcome bureaucratic resistance to reform, to Hsiao Pen's account of the defeat of reforms to abolish party core groups, to Chen Yizi's analysis of the ultimate undercutting of political reforms adopted at the thirteenth party congress, the impact of the party and of infighting within the party was ultimately decisive.

Western studies that do focus on the evolving force of the party in politics—such as those by Jowitt and Walder of Soviet and Chinese "neotraditionalism"—provide a healthy balance to studies that may exaggerate the segmentation of the system at the expense of factors that transcend or permeate bureaucracies.[31] The Lieberthal-Oksenberg study, in all fairness, does acknowledge the party's importance as an integrating mechanism in the Chinese bureaucratic hierarchy, but it notes that information on party operations within the energy bureaucracies has been impossible to come by and does not explicitly pursue the implications of this gap further.[32] Consequently, this is one area in which the émigré cadre literature makes an important contribution.

Problems of Change

Perhaps out of the ongoing work on all the above aspects and others may eventually emerge a portrait of the Chinese political system entitled *The Power Game—How Beijing Works.* Like Hedrick Smith's depiction of politics "inside the beltway," such a description of politics "inside the ring road" would have to build on an intimate understanding of the formal and informal processes at work in the Chinese political system. It would require study of many more pieces of the picture than are currently at hand, especially in policy arenas and aspects of the system in which prevailing models of explanation do not apply.

Composition of such a comprehensive and syncretic picture would allow more precise analysis of the larger trends of system change at work, aiding not only efforts to establish improved interpretations of the long-term evolution of both the history of the People's Republic specifically and modern Chinese history in general, but also better projections of the future evolution of China's politics. Such diachronic analysis would benefit from further comparisons with other political systems that have changed in qualitatively new directions.

The great value of examining the transformation of the Kuomintang-dominated Nationalist Chinese regime, for example, stems from the fact that both the Kuomintang (KMT) and the CCP began as Leninist systems,

that both regimes have pursued aggressive economic modernization programs that have had important effects on their respective political systems,
and that both are Chinese, a common basis from which they derive their
now quite different contemporary political cultures. The Nationalist regime
has been undergoing a process of transformation, at first incremental but
more recently quite rapid, from authoritarian rule toward some form of
political pluralism. Insofar as most analysts have seen a process of some
kind of political liberalization at work in the People's Republic of China
through the 1980s, the evolving pattern of Kuomintang rule, both during the
Nanjing decade from 1927 to 1937, and on Taiwan after 1948, seems to
offer useful perspectives for evaluating patterns of change in the PRC.

Not that scholarly consensus has been reached on some of these questions. Tien Hung-mao, for example, views the KMT as Leninist in its organizational principles and techniques throughout the Nanjing period,
describing the Nationalist regime as a "party-state," though he acknowledges that the KMT's organizational strength faded, especially in the face
of the growing power of military elites associated with Chiang Kai-shek.[33]
Only in its evolution on Taiwan, mainly in response to social and political
pressures growing out of the success of its developmental policies, did the
KMT regime lose its Leninist characteristics, abandoning resort to "coercion and control" in favor of tactics of "persuasion and conciliation." [34]
Joseph Fewsmith sees a different evolution, arguing that the KMT regime abandoned its Leninist foundations very early, as the core of Leninist organization—the KMT party—was subordinated rapidly to an
emerging authoritarianism built around Chiang and based on personal
networks and that co-opted major social elites through corporatist organizational mechanisms.[35]

Such differences in interpretation go to the heart of much of the most
interesting work in recent years on China in the traditional and Republican
periods, which examines the changing relationship of state and society.
Recent scholarship on the late traditional period casts doubt on the long
conventional Weberian-based picture of a strong imperial state presiding
over a subservient agrarian society. Recent work has shown instead an
imperial state that rarely intruded into local society. Increasingly through
the Qing, local nonofficial elites assumed more and more of the responsibilities for local order as well as functions previously performed directly by
the state. By the nineteenth century the foundations of the imperial system
had already been irretrievably corroded, and the multifaceted encounter
with the West only accelerated the emergence of new social groups beyond
imperial control with little stake in the imperial system and the usurpation
of formerly public functions by nonofficial and private elites.

From this new perspective, the 1911 Revolution is explained not so much as the result of successful conspiracies by anti-Manchu revolutionaries as the product of a complex social transformation under way for at least two centuries, which continued to percolate through the entire Republican period. Some scholars of the Republican period see an emerging, though still unevenly developed "civil society" in the 1920s, at odds with the authoritarian ambitions of the Nationalist state, crushed under Communist totalitarianism, and awakened again in the Dengist reform period and manifest at Tiananmen.[36]

These ideas, together with parallel insights into the process of transformation of KMT Leninist authoritarianism toward some form of political pluralism, open new avenues for understanding the evolving political sociology of the PRC. In this we may be handicapped by the difficulties of discerning with satisfactory precision the nature and direction of social change in China since 1949. The economic reforms of the Deng decade brought profound changes in China's social structure, and in significant respects the Communist state appears to have found itself struggling to react to unanticipated changes in the society it has sought to rule rather than itself acting as engine of social change. The events at Tiananmen, moreover, in many ways reflected some of the social tensions and pressures accompanying those changes. Disentangling the various threads of social change in the PRC—identifying those that are new with the Deng reforms, those that were set in motion by the policies of the previous three decades of Communist rule but hidden beneath the veneer of Maoist egalitarian idiom, and those that reflect trends of much longer vintage—is not a straightforward enterprise.

The émigré cadre's insight into the nature and direction of change under way in China's political system and its relationship with a rapidly changing Chinese society, of course, will be of great utility in assessing these problems. But with regard to longer historical trends, the assumptions of the émigré cadres about China's prerevolutionary past are strongly at odds with the thrust of the recent Western historiographic trends sketched above. Though there are few references among the papers in this volume, the view of China's historical evolution among émigré cadre scholars most frequently mirrors the May Fourth era historiography that informed both longstanding Western views of imperial and Republican history and PRC historiography itself. This outlook depicts a powerful autocratic state oppressing a weak, primarily agrarian society for two millennia and fostering an oppressive Confucian social and political culture that only began to be banished in favor of more progressive traits and attitudes during the New Culture movement criticisms of the May Fourth era.

Problems of Method and Interpretation

In conclusion, the émigré cadre literature brings several strengths and opens new points of departure in the study of Chinese politics and political history. It refocuses attention on the politics of the central leadership at a moment when interest in this topic has waned, as Western scholars, naturally enough, have eagerly and productively pursued insight into the long-denied area of Chinese society and subnational politics. It refocuses attention on the Communist Party at a time when much Western scholarly attention has focused on state bureaucracies, enterprises, and nonparty groups, thanks in part to the improved access to such organizations and in part to the continued difficulty of access to the party itself. In both respects, the contributions here may ultimately impel adjustments in views that overemphasize fragmentation, decentralization, and diffusion of party-state power.

There appear to be limits, too, to what the émigré cadre literature can tell us. One, as mentioned above, is the difference in historical perspective. Another is that while the émigré cadre analyses provide invaluable insight into the workings of the political system very close to the top, we do not appear to learn very much more about the interactions among the top leaders themselves. There are perhaps many reasons for this, but a major one may be the success of the elders and top leaders in shielding themselves from the routine observation of the bureaucracies over which they preside. None of the writers here worked on the personal staffs of the elders or the top leadership. They worked instead in permanent bureaucracies and ad hoc task forces that gave them occasional or even frequent opportunities to observe and make judgments about top leaders, but not an intimate knowledge of the leaders' work habits, schedule, or personal relations based on routine contact with them over long periods.[37]

We have a lot to learn from the experience and insight of our new colleagues that will enrich the study of contemporary Chinese politics in pathbreaking ways. Their contribution comes at a time when the avenues of inquiry and the varieties of information about China's political system are becoming both increasingly diverse and narrowly specialized and focused.

An ideal comprehensive analysis of the Chinese political system would combine the results of several analytical approaches in a complementary way. Use of the press along traditional lines of communications analysis can still provide interviewers with more insightful and potentially productive questions to ask official informants; conversely, insight from conversations with present and former officials into how the propaganda system links up with the ongoing political process can guide media analysis treating areas of the political system to which there is no easy direct access. Meanwhile, émigré cadre scholars are best positioned to offer insight into the interior workings of the system that help make sense of the public manifestations of the political process in the media and elsewhere.

Finally, a more empirically based understanding of China's political process may emerge that will help narrow the search for satisfying characterizations and models to describe and explain it. One of the most unsatisfying aspects of the successive approaches to understanding both the Soviet and Chinese political systems has been the degree to which they seem to derive from extraneous trends. The Soviet system was described first according to totalitarian models in the Stalin period, then conflict models under Khrushchev, then interest group and pluralist and corporatist models under Leonid Brezhnev, and finally according to more harshly authoritarian approaches thereafter. One cannot help but notice that these changes in approach correspond not only to apparent changes in the Soviet regime itself and its top leaders but also in some oblique measure to alternating phases of confrontation and détente in East-West relations. With a little reflection, one sees similar patterns in the successive models used to understand China's political system as well.

These recurrent revolutions in the Soviet and China fields naturally have had their origins not simply in changes within the former U.S.S.R. and China, respectively, but frequently in changing sensibilities that have little to do with China itself. Perhaps it is here that the émigré cadre literature challenges us most directly to sort out our assumptions and presumptions and to reassess our conclusions and judgments. At a moment when Western students of China see overwhelming evidence for the fragmentation and diffusion of authority, our former cadre colleagues see the pervasive presence of the party apparatus. At a time when Western students of China have begun to take a long view—spanning four centuries—of the "Chinese Revolution" and to search for signs of an emergent civil society and public sphere in the mid-Qing, early Republic, or the pre-Tiananmen PRC, many of our Chinese cadre colleagues perceive only halting progress in a revolution that has only begun to throw off an obdurately persistent "feudal" political culture that shored up imperial autocracy and Communist totalitarianism. Bridging these differences in perspective will be challenging and productive.

Notes

1. Andrew Nathan, *Chinese Democracy* (New York: Alfred A. Knopf, 1985), 228; A. Doak Barnett, "Ten Years After Mao," *Foreign Affairs,* 65, no. 1 (Fall 1986): 53;

Harry Harding, *China's Second Revolution* (Washington, D.C.: Brookings Institution, 1987), 174; and Zbigniew Brzezinski, *The Grand Failure* (New York: Charles Scribners' Sons, 1989).

2. Michel Oksenberg, "Politics Takes Command: An Essay on the Study of Post-Mao China," in *Cambridge History of China*, Vol. 14: *The People's Republic, Part I: The Emergence of Revolutionary China, 1949–1965*, ed. Roderick MacFarquhar and John K. Fairbank (New York: Cambridge University Press, 1987), 543–90.

3. Richard Sakwa, *Soviet Politics: An Introduction* (New York: Routledge, 1989), 137.

4. Jerry F. Hough and Merle Fainsod, *How the Soviet Union Is Governed* (Cambridge: Harvard University Press, 1979), 466ff.

5. Uri Ra'anan and Igor Lukes, *Inside the Apparat: Perspectives on the Soviet Union from Former Functionaries* (Lexington, MA: Lexington Books, 1990), 57–73.

6. A. Doak Barnett, *The Making of Foreign Policy in China* (Boulder: Westview Press, 1985), 19–32.

7. Zhao Ziyang, report to the Thirteenth CCP Congress, October 25, 1987, *Beijing Review*, November 9–15, 1987; "Revision of Some Articles of the Constitution of the Communist Party of China," *Beijing Review*, November 16–22, 1987.

8. Werner Hahn, "Who Ousted Nikita Sergeyevich?" *Problems of Communism* 40, no.3 (May–June 1991): 109–15.

9. State Statistical Bureau, *Zhongguo tongji zhaiyao 1990* (1990 Statistical Abstract) (Beijing: Zhongguo tongji chubanshe, 1990), 108.

10. Jin Chongji, ed. *Zhou Enlai zhuan 1898–1949* (The Biography of Zhou Enlai, 1898–1949) (Beijing: Renmin chubanshe, 1989).

11. Fan Shuo, *Ye Jianying zai 1976* (Ye Jianying in 1976) (Beijing: Zhonggong zhongyang dangxiao chubanshe, 1990).

12. Feng Jian, Cao Jianhui et al., *Zhongnanhai de chuntian* (Springtime in Zhongnanhai) (Beijing: Xinhua chubanshe, 1983).

13. *San zhong quanhui yilai zhongyao wenxian xuanbian* (Selected Important Documents Since the Third Plenum) (Changchun: Renmin chubanshe, 1982).

14. *Chen Yun tongzhi wengao xuanbian* (1956–1962) (Selected Draft Writings of Comrade Chen Yun) (Guangzhou: Guangdong renmin chubanshe, 1981); *Chen Yun wenxuan* (The Selected Writings of Chen Yun), Vol. 3: 1956–1985 (Beijing: Renmin chubanshe, 1986).

15. Li Rui, *Lushan huiyi shilu* (The True Account of the Lushan Meetings) (Beijing: Chunqiu chubanshe and Hunan jiaoyu chubanshe, 1989).

16. In addition to the narrower studies in this volume, there is a growing body of memoirs and broad-gauge analyses of the policy process in the Deng era. These include Chen Yizi, *Zhongguo: Shinian gaiming yu bajiu mindong* (China: Ten Years of Reform and the 1989 Democracy Movement) (Taibei: Lianjing chuban shiye gongsi, 1990).

17. Michael Schoenhals, *Doing Things with Words in Chinese Politics: Five Studies* (Berkeley: Institute of East Asian Studies, University of California, 1992).

18. Carol Lee Hamrin, "The Party Leadership System," in Kenneth G. Lieberthal and David M. Lampton, eds., *Bureaucracy, Politics, and Decision Making in Post-Mao China* (Berkeley: University of California Press, 1992), 95–124.

19 Michel Oksenberg, "Methods of Communication within the Chinese Bureaucracy," *The China Quarterly*, no. 57 (January 1974): 1–39; Kenneth Lieberthal, *Central Documents and Politburo Politics in China* (Ann Arbor: Center for Chinese Studies, University of Michigan, 1978); and Kenneth Lieberthal and Michel Oksenberg, *Policy Making in China: Leaders, Structures, and Processes* (Princeton: Princeton University Press, 1988).

20. Kenneth Lieberthal, *Research Guide to Central Party and Government Meetings in China, 1949–1975* (White Plains, NY: International Arts and Sciences Press, 1976); and Kenneth Lieberthal and Bruce J. Dickson, *Research Guide to Central Party and Government Meetings in China, 1949–1986* (Armonk, NY: M.E. Sharpe, 1989).

21. Aaron Wildavsky, *The New Politics of the Budgetary Process* (New York: HarperCollins, 1988), 8.

22. Hedrick Smith, *The Power Game—How Washington Works* (New York: Random House, 1988).

23. Peggy Noonan, *What I Saw at the Revolution* (New York: Random House, 1990).

24. One may also want to compare Frederick Teiwes's analysis of the seven "prudential rules" of leadership politics: (1) retain the leader's confidence—"don't cross the leader"; (2) maintain broad alliances; (3) "deliver the goods" even if violating directives is required; (4) protect institutional interests; (5) maintain *guanxi* networks; (6) develop patron-client ties; and (7) maintain PLA support. Frederick Teiwes, *Leadership, Legitimacy and Conflict in China* (Armonk, NY: M.E. Sharpe, 1984), 94–99.

25. Lieberthal and Oksenberg, *Policy Making in China*, 391.

26. Smith, *The Power Game*, 282.

27. Noonan, *What I Saw at the Revolution*, 102–3 and 107–8.

28. See, for example, W. Richard Scott, *Organizations: Rational, Natural, and Open Systems*, 2nd ed. (Englewood Cliffs, NJ: Prentice-Hall, 1987).

29. Hough and Fainsod, *How the Soviet Union Is Governed*, 531ff, and Lieberthal and Oksenberg, *Policy Making in China*, 30–31.

30. Smith, *The Power Game*, 160ff.

31. Kenneth Jowitt, "Soviet Neotraditionalism: The Political Corruption of a Leninist Regime," *Soviet Studies* 35, no. 3 (July 1983): 275–97; and Andrew Walder, *Communist Neo-Traditionalism: Work and Authority in Chinese Industry* (Berkeley: University of California Press, 1986).

32. Lieberthal and Oksenberg, *Policy Making in China*, 144–45.

33. Tien Hung-mao, *Government and Politics in Kuomintang China, 1927–1937* (Stanford: Stanford University Press, 1972).

34. Tien Hung-mao, *The Great Transition: Political and Social Change in the Republic of China* (Stanford: Hoover Institution Press, 1989), 4–16 and 72.

35. Joseph Fewsmith, *Party, State, and Local Elites in Republican China* (Honolulu: University of Hawaii Press, 1985), 181–95.

36. David Strand, "Protest in Beijing: Civil Society and Public Sphere in China," *Problems of Communism* 39, no. 3 (May–June 1990): 1–19.

37. Wei Li and Lucien Pye's description of the mediating roles of leader staffs—the *mishu*—in interactions among top-level leaders and among leaders and bureaucracies greatly illuminates how this separation and shielding comes about. Their study appears to draw primarily on the reminiscences of some *mishu* of past leaders like Mao Zedong, Lin Biao, and Zhou Enlai and on the small body of literature on *mishu* work published recently in China. See Wei Li and Lucien Pye, "The Ubiquitous Role of the Mishu in Chinese Politics," *The China Quarterly*, no. 132 (December 1992): 913–36.

19

The Structure of Authority and Decision-Making: A Theoretical Framework

Suisheng Zhao

Political authority and decision-making processes in the People's Republic of China (PRC) have long been a subject of scholarly inquiry. Scholars of Chinese politics such as Roderick MacFarquhar, Lowell Dittmer, and Avery Goldstein argue that political power in Beijing is highly personalistic. Hence, these scholars' inquiries have focused on the informal dynamics of the regime, looking at policy disputes, factional bases, and power contests mainly among a few individual leaders.[1] Other scholars like Kenneth Lieberthal, Michel Oksenberg, David Lampton, and Susan Shirk extend their inquiry beyond the top political elite and adopt an institutional approach to explore the decision- and policy-making process in China. Their studies pay great attention to formal government and party organizations and show that while power at the apex inheres in individuals, formal decisions are made in and implemented through the established bureaucratic institutions.[2]

Each of these two approaches represents a valuable focus for describing and analyzing China's policy-making process. While scholars are aware of the value of both, they have not clearly addressed when each approach is most valid. This confusion reflects the actual ambiguous relationship between the roles of informal personal power and of formal institutional authority. This concluding chapter attempts to use the findings in the book to provide a theoretical framework for delineating the circumstances in which personal power is likely to dominate the decision-making process, and when institutional factors are likely to play important roles.

Developing such a framework is now possible because personal and institutional authority has become more distinguishable in Deng Xiaoping's

China. The authority of the retired or semi-retired revolutionary elders is primarily personal and the authority of the younger generation of leaders is relatively institutional. Personal and institutional authority is hierarchically ranked in the policy-making arena.

The properties of different policies also give rise to differences in the role and influence of individual leaders and institutional actors, depending on the policy type and arena. As a consequence of the Deng era priority on modernization, and consequent reform and opening policies, the policy-making process is increasingly pluralized, as reviewed in Carol Lee Hamrin's study of the 1980s reform process.[3] This pluralization takes place primarily within the bureaucracy, so that both individual pluralism and institutional pluralism characterize decision-making in Deng's China, in spite of the lack of society-wide pluralism common in the West.

Leaders and Their Authority

Personal and institutional describe the two types of authority despite the considerable vagueness about the boundaries between them. The authority of most political leaders in the early period of the PRC was mixed. For example, Mao Zedong's authority derived from his unusual personality and his historical role in the revolution and could hardly be separated from his formal positions as lifelong chairman of both the Chinese Communist Party (CCP) and its Military Commission and, for a time, president of the PRC. Personal and institutional types of authorities have become more distinguishable in Deng's China since many powerful elderly leaders no longer hold any institutional positions.

In an overly simplified typology, China's political leadership at the top echelon is composed of three types of individuals: (1) the influential but elderly revolutionary leaders who have retired or semi-retired from their official posts; (2) top leaders in the CCP's Politburo, mostly its Standing Committee members; and (3) other top officeholders and bureaucrats, including State Council members, the top commanders of the military, and the leaders of the wealthiest and largest cities and provinces. Roughly speaking, the authority of the first type of leader is essentially personalistic while the authority of the third type is relatively institutional. The authority of the second type is a mix of personal and institutional, deriving respectively from their personal relations with patron elders and their holding of offices.

Personal authority revolves around the personage of leaders and derives from the charismatic nature of strong leaders, which supersedes impersonal organization in eliciting the personal loyalty of followers.[4] Such authority is rooted in the Chinese tradition of rule by man, not law. Its very basis in Chinese politics is the cultural pattern of personal patronage bonds and the Chinese concept of friendship as instrumentalist personal connections (*guanxi*).[5] In contrast, institutional authority derives from and is constrained by impersonal organizational rules. In an ideal type, such authority rests not on individual charisma but on formal position in an institutional setting. Insofar as a leader can issue commands under institutional authority, it is the function of the office he holds rather than of any personal quality.[6]

Why do the retired elders possess personal authority while the office-holders have to rely more on institutional authority? One answer to this question is that they have different career paths. As the war heroes and founders of the PRC, the former party and military leaders who helped Mao seize power not only have some "personal" charisma derived from the revolution and the party that they symbolize but also have broad and deep relations with key individuals and institutions in the power structure through a broad revolutionary career.[7] For example, Deng Xiaoping served as political commissar in one of the four People's Liberation Army field armies during war and revolution. He also held positions on the Central Military Commission in the 1950s, 1960s, and 1980s. He was the director of the CCP's Central Organization Department in the early 1950s, the general secretary from 1954 to 1966, and vice premier after the Cultural Revolution. This wide career path gave Deng vast connections in the army, the party, and the government.

The elders' revolutionary reputations and personal networks of colleagues and clients are both unmatched by the younger generation leaders. They have largely technocratic background with much narrower career paths, a good deal of which has been spent rising through the ranks of one of the three bureaucracies and building ties vertically within the organization, not horizontally with individuals and institutions within the wider system. Their careers, moreover, tend to be concentrated in a single sector (*xitong*), often associated with just one type of work (economic management, for instance) or one bureaucratic body (provincial administration). For instance, Zhao Ziyang had only provincial administrative experience before he became premier in 1982. Li Peng held positions only within the electric power sector before he took over the premiership in 1987. In particular, this generation of leaders lacks links to the military.[8]

From this perspective, whereas the revolutionary elders helped create the Chinese bureaucracy and institutions and hence stand above the state, the younger generation leaders are products of the state structure and are rooted within it. That is why the retired elders possess personal authority while the younger leaders have to rely on institutional resources. To some extent, this distinction of authority reflects longevity of posts at the center that are broader-ranging in authority. Since institutional resources can and are being used to build personal ties, the system may still produce new elders if the younger generation of leaders retain lifelong tenure in office.

The Hierarchical Line of Authority

If two types of authority are involved in the policy-making process, what are the structural relationships between them? In overly simplistic terms, the personal and institutional authority are hierarchically ranked. This may be observed from two aspects.

First, the influential elders with strong personal authority are supreme decision-makers, whereas the officeholders with institutional authority serve as the chief lieutenants to the powerful elders. In principle, the Politburo of the CCP is the top policy-making arena and the Politburo members, especially its Standing Committee members, are the top policymakers. In reality, however, the authority of the officeholders depends largely on the support and confidence of the powerful elders because the retired elders retain the power to select the Politburo members, assign them their duties, and give final approval to important Politburo decisions.[9] In an interview, one aide to Zhao Ziyang told me that when Zhao acted as the CCP's general secretary and chaired the Politburo meetings in 1987–89, he always went to Deng Xiaoping for instructions before a meeting was convened. The opening remarks Zhao made at Politburo meeting always mentioned "I have already talked to Comrade Xiaoping about this issue."[10]

Second, the authority at the apex of the China's power hierarchy is essentially personal whereas the authority below the peak is relatively institutional. Personal authority is used mostly as a means of controlling and mobilizing human resources via patron-client *guanxi* in a nomenklatura system. The institutional authority is used mostly as a means of controlling and mobilizing material resources through the bureaucratic bargaining process. Although most Chinese leaders suffered from Mao's abuse of personal power before the reform era, the post-Mao reformers have not been able to make real progress at depersonalizing political authority at the top level of the political hierarchy. It is true that the epoch of one superman's (Mao) near-total domination of the decision-making arena seems to have passed, but several elders still dominate and exercise greater influence than the younger officeholders, regardless of the title they hold.

The conflict between Deng Xiaoping and Chen Yun over reform and opening up policies after Tiananmen reveals the personalistic nature of authority at the very top level. Chen Yun retired from the Politburo and took a ceremonial position as chairman of the CCP's Central Advisory Commission at the twelfth party congress in 1982. Deng Xiaoping also retired from the Politburo in 1987 and resigned his last formal office (chairman of the Central Military Commission) after the Tiananmen crackdown in 1989. Yet their personal preferences have continued to affect policy.

Deng is known as the "chief architect of China's reform," and Chen favors a more orthodox planned economy. They have been at odds ever since they jointly defeated Hua Guofeng. Taking advantage of the Tiananmen crackdown, Chen Yun through his conservative supporters launched ideological attacks on economic reform policies by asking whether the reform was called socialism or capitalism. A three-year retrenchment of reform was enforced during 1989–91. To meet the challenge and "save" the reform, Deng Xiaoping made a highly politicized trip to South China, at the advanced age of eighty-seven, in early 1992, mobilizing reform-minded local leaders and waging an intensive policy battle in person with the conservatives. After this so-called Deng whirlwind, a new wave of bolder reform and greater opening up occurred in China.[11]

The dominance of personal authority at the top level is partly due to the tenacity of Chinese political culture and partly due to the systemic requirement for an ultimate authority outside the system, as reflected in the strategy adopted by the reform leaders. In traditional Chinese political culture, "status tends to imply power and is not treated as being merely symbolic."[12] The revolutionary elder (*geming yuanlao*) status with or without a ceremonial appointment can be readily transformed into actual power if a patronage network preexists and if the elder is not passive and exploits his potential for influence. Deng Xiaoping, while arguing strongly for the establishment of institutional authority, has resorted to invoking his personal authority to push through reforms resisted by the conservatives.[13] In doing so, Deng Xiaoping has in fact adopted a strategy of personalizing the reforms. Deng Xiaoping has been personally identified with the reform policy, thus his conflict with Chen Yun on the reform policy has become largely a contest between each other's personal status and guanxi networks.[14]

Authority below the very peak at the bureaucratic level is more institutional than it is at the top. As a result of the functional separation of party from government and of administrative decentralization, central government agencies and local governments are now much more influential in formulating economic and foreign policy than they were in the late Maoist period.[15] Government bureaucracy has acquired somewhat greater authority in other related areas, such as culture and education, or science and technology, which had previously been the exclusive preserve of the party apparatus. Regular administrative decisions have been made more and more within the bureaucratic apparatus without, or with very little, intervention of the elders or other top leaders. The rule of making policies at the bureaucratic level is what Susan Shirk calls "delegation by consensus."[16] The elders delegate administrative responsibility to the leaders. They further delegate to their subordinate bureaucrats the authority to make routine policy decisions. According to the rule of delegation by consensus, if the bureaucrats reach a consensus, the decision is usually approved by the leaders and may be further ratified by the elders. Only if there is a disagreement will the upper levels intervene.

Why do the elders delegate administrative responsibility to the front-line leaders and top bureaucrats? After all, the elders are very old and some of them are in poor health. While they know the general direction of their policy preferences, they have little information and few definite ideas about how to pursue them. The post-Mao reforms have created more vested interests among the bureaucratic and regional agencies, and the decisions on many policy issues have required more information and sophisticated calculation; therefore delegation of administrative responsibility to the bureaucratic institutions not only avoids responsibility for policy mistakes by the elders but also exploits the superior information of the bureaucrats and relieves the elders both of work under intense strain and of the political costs of constant intervention in the policy process.

Authority from the Perspective of Issue Areas

Variations in the relative weight of personal and institutional authority in the policy-making arena flow from the characteristics not only of the hierarchical structure but also of different issue areas. In other words, "policy determines politics."[17] Differences in the properties of policy itself give rise to differences in the organization of politics and, consequently, in the role and influence of individual leaders and institutional actors.

The importance of issue-area characteristics may be observed by comparing policy-making in economic and ideological issue areas. It is striking that the authors of the major works that have adopted an institutional approach in the study of China's policy-making process have focused primarily on the economic issue area. Lieberthal, in a recent study, recognizes that there is far less evidence of the institutional bargaining relationships in a number of noneconomic issue areas than has generally been found in the economic issue area.[18]

Indeed, in the economic issue area, not only is policy-making power increasingly fragmented and diffused but also the policy debates and bargaining are increasing among bureaucratic institutions, involving technical criteria. A recent study of the policy-making process in China's energy sector found that, no matter how powerful individual leaders at the top may appear, they lack the time, interest, and knowledge to manage and coordinate all the activities in the energy sphere. Not even the handful of top energy specialists can manage the vast petroleum, coal, and electric power industries. Inevitably, much of the critical activity in shaping and implementing policy takes place within the bureaucracies and through intensive bargaining among central bureaucratic agencies (in the energy sector, for example, the State Planning Commission, the State Economic Commission, the state Science and Technological Commission, Ministry of Finance, Ministry of Petroleum, and Ministry of Coal) and between central agencies and local governments.[19]

By contrast, the ideological policy area, considered broadly to include media, education, culture, and scientific research, has become somewhat more pluralistic, but authority for making decisions about sensitive political issues remains concentrated more in the hands of a few top leaders than in institutions, and the war over ideological issues is still waged primarily among individual leaders. For example, the ideological controversy over the "truth criterion" (*zhengli biaozhun*) in 1978–79 was primarily between Deng Xiaoping and Hua Guofeng.[20] The battles over "spiritual pollution" in 1984 and "bourgeois liberalism" in 1987 were fought out mainly among a few top leaders, with Hu Yaobang and Zhao Ziyang, supported by Deng Xiaoping, on one side, and Deng Liqun and Hu Qiaomu, backed by Chen Yun, on the other.[21] Even the controversy over a highly critical six-part television program, *Heshang* (River Elegy), evolved primarily between Wang Zhen (an elderly vice president of China) and Zhao before the Tiananmen crackdown in 1989.[22]

The characteristics of economic and ideology issue areas appear to influence the role of personal and institutional authority for many reasons. First, in China, where socialism is held as the official ideology, an ideological policy issue becomes a "high politics" arena that has direct implications for the status and power of the top leaders or their factions, whereas an economic policy issue is a "low politics" arena that usually does not directly affect individual leaders. Therefore, the top leaders are more sensitive to the consequences of ideological policy debate than to those of economic policy debate. They get involved personally in economic policy debates only if the policy becomes ideologically sensitive. Such has been the case with the dismantling of the communes, the radical price reform of 1988, and Deng Xiaoping's war with Chen Yun in early 1992 over the decision to accelerate market reforms.[23]

Second, economic policy issues involve ever more specialized knowledge and information and have required increasingly sophisticated technical calculation since market-oriented reform began in the late 1970s. The top leaders, especially the elders, either lack interest or feel incapable of intervening in regular economic policy decisions. It is a different story regarding ideological policies, on which all Chinese leaders claim to be experts. They are not only highly sensitive to any ideological debate but also clearly understand the political implications of such debate.

Third, the reforms of the past decade have consciously decentralized decision-making power and have given lower bureaucratic levels more control over their resources (financial and material) in the economic sphere. In the ideological issue area, nevertheless, power has been decentralized to a much more limited extent, so that lower-level institutions still cannot make major decisions.

National security policy, especially internal security and military issues, also remains highly centralized.[24] In foreign policy, while decision-making authority on secondary bilateral relations, and foreign economic and cultural relations has been delegated to lower levels and to different institutions, the decisions on strategic issues are still held tightly by a few top leaders.

The continuing concentration at the apex of decision-making authority over such sensitive issues confines policy contention mostly among a few leaders, whereas the decentralization of decision-making authority over less sensitive issues gives rise to bargaining relationships among institutions. Organization and personnel matters fall somewhere in between, with considerable decentralization of authority for positions below the Central Committee level in the mid-1980s, reforms that were reversed after Tiananmen.

Growing Pluralism in Policy-Making

The policy-making process became so much more pluralistic than it had been before the reform decade that scholars such as Kenneth Lieberthal developed a "fragmented authoritarianism" model to describe the Chinese system.[25] During the Maoist era, the power to make important decisions was extremely concentrated in the hands of Mao and a few of his close aides. Input into this process was restricted to a few individual leaders, not bureaucrats or intellectuals, and policy debates were rare even internally, let alone openly. This pattern of policy-making has changed, as more input comes from the burgeoning policy research institutions and bureaucratic agencies. Numerous work conferences and meetings, at which policy issues and solutions are discussed, bring together governmental officials from relevant ministries and experts from relevant research institutes of the Chinese Academy of Sciences, the Chinese Academy of Social Sciences, and universities. Policy debates thus are more open and more frequent, and the results of these debates often have a greater effect on final policy decisions than was the case before the reform decade.

To the extent that a diversity of actors has been involved in policy-making, it is reasonable to say that China's policy-making process is increasingly pluralized within the framework of bureaucratic authoritarianism. It is worth noting that the growing pluralism in China clearly differs from classical pluralism in the West.[26] Classical pluralism allows all citizens to choose between the policy programs of competing elites in elections and to form new pressure groups or parties to advance their political interests. In China, pluralism is restricted primarily within the bureaucratic elite. Those who want to affect policy change must, with a few exceptions, work through personal connections with individual leaders or work within the official institutional or bureaucratic framework. Although any citizen can make appeals or suggestions regarding official policies, the leading participants in the policy process are still always the individual leaders and top bureaucrats. Therefore, two new terms, *individual pluralism* and *institutional pluralism,* might be used to characterize the growing pluralism in China and to distinguish pluralism under bureaucratic authoritarian rule from pluralism in the West.

Individual pluralism is defined as a situation in which individual leaders, whose power is not primarily institutional but personal, compete for their policy preferences and in which no single leader dominates.[27] This is the case in Deng's China, where no single leader enjoys the unrivaled personal authority that Mao used to wield. Even Deng Xiaoping is only first among equals; other senior statesmen also exercise great personal authority. Deng has to rely on a mix of persuasion, cajolery, compromise, and threats. On several occasions, he was forced to make concessions to Chen Yun and other elders on important policy issues and even on crucial personnel appointments. This was the case with the forced resignations of Hu Yaobang and Zhao Ziyang in 1987 and 1989.

Institutional pluralism is characterized by conflict among political leaders and bureaucrats who must be reckoned with mainly according to the institutional resources provided by their offices.[28] In China, institutional pluralism is structurally based on the functional division of authority among officeholders. At the apex, each member of the Politburo Standing Committee is in charge of one segment of governance (such as economic affairs, ideological and cultural work, or personnel affairs). At the bureaucratic level, both party and government bureaucracies are organized by sectors (agriculture, coal, machinery) and functions (education, culture, public security).

Since most of the younger generation leaders in post-Mao China have been associated with only one type of work in one bureaucratic sector and lack strong personal influence within the power structure, their authority is often confined to their institutional resources. When such a leader comes to office, he usually creates new institutions that may be used to strengthen his authority. For example, Zhao Ziyang created six high-ranking policy research centers immediately under the State Council while he was premier.[29] The creation of these high-ranking centers reflected Zhao's purposes "in both a policy and a power sense."[30] These centers provided Zhao Ziyang, an outsider (a former provincial leader) facing entrenched bureaucracy, not only with a more effective personal staff but also with badly needed institutional resources to establish his own policy priorities by eliciting more information and coordinating policy deliberation. This type of strategy promotes the development of institutional pluralism.

Operational Consequences

In conclusion, let me indicate three operational consequences of the authority structure analyzed above (see table 19.1), with respect to policy outcomes.

1. At the top levels and in the ideological and national security (including internal security and military) policy issue areas, decisions are relatively unconstrained by institutions at lower levels. In such situations, decisions are made mostly in the context of personal factional competition, in relative isolation from information and advice regarding the interests of the various bureaucracies and localities. One or a few top leaders can bring about a drastic change of policy direction unanticipated by outside observers. The Beijing massacre of June Fourth, 1989, is a recent important example of this type of decision.

2. At the lower levels and in the economic and related foreign policy and science and technology issue area, where policy-making is characterized by institutional pluralism, policy change tends to be incremental. Dramatic changes in policy direction or massive shifts in the allocation of resources are inhibited by the requirement that every affected agency and local government agree to them. In this situation, making decisions can be a difficult, protracted process. Nonroutine decisions can be kicked around at lower levels for years without being resolved if no consensus can be reached or the top leaders do not want to take positions or do not know what position to take. That is one reason why it was so difficult for the conservative leaders to reverse the economic reform policy even after the Tiananmen

Table 19.1

Summary of the Major Findings

	Personal Authority		Institutional Authority
Leaders			
elders	More		Less
top leaders		Mix of both	
officeholders	Less		More
Power hierarchy			
at the top	More		Less
under the peak	Less		More
Issue areas			
economic and foreign policy	Less		More
ideology and national security	More		Less
Pluralisms			
individual	More		Less
institutional	More		Less

massacre. The decades-long debate over the Three Gorges dam is another outstanding example.

3. A long-term trend toward more institutional pluralism wherein formal institutional positions and the trade-off of organizational interests predominate seems inevitable because the rising younger generation leaders have less power vis-à-vis bureaucratic interests than do the revolutionary elders. The necessary but insufficient requirement for more institutionalized patterns to take over fully is the complete passing away of the revolutionary elders. Rising through the bureaucratic ranks and unable to draw on the heroic legacy of the past, new generation politicians will increasingly stake their policy positions on bureaucratic trade-offs. As a result politics will be based more on persuasion and compromise and bold new initiatives harming entrenched bureaucratic interests will be less likely. When this happens, personal politics focused on short-term interests will give way to more institutional politics that take into account long-term interests to a greater degree, and a new structure of authority and rule of decision-making may develop for us to explore.

Notes

1. See Roderick MacFarquhar, *Origins of the Cultural Revolution,* vol. 1 (Cambridge, Mass.: Oelgeschlager, Gunn, and Hain, 1981); Lowell Dittmer, *China's Continuous Revolution* (Berkeley: University of California Press, 1987); Avery Goldstein, *From Bandwagon to Balance of Power Politics* (Stanford: Stanford University Press, 1991).

2. See Kenneth Lieberthal and Michel Oksenberg, *Policy Making in China*

(Princeton: Princeton University Press, 1988); David Lampton, ed., *Policy Implementation in Post-Mao China* (Berkeley: University of California Press, 1987); Susan Shirk, "The Chinese Political System and the Political Strategy of Economic Reform," in Kenneth Lieberthal and David Lampton, ed., *Bureaucracy, Politics, and Decision Making in Post-Mao China* (Berkeley: University of California Press, 1992).

3. Carol Lee Hamrin made a valuable attempt to identify the suitability of rational actor, power, and bureaucratic models in terms of different levels of politics—international, leadership, and elite. This study further develops analysis along the lines of hierarchical structure, generational background, and issue areas. See Hamrin, *China and the Challenge of the Future* (Boulder, CO: Westview Press, 1990), 2–32.

4. Lucian Pye described this type of authority in terms of "the mystique of leadership"; see Pye, *The Mandarin and the Cadre: China's Political Culture* (Ann Arbor: University of Michigan Center for Chinese Studies, 1988), 135–97.

5. Lucian Pye discussed the personal bond and *guanxi* in his book *The Spirit of Chinese Politics* (Cambridge: Harvard University Press, 1992).

6. Institutional authority is compatible with Max Weber's legal-rational authority. See Weber, *The Theory of Social and Economic Organization* (New York: Free Press, 1964), 328.

7. In an interview with Edgar Snow in 1960, the late Premier Zhou Enlai disclosed that China had been governed since 1949 by a group of approximately 800 key party and military leaders who had helped Mao to seize power. Most of these 800 are dead, or, in some instances, in political disgrace. About 150 members of this group survived the Cultural Revolution and became the elders during the reform decade. See Parris H. Chang, "The Changing Nature of Elite Conflict in Post-Mao China," in *Chinese Politics from Mao to Deng,* ed. Victor C. Falkenheim (New York: Paragon House, 1989), 117.

8. David Bachman, "Domestic Sources of Chinese Foreign Policy," in *China and the World: New Directions in Chinese Foreign Relations,* ed. Samuel Kim (Boulder, CO: Westview Press, 1989), 37.

9. It is based on this fact that, in the view of some China scholars (as well as many politically knowledgeable Chinese), the front line officeholders are merely puppets controlled by the retired party elders who are behind the scenes. In this view, the younger generation leaders' power, if any, mainly comes from the elderly patrons backing them.

10. Author interview of a high-ranking Chinese official involved in the decision process, San Diego, summer 1988.

11. For details, see Suisheng Zhao, "Deng Xiaoping's Southern Tour: Elite Politics in Post-Tiananmen China," *Asian Survey* 33, no. 8 (August 1993): 739–56.

12. Pye, *The Spirit of Chinese Politics,* 225.

13. For example, Deng Xiaoping, in a speech at an enlarged meeting of the Politburo in August 1980, said, "A sound system can prevent would-be evildoers from running amok; under a bad system even good people will be unable to do things well and may, in fact, move in the opposite direction." Referring to the decision-making process, he claimed, "Major problems must be discussed collectively and the decision-making must strictly follow the majority principle. One person, one vote, and no decisions may be made by the first secretary only." See Deng Xiaoping, "Lun dang he guojia lingdao zhidu de gaige" (On Reform of the Party and State Leadership System), *People's Daily,* July 1, 1987, 1.

14. *Renmin ribao* (People's Daily, overseas ed.), April 3, 1992.

15. Suisheng Zhao, "From Coercion to Negotiation: Changing Central-Local Economic Relationship in the People's Republic of China," *Issues & Studies* 28, no. 10 (October 1992): 1–22.

16. Susan Shirk uses this term in her new work, *The Political Logic of Economic Reform in China* (Berkeley: University of California Press, 1993), while she used the

term *management by exception* in her earlier works to express the same meaning (see, for example, "The Chinese Political System and the Political Strategy of Economic Reform," in Lieberthal and Lampton, ed., *Bureaucracy, Politics, and Decision Making in Post-Mao China,* 76).

17. Theodore J. Lowi, "American Business, Public Policy, Case-Studies, and Political Theory," in *World Politics* 16 (July 1964): 677–715. Also see John Ikenberry, "Conclusion: An Institutional Approach to American Foreign Economic Policy," in *The State and American Foreign Economic Policy,* ed. Ikenberry, David Lake, and Micheal Matanduno (Ithaca: Cornell University Press, 1988), 236.

18. Kenneth Lieberthal, "Introduction: The 'Fragmented Authoritarianism' Model and Its Limitations," in *Bureaucracy, Politics, and Decision Making in Post-Mao China,* ed. Lieberthal and Lampton, 17.

19. Lieberthal and Oksenberg, *Policy Making in China,* 63–134.

20. See Michael Schoenhals, "The 1978 Truth Criterion Controversy," and Merle Goldman, "Hu Yaobang's Intellectual Network and the Theory Conference of 1979," in *The China Quarterly,* no. 126 (June 1991).

21. Ruan Ming, *Lishi zhuanze guantou de Hu Yaobang* (Hu Yaobang at the Turning Point of History) (New York: Shijie chuban she, 1992).

22. Andrew Nathan, *China's Crisis,* (New York: Columbia University Press, 1990), 122.

23. Zhao, "Deng Xiaoping's Southern Tour."

24. Because scholars have very limited access to internal and military decision areas in China, this is only a logical hypothesis.

25. Lieberthal, "Introduction," 1–32.

26. Hamrin, in *China and the Challenge of the Future,* highlights the pluralizing of the system to include intellectuals (professional experts) in the policy process via "think tanks." This is the first involvement of "society," although it took place through bureaucratic institutions rather than autonomous or electoral channels. Since 1988–89, social pluralism has been occurring through the development of semi-independent polling organizations and news media such as the *World Economic Herald.*

27. Here individual pluralism is adopted from *individualized pluralism,* a term used by Samuel Kernell to describe U.S. presidential politics in the 1980s in which independent politicians had few group or institutional loyalties and were generally less interested in sacrificing short-run, private career goals for the longer-term benefits of bargaining. See Kernell, *Going Public: New Strategies of Presidential Leadership* (Washington, DC: C.Q. Press, 1986).

28. Jerry F. Hough used "institutional pluralism" as a model to describe the post-Stalin system in the Soviet Union. According to this model, "ideas and power flow up the administrative hierarchies as well as down, and they do not see immobilism in the process of policy formation." Hough, *The Soviet Union and Social Science Theory* (Cambridge: Harvard University Press, 1977), 22.

29. The six high-ranking policy research institutions established during 1980 and 1982 are the Economic Research Center, the Technical Research Center, the Price Research Center, the Rural Development Research Center, the Economic Legislation Center, and the Center for International Studies. The first three centers were combined in 1985 into a Economic, Technical, and Social Development Research Center. I worked as a research fellow at the Economic Research Center in 1984–85.

30. Nina Halpern, "Information Flows and Policy Coordination," in *Bureaucracy, Politics, and Decision Making in Post-Mao China,* ed. Lieberthal and Lampton, 131.

Index